Living and Touring with

Alice Cooper

and Other Stories

MYSTERIOUS TALES FROM THE EARLY YEARS

Michael Allen

MANHATTAN
BOOK GROUP

These stories do not follow a strict timeline. My brain isn't that good. I felt it was better to tell my stories than attempt to arrange them in exact chronological order. Plus, it was driving me nuts trying to do so. I have written this book from memory. I recognize memory is flawed, especially mine, and I may not recall exactly the circumstances of some events, but I have tried as best I could. There may be embellishments of some events and, imperfections in recreating conversations, but the essence is there. The stories, events, and experiences are my own recollections, and others mentioned in the book could have their own.

Published by Manhattan Book Group
447 Broadway | 2nd Floor #354 | New York, NY 10013 | USA
1.800.767.0531 | www.manhattanbookgroup.com

Printed in the United States of America
ISBN-13: 978-1-958729-90-8

Dedication

Thanks for taking me along on your trip
through the Looking Glass.

Preface

A Book, a Movie, and a Funeral

Three things led to writing this book. I very rarely talk about my time with the band, figuring nobody would be interested or that it would come off as bragging. I thought that was then, and this is now, and it was time to move on. I doubt that a dozen people outside the family know my history.

I was drawn back into my past when Dennis Dunaway was writing his book, *Snakes! Guillotines! Electric Chairs!* He contacted me to ask if I could remember particular events from the time I worked for the group. When Dennis's book came out, I read it, and it took me back in time. Through his stories, I started to relive the past. I began to remember more and more things. The further I read, the more I remembered. I recalled events that weren't in his book and additional details to stories that were. In short, Dennis's book made me think about the past. Memories that had lain dormant in my brain for more than fifty years were now back in the forefront.

And I started to enjoy thinking about those times.

Taken at the World Premiere Live at the Astroturf, Alice Cooper
April 4, 2019

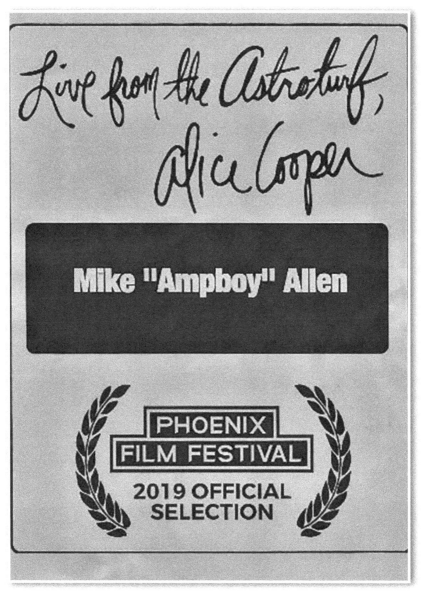

My seat holder at the Premiere

The second thing that happened was at the world premiere of *Live from the AstroTurf, Alice Cooper*. Dennis had invited me and my wife to attend the movie and, in a word, it was terrific. It won Best Short Documentary at the Phoenix Film Festival. It seemed, after all the years that had passed, the original band members really enjoyed playing together again, and it showed on screen.

After the movie, Dennis introduced me to two individuals, Paul Brenton and his wife Kendall, who were self-proclaimed keepers of the history of the Alice Cooper group. I stood outside the movie theater for close to an hour while they asked all sorts of questions about the early years of the band. The entire time I wondered why these people wanted to talk to me about my history with the Alice Cooper group. With each story I told, they said, "I didn't know that happened. You need to write this down." They even asked me sign their copies of Dennis's book as Mike "Amp Boy" Allen.

"You don't want me to autograph these books," I said.

"Yes, we do. You are part of the history of the group."

I was taken aback. "I'm not part of the history of the group. The band made history, not me."

"You were mentioned in Dennis's book a number of times. Please sign our books. And tell us more stories."

I signed their copies feeling self-conscious and went on to recount more of my experiences until my voice started to give out.

They kept repeating, "These stories are great!"

The third reason for writing the book was a funeral. My wife's uncle had died, and relatives came from out of state to attend the service. The evening before the service, we invited the family to our house to relax, get together, and share a meal. After the funeral, we gathered one last time for dinner and to decompress from the day's events.

We reminisced about the family and our youth, and then my wife's cousin Ray asked the question.

"Who here worked for a band?" Sheepishly, I raised my hand.

"What was that like?" he asked.

Normally, I would have said it was okay without much detail. We traveled around, saw some things, and met some people, but this time I didn't. Everyone wanted something to take their minds off the day's events, so I told them stories of working for the Alice Cooper group.

After an hour of storytelling, one of my wife's brothers, Danny, spoke.

"I've known you for more than forty years, and this is the first I've ever heard these."

"It was a long time ago. I didn't think anyone would want to hear stories about a band from years ago," I replied.

"You're wrong. This is music history. You know about and remember the history of one of the most famous rock bands ever, practically from the beginning of their existence. You just didn't know the significance of it at the time. You experienced it with the band, literally as it happened. Lots of people would want to hear these stories. You need to write this down. You need to write this stuff down."

I then told them about meeting the Brentons at the Alice Cooper premiere of Live from the AstroTurf.

"See, people want to know these things. You need to write the stories down," Danny said again.

Four months later, I thought, *why not?*

And that's just what I did.

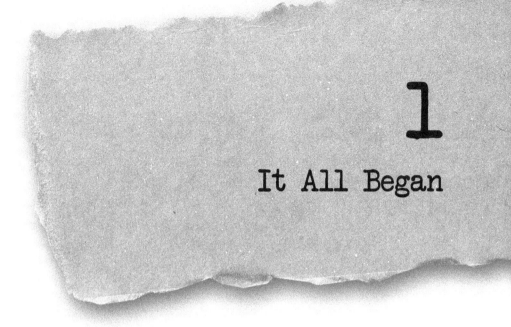

1

It All Began

Glen Buxton. He got me my job with The Spiders, who became The Nazz and later Alice Cooper.

Hold on there. Don't you think you should tell people a little something about yourself first, leading up to starting to work for the band? my inner voice asked.

"Okay, but why?"

So, they might get an understanding of what makes you, you.

"I don't even know what makes me, me! I guess it would be experiences and how I dealt with those experiences."

Exactly. Tell the people about some of those experiences.

With that I started to type.

My Story

My father was from Mississippi and had a career as a Marine. My mother was a housewife from North Dakota. The day I was born, Dad decided to go duck hunting near Escondido, California. Mom went along with him, she said, to retrieve the ducks, and so did I.

When she went into labor, my dad hadn't gotten his limit. Along with that, he was disappointed my mother couldn't hold off so I would be born on the Anniversary of the Marine Corps, which was only two days away. But I was having none of that. I wanted out, and I wanted out now! No amount of my father's pleading, "if you could just wait a couple more days," was going to change anything. Despite not getting his limit of ducks and not having me born on the Marine Corps anniversary, my dad, forced by urgent circumstances, gave in, and off to the hospital we all went.

I was their only child. I like to think they stopped at perfection: me. I'm going to stick with that answer. Dad swore my very first words were "pressure cooker." I was either a very gifted baby, or I just didn't speak until I was ten.

Yes, that's me in 1947 at four months with my gallant father and stalwart mother, and the radio operator who's attempting to teach me how to make a wireless call across the world. You can see why my parents stopped with just me. I was perfect. I eventually grew out of those cheeks.

In the 1950s, my dad was assigned to a duty station in Virginia. We lived in base housing, as was common. One of the greatest days on base that military kids and parents looked forward to was the arrival of the DDT sprayers. Once a month in spring and summer the military would fog the base for bugs. In today's world, spraying a neighborhood with a poison like DDT would make people duct tape their windows and retreat to a safe room, not to mention call the authorities! Life was much simpler back then.

We could hear the tractor coming, pulling its 60-gallon tank with two magic nozzles protruding from the sides that made those wonderful clouds of poison. Every kid and adult on the block ran to the door to witness the wondrous sight.

Parents, instead of recoiling in horror, said, "Why don't you go out and play in the fog?"

And every kid in the neighborhood ran joyously behind the tractor that sprayed white clouds of DDT over everything and everyone.

I'm sure you're thinking, *Wait a minute! Parents told you to go out and play in the DDT spray?*

At the time it was thought that DDT wasn't harmful to humans or animals, only bugs. Nobody ever considered there just might be a correlation between killing bugs and other living, breathing things.

We fastened towels on as capes and we were Superman flying through the clouds, or played at war, on our bellies inching our way through the fog ready to attack the enemy. My dad even found a military gas mask that I ran around in the spray with. That may actually have saved my life. As an added bonus, the dogs would frolic in the fog with us, and unsurprisingly they wouldn't have ticks! There was just a small problem: the dogs were dying way too young. Nobody could ever figure out why. I don't think the DDT clouds had much effect on me, except I can't do simple math.

When I was in the six and seventh grades, my dad was transferred to a hazardous-duty station overseas. This meant no wife and no children. My mother and I packed up our belongings and moved into her parents' home in North Dakota. For the next two years we lived in the small town of Lidgerwood, population 1000. Lidgerwood was a typical farming town located in the southeast corner of North Dakota. It had four churches and four bars, a bowling alley, a bank, a grocery, a movie theater, other businesses necessary to basic survival, and requisite for a farming town, a railroad track and grain elevators.

The house was a tiny one-bedroom asphalt shingle-sided structure. The shingles slightly resembled gray stone blocks. Mom and I used the screened-in front porch as a bedroom. Every child should grow up in a small farm town in North Dakota. Living there taught me self-reliance, a work ethic, appreciation of nature, survival skills, not to take farmers for granted, and most important of all to wear two pairs of socks in the winter.

I fished and hunted. I skated, rode my bike all over town and down county roads, and joined a bowling team. Lidgerwood had a pretty good baseball team for a small town. I played catcher, first base, or second base. I also took piano lessons from a lady down the street.

My grandfather taught me to drive his 1951 stick-shift Crosley station wagon. Sometimes he let me drive him to work. I had three jobs for spending money. One was "picking rocks" off farmland before plowing—I don't recommend that as a career move. I also worked at my grandfather's Skelly gas station cleaning up and pumping gas, and then I stocked shelves and delivered orders on my bike for tips at my uncle's Red Owl grocery store. I even got to run the cash register on occasion.

One day two strangers came into the Red Owl. I knew they were strangers because they weren't wearing jeans or overalls. As they approached, I recognized them: they were Yogi Berra and Mickey Mantle. I was so shocked to see them that I hid in the back of the store. They were my gods. I followed the Yankees religiously.

They called out, "Anybody here?"

I was frozen in place, mouth hanging open, unable to make a sound. The only thing better would have been if Roger Maris had strolled in with them. My uncle Fritz came out from the back room and gave them directions to the farm they were looking for.

I asked him, "Do you know who these guys are?"

"They look familiar," he said, as he watched them getting into their car.

"That was Mickey Mantle and Yogi Berra!"

"They seemed nice" was his reply. Such was life in a small Midwest farm town.

Red Owl in Lidgerwood, N.D. circa 1960

The sixth and seventh grades were taught in a single classroom at the same time. Besides the usual curriculum, the program included lessons on farming. Joining 4 H, which I did, got you extra credit. We learned about crops and crop rotation, the best price to get for soybeans and corn, and what kind of cow is the best for milking. For your information, it's a Holstein, and no other answer will suffice. If somebody walks up to you and tells you the Guernsey is a better milking cow, smile and just walk away. We also learned about the best breed for a laying hen. Now, this subject can cause a deep division in families because everybody has their favorite. Discussing the best laying chicken was akin to discussing politics or religion. For your own knowledge, the best laying chicken is a Leghorn. Some people may say they prefer the Rhode Island Red, but what do they know?

After North Dakota, my dad's next duty station was Camp Lejeune, North Carolina, outside of Jacksonville. I lived and went to school on base. On weekends and all summer, I worked for tips as a pinsetter at the base bowling alley. It must have been that North Dakota work ethic kicking in. This was long before the age of automatic pin setting machines.

A job as a pinsetter should have qualified for hazard pay. The pinsetter had to be smart and quick, dodging flying pins and bowling balls while setting up for the next frame. On the other hand, if he survived, a kid could walk out of the bowling alley with five to eight dollars in his pocket. Being that the average minimum wage back then was a little over a dollar an hour, that was big money, and it was all cash. If you worked on a league night, the sky was the limit. In one night, you could make enough money to buy a bike.

On those nights, the air hung heavy with cigarette smoke and the smell of beer—lots of beer, testosterone, and the spirit of competition. Seeing which team wore the loudest bowling shirts was a large part of the night's entertainment. Two five-man teams bowled three games on league nights, which made for a very good payday. The bowlers would slide a fifty-cent piece, along with any other change they had in their pocket, and the occasional set of car keys, down the alley for the pinsetter. Did I fail to mention the abundance of drinking? It was extra exciting when I'd find dollar bills stuffed into the finger holes of a bowling ball that had been sent down the alley at the end of a full night of drinking.

Occasionally, my mother would open the desk drawer in my bedroom to find lots and lots of money in change and dollars bills.

Surprised, she'd ask, "Where did you get all that money?"

I told her and she was relieved. She hoped I hadn't held up a liquor store. Every few weeks Mom would take me to the bank and I'd put all the money in my savings account. I guess that was a good idea, but I did enjoy looking at it in the desk drawer.

"We can come to you for a loan and get better interest rates," my dad joked when he found out.

Eyeing him I'd answer, "Don't be too sure of that."

At any base, the thing about the Marines is that they may be the best fighting force in the world, but they can't hide anything from 12-to-14-year-old boys. The Marines held maneuvers in the woods behind our base housing. At the end of the day, the neighborhood kids went to ferret out where the troops had hidden their equipment and supplies. We'd lug the treasure back to our houses. The very next day my dad, along with all the other dads, would pile it all in their cars and lug it back. Some of the booty was ammo boxes filled with rifle and machine-gun ammunition, all blanks of course, field phones, dummy hand grenades, medical supplies, and K-rations, which are whatever stuff you can put in a green can. The bacon was mostly fat, the stew was passable, and the pudding was good depending on what flavor you got. The fruitcake could double as a hand grenade. It was heavy and eating it was unpleasant.

The only bad experience I had at Camp Lejeune was the day I blew myself up while playing in the woods. Being the curious and inventive kid I was, I had emptied a bunch of gunpowder from ammunition I'd found into a glass bottle and screwed the lid on it. Then, I built a fire, put the bottle with the powder on it, and hid behind a tree with our dog Rex, who would accompany me when I went to the woods, and any place else for that matter.

Rex was a very large and intimidating German Shepherd, and he was a good companion. My dad sometimes took him to his office where Rex would lay hidden under his desk. When someone came into the office and saluted him, a low, deep growl was heard. This always caused great fear in the person doing the saluting and amused Dad greatly.

Sorry, back to the gunpowder story. After a while I grew impatient and walked back to the fire with the bottle of gunpowder sitting in it. I started to put out the fire, crouching down to throw dirt on it, when the bottle suddenly exploded, enveloping me in smoke and fire. Pieces of broken glass peppered my face and chest. I smelled my hair burning and slapped it out with my hands. I was almost blinded by the blood running down my face into my eyes. The dog was going crazy barking and jumping around. He seemed quite prepared to knock me down and drag me home. Sometimes when we played, I pretended to be injured and would fall down. Rex would run to me and push me over on my side and grab my pant leg and yank me toward the house.

I ordered Rex to go home. I held onto his thick coat as he walked a few steps. I followed him, he walked up some more, and I would follow him again. It was slow going. When I finally reached the house, I went through the back door into the kitchen. My mom was at the stove with her back to the door. Hearing me come in, she turned.

Startled she said, "What did you do?"

I muttered that I would be fine and just needed to lie down.

"You're going right to the hospital!" she said.

She wrapped my face in a towel so I wouldn't bleed all over the car's upholstery. Mom was practical even in an emergency. At the base hospital, I was taken into the ER where a nurse unwrapped the towel from my face and assessed the damage.

In a calm, professional voice the nurse said, "Doctor, can you come over here and look at this?"

He walked to the bedside and in a not too professional voice said, "Jesus Christ! What the Hell did you do to yourself?"

I was taken straight to the operating room where somebody asked if I'd had anything to eat. That was very nice, but I really wasn't hungry. The person said it was time to take a nap. I couldn't have agreed more. It was during this nap-time that they attempted to sew my face back together.

In the meantime, my dad had come home from work and probably said the usual, "What's for dinner?" He walked into the kitchen expecting to find my mom at the stove. Instead, what he saw was blood everywhere and the dog that was still going crazy. Dad ran through the house searching for us, then drove to the hospital, where he found us in the recovery room. My mom told him what happened and to take it easy on me—I had been through a lot. He did.

A few days later I was back at the doctor's because I still couldn't see out of my left eye and there was a scratching pain every time I blinked. The doctor asked what the problem was. I told him.

"Let's have a look," he said.

He shined a bright light in my eye and muttered, "Oh darn!" (I cleaned that up for the children), which was not encouraging to me or to my dad. The doctor looked very concerned.

He said, "There's a sliver of glass that goes from your pupil to the back of your eye, and it's very close to causing a rupture. It has to come out before permanent damage is done."

He called more people into the room, put me in a rigid chair with my head in some sort of metal contraption where I could rest my jaw and strapped my forehead to it. "Don't move your head," he repeated over and over again.

His hands rested on the bar in front of my face as he squirted a liquid from a small bottle into my eye. It made my eye burn. He put something under my eyelid to keep me from blinking and reached in with an instrument to remove the shard of glass. My dad said the doctor's hands were shaking after he finished. The doctor told me I was very lucky, I could have easily lost my eye. It seemed that the shard of glass was literally resting on the back of my eye. If it had continued through, let's just say it would not have been good.

All in all, everything worked out fine. I received a lot of attention at school with all my facial stitches and the eye patch and burnt hair, and I even got to tell my story in class. Before I began however, the teacher pointed out to the class that, "This is an example of what not to do in the woods."

In 1963, I was sixteen and my dad retired to Phoenix, Arizona after the military. I finished my last two years of high school there. On weekends I worked at Cactus Stables in Sunnyslope saddling horses, cleaning up after the horses, grooming, and riding them. Again, it must be that North Dakota work ethic.

I also devoted some of my time to trying to impress girls. I even wrestled a bear once in an attempt to impress one. Yes, it was a real full-size bear. It was for a promotion in Phoenix for a local car dealership. Wrestle a bear, pin it down, and win a car, or wrestle it for ten minutes and win one hundred dollars. That was a nice chunk of change back then. I took the girl I wanted to impress to watch someone wrestle the bear.

"Okay," she said, "Maybe someone will get hurt."

I hope not, I thought.

At the dealership a crowd had gathered, but nobody was wrestling the bear. Maybe everyone who already wrestled it had been taken away in an ambulance. I sized up the bear, which didn't look that big. It was on all fours and pacing. He had a muzzle on, which was reassuring, and had padded covers on its feet.

"I'll wrestle the bear," I volunteered.

The crowd cheered. I don't know which of us the crowd was cheering for, me or the bear. The girl I brought mouthed, "Are you nuts?"

I paid the five-dollar fee and signed numerous forms affirming that I was making this choice with a sound mind and wouldn't hold anyone responsible in the unlikely (or maybe likely) event something happened to me. I figured the papers wouldn't be legal because I wasn't 21. The joke's on them. Not to brag, but I was six-foot-five and had played a little high school football and basketball. Although I was still pretty much a stick-figure at 185 pounds, I believed I had a height advantage and calculated if he walked on all fours I could grab a paw, lift it up and out, turn him on his back to pin him, and drive away with a car and a very impressed girl. I could already hear her exclaiming, "My hero!"

The owner of the bear took me inside the metal fence to the middle of the ring. He said he wanted a good clean fight. I hoped the bear was listening. He told me to wait for the bell.

"Most importantly," the bear's owner said, "don't hit the bear. He doesn't like that."

That sounded like a good thing to know. Fact is, I could use that phrase as a mantra on how to live my life. The bell rang, and to my surprise the bear stood up, straight up. He was more than six feet of thick brown fur, muscle, and bone. He looked me over making a quick appraisal, dismissing me instantly as a capable adversary, it seemed. It turned out that not only was he was taller than I was, but he had at least 200 plus pounds on me. To make matters worse, when he put his front paws on my shoulders to steady himself, my knees buckled and I almost went to the ground. It took a tremendous effort, but I straightened myself up.

The crowd was cheering, though I still didn't know for which of us. Stepping to the side of the bear, I put one arm underneath his front leg, and my other arm around his neck. My plan was to pull him over and onto his back. We looked like we were buddies posing for a photograph. Using all my strength, I tried to pull him backward, but the bear was not budging. He looked distracted, like he was thinking about something else, then he decided to go back down on all fours. The unexpected movement sent me tumbling to the ground. The crowd cheered. I now understood which of us they were rooting for. Log-rolling myself across the ring, I felt something wet. To this day I hope it was just water. I got up on one knee, trying to catch my breath. The bear was heading for me. He moved more quickly than before. I stood up just before he hit me from behind, knocking my legs out from under me and pushing me to the ground. He lumbered over and sat on my legs.

It was over. I had lost. As I left the ring, the bear got his reward for this five-minute rumble, a large bottle of Coke. He laid on his back, held the bottle with all four paws, and poured the soda into his mouth. I thought at least I had impressed the girl, but it did me no good.

On the way home she said, "You need to take a shower. You smell bad."

I guess I didn't impress her as much as I'd hoped.

The next girl I hoped to make an impression on at least didn't involve putting myself in mortal danger. I invited a girl to ride in the Phoenix Rodeo Parade. What girl didn't like horses? This one didn't, but she liked the idea of being seen by thousands of people lining the street. Also, it was being televised, so a lot more people would be watching.

On the day of the parade, I had two horses brought down from the stable—a flashy Pinto for me, and a horse that had one speed—walk—for her. It was oblivious to anything and everything. She thought she would look better on the Pinto and said so.

I said, "That might be a bad idea." She ignored me.

I had picked the horse especially for her. I didn't tell her it would walk through a wall of fire without a care in the world.

I wore a pair of pressed jeans—I preferred Levis over Wranglers—and a starched white shirt and cowboy hat and boots and a borrowed a pair of chaps. For extra effect, I had a six-shooter strapped to my leg, and a 30/30 Winchester in a scabbard on the saddle. The girl wore an outfit you might wear to the Grand Ole Opry: a white hat and a rhinestone and fringed shirt with embroidered flowers, tight jeans, and what I believe were a pair of white go-go boots. She was a big hit. People lining the sidewalks waved, and I smiled and waved back. They would yell, "Not you. I'm waving at the girl."

After the parade was over, she thanked me and rode off into the proverbial sunset. Actually, her parents picked her up and drove her home. She called later and told me that all her friends had seen her on TV and said she looked great.

So much for my dating life.

2

Then There Was Glen Buxton

Glen, he got me the job with the Spiders, who became The Nazz and then Alice Cooper.

I first met Glen at Glendale Community College in Glendale, Arizona. The college was definitely not named after Glen. We were taking the mandatory freshman classes until we could decide what we wanted to do with our lives. I didn't have a clue, and Glen was just going through the motions. Between classes and after school we'd go to his parent's house to listen to music, and he would play his guitar. He had his Gretsch guitar plugged into a bunch of tubes and wires that were stuck inside his nightstand, with more wires running to a speaker without its box. I was amazed at the setup.

I asked him, "Did you make that?"

"Yes, I did," he said coolly.

Later, I learned it was just an old AM receiver without the case, and he had plugged his guitar into the microphone jack.

He told me he was in a band and hoped it would lead to something in the future.

"That would be great. I could say I knew you when," I said.

I asked him who his favorite group was. He said his favorite group wasn't a group; it was a person, and that person was Chet Atkins.

"Chet Atkins, the country guitar player?" I asked.

Glen nodded. "Yes, he is the best guitar player I've ever heard."

He put an Atkins's record on the machine, playing along on his guitar, stopping every once in a while, to mutter to himself, "How does he do that?"

I said, "He does have a certain style."

"Yes, he does. And the ability and talent to play rock and roll, or any style, and blow every guitar player away, too," Glen replied.

I had no means to argue that fact, because he was probably right. I recently saw a video of Chet Atkins playing "Dixie" and "Yankee Doodle Dandy" at the same time. It was pretty amazing.

We continued to see each other, going to classes, listening to music, and generally just hanging out. One day he asked me what type of car I drove. It was a funny question because for a month I had driven him everywhere. We almost got in an accident once when another car ran a red light. We actually may have been in an accident, but didn't notice because the car was built like a tank. It was a 1960 Plymouth Fury station wagon painted Earl Scheib blue, because Earl Scheib painted it blue. He would paint any car for $19.95.

I asked him, "Why the interest in the car?"

"The band is starting to get noticed, and we're lining up jobs at the VIP Club on weekends," he said. "We also hope to start playing in Tucson and we need someone to drive our equipment and us around. If we can fit in your car, you can set up our equipment, take it down, and drop us off at our houses."

I shrugged. "And that's all?" I said with a hint of sarcasm.

"Yes, and we can pay you. We've changed our name to The Spiders from The Earwigs."

I thought that was a good choice. Anything would be better than The Earwigs.

The Earwigs were a little before my time. It all started with a few guys wanting to be in a talent show at Cortez High School in Phoenix. Vince Furnier and Dennis Dunaway recruited Glen Buxton, who was the only one who knew how to play an instrument. John Tatum and John Speer joined them. Vince, Dennis, and John Speer donned cheap Beatle wigs, but they could not convince the cooler Glen or John Tatum to put one on. They caught the band bug, no pun intended, after receiving a standing ovation for their performance, which consisted of singing Beatle songs with made up lyrics about Cortez High School and the people who worked there. They were "Weird Al" before there ever was a "Weird Al."

Photo by Scott Ward courtesy Jane Ward

Vince and Dennis liked what they saw and heard and asked the others to form a real band. This was the beginning of something that was going to be remarkable. The birth of what was to become the Alice Cooper Group.

Photo by Scott Ward courtesy Jane Ward

Dennis tells a story about one the Earwig's first paying gigs. They weren't to be paid in money but in pizza. To five teenage boys, that's the equivalent of being paid in gold. The pizza payment being offered was for "any kind you want, and as much as you can eat." They had hit the mother lode.

With thoughts of delicious, piping hot pizzas swirling in their minds, they showed up at Village Inn Pizza on Bethany Home Rd, next to the Bethany West Theater. A movie theater next door meant there was bound to be a good-size crowd for their show.

They saw the stage, such as it was, basically just a rectangular box raised off the floor, and decided it needed improving to make it more theatrical. They got busy building a tri-level stage by stacking beer kegs and benches. Vince and John Speer the drummer would be on the main stage, which was six inches off the floor. Glen and John Tatum were on opposite ends of the stage standing on benches that could have doubled as balance beams in gymnastics. Glen started out trying to balance himself on top of a beer keg and playing rock and roll all at the same time. He reluctantly gave the keg up for the relative safety of a bench. The stacked-up beer kegs were left there for show and to break their fall, if that were to happen. I don't know what Dennis was on top of, it was probably a table, but he should have been wearing a safety harness. He towered over John Tatum, who stood on his own bench, and his feet were higher than John Speer's head sitting at his drums. I'm sure of one thing: it wasn't safe.

The show went off without a hitch, except for a few balance issues, perhaps. Now, it was time for the big pizza payoff. Everybody had their order ready. The guy who made the pizzas was going to be quite busy. They expected the owner to congratulate the band on their set, except for one thing, he didn't. What he said was. "No pizza!"

It seemed one of the restaurant patrons didn't like the band's name. He complained it had made him nauseous so he couldn't enjoy his pizza and wanted his money back.

"That's his problem," Glen retorted.

The owner's response was, "No, it's your problem! No Pizza!"

He disappeared into his office. Glen tried to work out his frustration by attempting to tap into the beer keg he had previously been standing on, which would have been interesting to see if he had done it. Beer kegs are pressurized. If Glen had succeeded, he would have gotten all the beer he could drink and wear all at the same time.

A meeting was called and they decided to send in the band's two enforcers: Glen and John Tatum. They probably didn't weigh a hundred pounds between them. Neither had adopted the Beatle hair style yet. Their hair was Brylcreem-slicked back. The Brylcreem slogan was "A little dab will do you." Apparently, a lot would be so much better.

After some tense closed-door negotiations, the two emerged, triumphant grins on their faces. They would share one large pizza for the evening's work.

The pizza arrived at the table bubbling hot. Melted-mozzarella-burn-your-mouth hot. The kind of hot pizza that nobody, with the exception of John Speer, could touch, let alone eat. Therefore, John ate most of it before the others had a chance.

When the band had finished the pizza—sorry, when John had finished the pizza—they got their equipment and raised a ruckus as they exited the restaurant muttering things like, food poisoning, cockroaches, flies, Earwigs. They were never asked back.

John shared with me his secret to eating scalding hot pizza. Try this at your own risk. First, fold the pizza slice in half lengthwise, then wave it around for a few seconds. This allows the pizza to cool a little, and at the same time your mouth has time to fill up with saliva, or you could take a sip of soda and hold it in your mouth. Be careful not to spill the soda out of your mouth. Then, carefully insert as much pizza into your mouth as you can chew and swallow as quickly as possible. Sounds appealing, doesn't it? John's technique gave him a 3 to 1 slice advantage over the competition.

The moral of the story: Change the band's name to something more appealing, like The Spiders, that won't make people sick, and don't order pizza when John Speer is around.

Earwig tambourine painted by Vince
Courtesy Paul Brenton

Earwigs at their first show Cortez High School cafeteria
Photo by Scott Ward, courtesy Paul Brenton

The following photos by Scott Ward courtesy Jane Ward

Glen, John Tatum, Vince, Dennis

Dennis, Vince, John Tatum, Glen

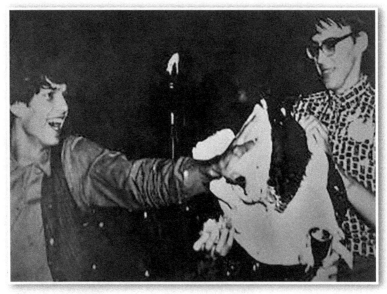

Dennis throwing a pie at John Speer, friend Ray Sadowski

John Speer, pie faced   Vince and John Tatum   Vince, Glen and Dennis

Vince

Now, back to how I was hired. Glen was really psyched about having an equipment guy, and I didn't want to dampen his excitement. I was flattered he wanted to include me in his dreams and work for the band.

I said, "Why don't we all sit down and talk about it?"

"Great!" Glen smiled at me. I didn't know if I should be happy or worried. "Tomorrow you'll meet the rest of the band at Christown for an interview. Can you pick me up?"

John Tatum, Vince Furnier, Dennis Dunaway, John Speer
VIP Club
Photo by Tom Buxton courtesy Janice Buxton Davison

The Interview

The following day, I picked Glen up and we headed to meet some Spiders, formerly the Earwigs, at Christown, which was the first enclosed air-conditioned shopping mall in Arizona. The Earwigs had won a "Battle of the Bands" at the mall a couple of months earlier and were awarded a loving cup for their effort. Emblazoned for all the world to see were the words "First Place, Combo Contest." The mall owners couldn't bring themselves to inscribe "Rock and Roll Band" on the trophy for fear of summoning the Devil, because he was deeply involved in destroying the youth of America with rock and roll music at the time.

When we entered the mall, Glen spotted the guys sitting on a bench, and we headed toward them. The band members were Vince Furnier (Alice in the future), Dennis Dunaway the bass player, and John Speer the drummer. I'm not sure if John was there. Introductions were made.

My first impression was these guys needed to eat something. Whatever expression you could come up with to say somebody was thin would apply to these guys: rails, sticks, twigs. I've seen shadows with more meat on their bones. I later learned Vince, John, and Dennis were track and field runners at Cortez high school. Go Colts! This calmed my fears of the starving artist syndrome. Vince asked the most questions.

The first one was, "What type of car do you own?"

I'm thinking, *Glen, don't you ever talk to these people?*

"I have a station wagon," I replied, glancing at Glen.

Well, my dad and I had a station wagon. My dad wanted a second car. He already had a nice 1957 Oldsmobile 98. I wanted a vehicle for myself, so I wouldn't have to borrow his all the time. His objective was to use the new car for hunting and fishing, and mine was to drive around and look cool. My dad said he'd handle everything—I would just have to hand over my share of the cost. I agreed. I was imagining myself cruising around town in something sleek and sporty. He was thinking about something he could throw a dead deer, ducks, or fish into.

What he eventually brought home was a dark blue 1960 Plymouth Fury station wagon in need of some love. My dream of picking up girls evaporated. The car was monstrous, all fins and chrome. It was probably the base model or a model under base. If there was such a thing, it was that one. He bought it for the princely sum of $300.00. He wanted to name it the Blue Goose. Secretly, I called it My Despair.

It was wide, long, and could just about fit in a space reserved for a Greyhound bus. A family of six could sleep comfortably on the two extremely large bench seats. There was more room than a New York City apartment and more glass than your typical house. It wasn't spacious; it was cavernous. A push-button transmission was mounted on the left side of the dash, which was great if you were left-handed. The AM radio only worked sporadically. To be honest, all AM radios at that time worked sporadically. The car, instead of having plush carpeting, had a floor lined with rubber. My dad was excited about that because he would be tossing dead animals on it. Under the rubber floor, the car had built-in vents that could be opened to hose down the interior—all the water would wash out through the vents. Perfect if you were cleaning up after a murder.

This car was like a person with a weak bladder—it wanted to stop at every gas station. Fuel at that time was an ungodly 32 cents a gallon. For the longest time I thought the gauge was broken, it sat on E constantly. I felt the only redeeming feature was the car had air conditioning. I mean, it had great air conditioning. It could easily cool a 4-bedroom house. With the exception of the air-conditioning, I intensely disliked my dad's choice, because it didn't fit my needs. I wanted something to look cool in. I didn't want to drive a bus.

The importance of that car is not lost on me. Even though I grudgingly accepted the vehicle as partially mine and eventually totally mine, it turned out to be the most consequential car I've ever owned. I literally owe the greatest adventure I ever lived to that big beautiful hunk of blue steel, for without it there would have been no adventure. It's amazing such a seemingly insignificant thing could change a life.

My dad told me, "That car isn't much, but it will get you where you want to go. And that's what is important." So true. So very true.

Dennis asked about my availability to work on weekends.

"That should not be a problem. I'm not working at present." They wanted to know what my last job was. "I worked at a riding stable, saddling horses, cleaning up after horses, etc." I believe these skills were not necessarily what they needed.

"Do you know anything about musical equipment?" Vince asked.

"Not a thing," I admitted.

"Well, you can show up at the VIP Club this weekend and we can show you," he said.

"Okay. I'll do that." I sounded more confident than I felt.

The interview was over. I got the job, I think, but did I really want the job? They talked about their hopes and dreams: they wanted to be the first group to have a hit record in Arizona. I didn't say anything about Marty Robbins, Duane Eddy, or Wayne Newton already having hit records, but the category was musical groups, not individual artists. They wanted to move to Los Angeles and sign a recording contract, make hit records, and live in a big house with a practice studio.

They had great plans. I hoped their dreams would come true for them. I liked these guys: Vince/Alice, Dennis, Glen. It was dream big or go home for them, and I could buy into that. They admitted why they wanted somebody to haul their equipment. It was because no other group in Phoenix at the time had somebody who did that, and they wanted to be the first.

I was their status symbol. Never in my wildest dreams did I think that I would be a status symbol. *I'm in*, I thought. As a plus, maybe

I could meet some girls. I'd heard girls went for guys in bands, and maybe they went for the people who worked for bands, too.

There was an idea, put forth by Vince, that the Plymouth should be called "The Spider Mobile." *You can call it whatever you want*, I thought. Dennis said something about painting webs on the car and a giant spider with fangs dripping blood. I intervened before they put it to a vote. I didn't want a bloodthirsty arachnid painted on my car, and I was pretty sure, 100% positive in fact, that my dad would share the same feeling.

"Why don't we hold off on that for a while," I said.

I saw the disappointment in their eyes. Despite the setback about painting the car, their excitement was contagious. They had me believing in them, that they might actually pull it off. If the music thing didn't work, they could have a future selling used cars. They had the dream. They had the desire.

All they needed were the breaks. But a lot of groups shared the same dream.

Courtesy Paul Brenton

Photos by Tom Buxton courtesy Janice Buxton Davison

Spiders with John Tatum at the VIP Club, Phoenix, AZ

Dennis and Glen

3
The Beginning

That weekend I went early to the VIP Club to see how the equipment was set up. It wasn't complicated since I didn't have to deal with a lot of microphones. I just had to place the equipment on the stage.

Facing the stage, Glen's amplifier was on my left. He had a Fender Deluxe and his beloved Chet Atkins Gretsch guitar that he alone touched. Four months after I started working for them he allowed me to carry it, but always within his sight.

Next would be Vince up front with a microphone. He needed a tambourine, maracas, and a harmonica, depending on the song.

John Speer on drums was directly behind Vince. He had a combination of Ludwig Drums and Rogers cymbal stands and Zildjian cymbals. He liked Rogers' stands because they were sturdier and had heavier bases with better locking mechanisms.

John imagined himself a ladies' man and was always after girls. There was talk that he would sneak into the ladies' bathroom at the VIP Club, and likely others, and write on the bathroom walls. Clever things like, "John Speer is good in the sack" or "John Speer is a good lay." It pays to advertise, I guess. The girls who frequented the bathroom might have caught on, because underneath his scribbling someone had written, "John has the clap" and "John has crabs."

Or had they? It was rumored, but never proven, that his fellow band members might have dissed him as a joke.

In any normal conversation, John liked to insert cuss words for effect or to punch up a story to give it more gravitas. Whenever this girl, Ellen, who was gorgeous and way out of my league, was there, John always apologized for swearing in front of her, because in those days she was a shy and reserved teen. I guess he thought she'd be embarrassed. Instead, she thought it was cute when he apologized, but never said so.

Then, there was Dennis Dunaway on bass. He had a Fender Bassman amplifier head with a Fender speaker cabinet. He played an Airline bass guitar, purchased at Montgomery Ward, which he would decorate from time to time.

Dennis proved to be my problem child on stage. Glen stood within a 4-foot radius of his amplifier. Vince would go as far as the microphone cord let him. John sat on a stool behind his drums. Dennis, on the other hand, liked to travel across the stage, into the crowd, outside to check if he'd left the lights on in his car. He would test the tensile strength of each and every cord I gave him. I traveled with two types of guitar cords: ones that needed repair, and ones that were going to need repair. I would splice two or three cords together, but that just encouraged him to see what was going on down the street. I bought solder in bulk. I briefly considered putting wheels on his amplifier so he could drag it with him.

Come to think of it, Vince was hard on his harmonicas, too. He preferred the Hohner harmonica, particularly the Marine Corps Band model. I'm sure the Marines appreciated his patronage, and might have hired Vince as their spokesperson if only they had known.

Instead of setting the harmonica gently down somewhere, he would throw it onto the stage floor and end up stepping all over it. After Vince located the harmonica on the floor, he wiped it on his shirt or pants, whichever was the cleanest, and brought it to his mouth and started to play. At least he wasn't afraid of germs. I found a nice little wicker basket for him to keep his harmonicas and maracas in. It lasted one night before Vince destroyed it during the show. Old habits die hard.

When a harmonica went bad, it was always the C-reed. Why just the C-reed? Maybe every reed in a harmonica is a C-reed…I didn't have a clue.

I began acting like an umpire in a ball game. When the pitcher did not like a certain baseball, he tossed it to the catcher. The catcher would give it to the umpire who put it in his pocket. Sometime during the game, the umpire would throw the same ball out to the pitcher, the pitcher would throw it, and it would be just fine. I tried this technique with Vince and the harmonicas many times—sometimes it worked, and sometimes it didn't.

The rhythm guitar player would be next to Dennis, only there was not one. John Tatum had left the group. This was throwing off my learning process. Glen said a few guitar players were coming down to try out for the band. How was this going to impact the group, and even me for that matter?

Several people auditioned and a unanimous decision was made: the multi-talented Mike Bruce would be the new rhythm guitar player. He started out playing a Gretsch guitar like Glen's, except his was orange. Later, he would switch over to a Gibson SG, the same color as Glen's Gretsch guitar. He changed his amplifier to a Fender Deluxe amp like Glen's and, being the same size, it was easy to pack in the Plymouth. Mike could sing and harmonize, which was another plus. He could also play the piano, which was a bonus for versatility, but a negative for me if I had to haul a piano around.

Visually, Mike was another thing altogether. Most of the band were on the lean side and hadn't seen the sun for a while, if ever. Mike Bruce, on the other hand, looked like he could be a fullback on a football team, and he had a deep tan.

The important thing was that once again the group was complete, and all that lay ahead were fame and fortune. I wondered if now would have been a good time to ask, "What are you going to pay me?"

Glen and I started going out on dates. Let me rephrase that. Glen went on dates with girls, and I would come along. For some unknown reason, he'd arrange with his current girlfriend to bring a younger or older sister, or a girlfriend of hers to be my date. I didn't mind. Since becoming associated with the band, I wasn't having any problems getting girls to go out with me. There was even a girl who would call me up at 2:00 in the morning to chat, which was kind of embarrassing since the phone on that side of the house was in my parent's bedroom. My dad would yell to me to come to his room, or he'd come into mine.

"Some girl is very excited to talk to you," he'd say.

My side of the conversation was usually brief, filled with one-word sentences. "Yes," "OK," "Great," and ending with, "Thanks for calling."

After hanging up, I'd hear dad muttering, "Do you think she could call later on in the day?" or "You're not much of a conversationalist."

I can think of no rational reason why Glen would want to fix me up with girls for his dates. There were a few possibilities, though. Either it was because I did most of the driving, probable, or because Glen was afraid of the girl he was going out with, improbable. The girl might have been afraid to go out alone with Glen, also probable. Maybe the parents didn't want their daughter going out alone with Glen, highly probable.

This double-dating scenario only lasted a few months. The end coincided with the time we started going down to Tucson on a regular basis. It was fun while it lasted.

Spiders with Michael Bruce
Photo by Tom Buxton courtesy Janice Buxton Davison

Wallace and Ladmo

The Spiders were in a local stage production of *Bye Bye Birdie* starring Jan Murray as the father.

They were Conrad Birdie's backup band. Doing the play ignited the idea of having a more theatrical presence, and they began using various props hoping to make the shows more interesting and entertaining, or at least make the audience curious about what was going on. At the VIP Club, they used props like rope spider webs, pieces of fencing, tires, and whatever could be dragged in from behind the building, and there were go-go girls. Those were nice touches.

One-night Toodie Mueller, a good friend of the band and myself who figured prominently in our lives, had the idea to apply fluorescent paint to their faces. When a black light was turned on, the effect was quite dramatic and shocking at the same time, and it had a nice effect on the audience, too. Was this stuff toxic? Probably, but who knew or cared? Just look at the crowd's reaction: they were wild.

There was even the occasional toilet that I'd set on the stage, and the band would throw full and half full rolls of toilet paper from it into the audience. I was very relieved that no one ever attempted to use the toilet during the show. I would pick up a roll of TP when I needed to use the restroom, because I knew where it had come from. Sometimes a TV, probably tuned to the *Wallace and Ladmo Show*, was brought out on stage.

The Wallace and Ladmo Show was a Phoenix television institution for thirty-five years. The Spiders were invited to the show several times as guests. Initially, the show was geared toward entertaining children, with cartoons as the main feature. But as the show grew in popularity, and cast members were added, it became more sophisticated, drawing a larger and older audience.

Teenagers and adults became huge fans due to its often irreverent and timely social commentary.

The show regularly featured props and skits with a variety of oddball characters. Vince and the rest of the band watched and learned. The antics were really funny, and the cartoons weren't bad either. The Spider's favorite was "Roger Ramjet."

A Ladmo Bag, which was a paper grocery bag filled with toys and candy, was awarded to one lucky guest, usually a kid, every show. The bags were highly prized, and even today when the *Wallace and Ladmo Show* is spoken of, recipients proudly retell their own story of receiving one. On the 35th anniversary show Ladmo handed Alice a coveted Ladmo Bag.

During the final show in 1989, Ladmo presented Wallace with the very last Ladmo Bag. After the show ended, two plays were written and performed at a local theater. During one performance, Alice popped up as a celebrity guest in a "time machine" skit.

One of Vince's stage props was a book, but not just any book. During a song, he would stop and grab a Catholic Missal or a Gideon Bible and, in a fire and brimstone preacher's voice, he read passages from the book. When he finished, he slammed the book down on the floor or a table with such a force that people in the audience jumped in surprise, or was it alarm? Great, now we're all going to Hell! Just remember, God, it wasn't me who threw down the book. It was Vince, the son of a preacher.

Note to self: don't stand too close to Vince during the show.

Glen Buxton, Dennis Dunaway, John Speer,
Vince Furnier, Michael Bruce
Photo by Tom Buxton courtesy Janice Buxton Davison

I Almost Quit

Everything was going well. Setting up at the VIP Club was easy. They could practice there if they wanted, and I could leave everything set up for the show on the following weekend. They weren't quite the house band just yet, but they were getting there.

Two things happened during this time. The first was Vince started calling me "Amp Boy." I thought it was because he wouldn't have to remember my name or get me confused with Mike Bruce. Then a lot of people started calling me by that name.

The second thing was they booked their first job outside the VIP Club at the Red Dog Saloon. Most of the time, the Red Dog Saloon was a western-themed bar in Scottsdale, Arizona, which called itself "The West's Most Western Town." The place came complete with a wooden bar and a naked lady painting. Once or twice a month on a Friday, they would turn the bar into a place where teens could dance. The liquor was locked up and the naked lady painting was covered with a sheet.

On a side note, one night we all snuck into a porno, I mean an art movie, near the Red Dog Saloon in Scottsdale. The movie was called *Stewardesses*, and was in 3D, and was quite an eyeful. The fact that we were all underage made it all the more exciting. Back to the story, lest I bore you talking about a movie filled with lots of naked women all in 3D.

The Spiders were booked to play at the Red Dog Saloon. This was my first big test, and I was ready. Arriving two and a half hours early, I walked inside. The staff was busy moving tables and chairs off the dance floor and covering up the naked lady. I asked where the stage was, thinking that it must be in the back of the building. They pointed straight up behind me. I turned around and looked up to see a platform located above the double front door. It was what I can best describe as something a window washer would use on a high-rise. A ladder bolted to the wall led up to a trapdoor on the underside of the stage, which was about nine feet above the floor. *What the ......?*

I asked the bartender, "How do you get musical equipment up there?"

"You bring more people," he answered wryly.

Very funny, I thought. Undaunted, I unloaded the equipment from the Plymouth and studied the situation and came up with a plan. I took the smaller pieces like the drums, cymbals, stands, Dennis's bass head, cords, harmonicas, tambourines, and things like that up first. For the larger and heavier pieces, I hauled them one at a time up the ladder, hoisting myself up the ladder with one arm while holding onto whatever I was carrying with the other. I lifted the piece through the trapdoor onto the stage floor and shoved it away from the opening. Finally, I just had the amps to bring up. I dragged a tall table and a chair underneath the trap door, put the chair on the table, and pushed it next to the ladder. I put Glen's amp on the chair and climbed the ladder through the trap door. Lying on my stomach on the floor of the stage, I reached down and grabbed the handle that was attached to Glen's amp. The Fender Corporation must have foreseen this situation and thoughtfully provided a handle on the top of the amplifier. I guided the amp up the ladder and pulled it up through the opening. I followed the same procedure with Mike Bruce's amplifier. Dennis's amplifier was a little different. The speaker box was rectangular, and the handle was on the long side. I had to come up with something else for that.

By this time, the Saloon staff had stopped working and were watching intently as I struggled. They were taking bets to see if I was going to make it, fail, or die. I would have placed money on die.

I lifted Dennis's speaker box, tall side up, to the chair on top of the table, and tied one of his broken guitar cords that I had been meaning to fix to the handle. Once more, I climbed the ladder and went through the trap door pulling the speaker cabinet behind me as high as I could. Using one hand I grabbed onto the handle while with my other hand I steadied the box and scooted backward on my stomach until the cabinet was partly through the opening, then I grabbed the cord and dragged the amp onto the stage. Success! I rested for several minutes before setting up the equipment. When I finished I went down the ladder, and moved the table and chair back where they belonged.

I was drenched in sweat, which is quite common in Arizona. The bartender motioned me over and gave me a glass of Coke. I drank it, thanked him, and asked for a couple glasses of water and drank them both down.

The bartender remarked he had seen three guys struggle to do what I had just done by myself. He explained that the owner prohibited any of the staff from helping people with the equipment because of the liability issue. I said I understood.

Forty-five minutes before the saloon opened, the band arrived and looked up in disbelief at the stage.

"How did you get that equipment up there?" Dennis asked, craning his neck to see the stage.

"You'll find out when you're finished playing tonight," I said in a not-so-pleasant voice.

They all helped me take the equipment down after the show.

The following photos by Tom Buxton
courtesy Janice Buxton Davison

Dick Phillips, John Speer, Vince Furnier, Me
(partially hidden), Dennis Dunaway, Glen Buxton

Glen, Dennis (partially hidden by me), Vince, John, Michael

Glen, John, unknown girl, Vince, Michael, Me, Dennis

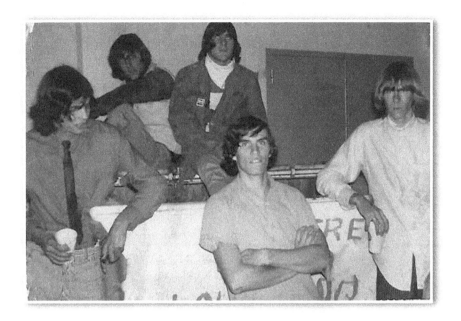

Tucson

The Spiders were becoming more successful. They were playing in
Tucson quite a lot, at least a couple weekends a month. Glen and I
would drive to Tucson on Friday night, leaving just before midnight,
because we'd found a motel that would let us stay through Sunday for
the price of one night. We would arrive at the motel around 2:00 a.m.
Saturday and check in. We stayed at the same motel most trips. The
location was off Speedway, the main cruising street in Tucson for teens.

The rooms, let's just say were not as clean as they could or should
have been, and the motel catered to a specific type of clientele. We
always hoped, and sometimes prayed, the bed sheets had at least been
washed. There was a paper tape around the toilet seat to convince
guests it had been sanitized, but we had our doubts. The paper tape
did look new, though. One thing about the motel, along with the
Gideon Bible, was that the rooms were stocked with a good supply of

well-used porno magazines. The magazines were a typical feature in many motels where we stayed. I guess that meant we were not staying at the best places in town.

Glen's standard reaction on entering the room was to take a deep breath and say, "Ah, just like home!"

Well, maybe your room, I thought. After a few hours of sleep, we would get up around 10:00 to see the sights and wait for the rest of the group to get into town, which was usually around 2:00 in the afternoon.

The road to Tucson from Phoenix was basically deserted at night, and it was an easy drive. You only had to watch out for the drunks and the crazies. We frequently stopped at the Stuckey's along the way. Stuckey's had a gas station, a restaurant, and most importantly a bathroom. Stuckey's was famous for its nut log roll. We never bought one. We would just get gas, a Coke, and some snacks before taking off. Two incidents happened on our drives to Tucson. One involved the Stuckey's and a tire, the other involved a ghost.

The first occurrence was when we saw a car had broken down on the side of the road. We stopped to see if we could help or at the very least take them to the Stuckey's, which was about eight miles away. The family looked warily at us. I told them who we were, that Glen was a musician, he was in a band called The Spiders, and we were heading to Tucson to play at a club the next night. The two children said they'd heard of them. One of them asked if I was in the band. I would get that a lot.

"No. I'm *with* the band," I said.

They looked puzzled. I would also get that look a lot. Glen told them that I was Amp Boy. This likely confused them more.

Their problem was that they had a flat tire, and there was no spare. I said, "It's possible my spare might work for you. The bolt pattern looks the same as I have on my Plymouth."

They had a Dodge, so maybe. I unloaded the equipment to get at the tire. My spare would work on the Dodge. Although my tire was bigger, the bolt pattern was the same. The driver put my spare on and removed the jack.

"How can we get your tire back to you?" he asked,

"There's a Stuckey's about eight miles down the road. We will meet you there and get the spare back, and somebody might be able to fix your flat."

"Great! We'll meet you there."

They headed out as we put the equipment back in the Plymouth. Arriving at Stuckey's to pick up my spare, we pulled into the parking lot and noticed that their car wasn't there. I drove around to the side and back to see if that was where they had parked. It wasn't. I walked over to the gas station to ask if a family with the two kids had gotten air in their tire or had gotten it fixed. The station attendant said nobody had come in to change a tire. It appeared they had just kept going. So much for helping people stranded in the desert. Live and learn. We never found them. At least I would have plenty of time to buy a tire while I was in Tucson.

The ghost was something neither Glen nor I could explain. I'm not quite a believer, but anything is possible, and I try to keep an open mind. Once again, we were headed to Tucson. As usual, I was driving and Glen was riding shotgun. We were a few miles south of Picacho Peak, about halfway between Phoenix and Tucson. An interesting fact about Picacho Peak is it was the site of the only Civil War battle fought in Arizona with loss of life.

It was around one in the morning when we saw something on the road ahead. It was sort of a gray mist that had a subdued light coming from it. I asked Glen what he thought it was.

"It looks like a man walking with a dog," he replied squinting to see better.

I thought that's what it looked like, too. It was sort of like when you look at fluffy clouds on a beautiful day. You can see all sorts of things in those clouds: animals, planes, ships. You see the shape but not any definition, and that was how it was with this. We didn't see a 6-foot-tall man in a gray suit with brown hair walking with a German Shepherd. We saw the shape of something that could be perceived as a man and a dog moving across the road before disappearing.

We tried to figure out what caused the image. There can be fog in the desert, but there was no fog. Light reflecting from somewhere else, or perhaps even a prank played on travelers by someone with a little bit too much time on their hands? The best non-spooky explanation we could come up with was a car on the side of the road had pulled back onto the highway leaving a dust cloud that was lit up by our headlights.

We knew what we saw, but we didn't know that what we saw was what we saw. I'm sure there was a logical explanation for it, but on the other hand, who knows? It's been said travelers encounter strange things in the desert at night.

Traveling to Tucson from Phoenix even though it's only a hundred miles could get pretty boring, with the exception of seeing ghosts and having your tire ripped off. Glen and I spent the time listening to Kriz or Krux, which were rivals on local Phoenix AM radio stations. That's right, FM hadn't been developed yet. We listened until the station faded away, which unfortunately was about thirty miles outside of Phoenix.

If we were lucky, we could listen to Wolfman Jack on a broadcast coming from Mexico, broadcasting literally over the entire country— no FCC regulations there. Actually, Wolfman recorded his shows in Los Angeles, and they were shipped to Mexico for broadcast. If I was not so lucky, Glen would do his own Wolfman Jack impersonation, and his version of the Wolfman seemed to go on and on forever.

When I was very lucky, Glen and I talked about music, and what songs the band should be playing. I know he wanted to do "19th Nervous Breakdown," by the Rolling Stones. After listening to his Wolfman Jack impersonation, I could relate to having one.

One time while driving to Tucson, he began talking about what he would do if the Spiders made it big.

"I'm going to get a chauffeur," he announced matter of factly.

"Really?" I said sarcastically, glancing sideways at him.

"Yes. He or she would pick me up—a girl driver would be nice, take me wherever I wanted to go, and then take me home. I don't like to drive that much," he explained.

"Really," I said again. This time it was not a question. My sarcasm had been lost on Glen.

"Yes. It would be great." Then, he caught on.

"Well, you're different," he said.

"How so?" I asked. I was very curious to hear his reason.

"I would have to pay her!"

"Maybe I'll apply for the job when it opens up. I have a lot of experience driving you around."

"That's true. But I really like the idea of a girl driver," he said, smiling.

Every once in a while, Glen wouldn't ride back with me to Phoenix from Tucson. His girlfriend Denise, who had gone to Tucson for the show, would drive him home. Why he would rather ride home with a cute girl instead of me I'll never know. Well, actually I do know. I would have done the same thing.

When Glen bailed on me, I picked up two new passengers, Mike Bruce and John Speer. Mike would spend the two-hour drive trying to teach us to harmonize to Beatles songs. I have to admit by the time we got to Phoenix we weren't bad, but we weren't that good either.

Tucson, to me, was this great strange exotic place. I was still a teen-
ager, and we were on our own: no parents, staying in a motel room
with porno magazines in the drawers. Going and doing whatever we
wanted. The good life.

The band played at several clubs and continued to build a following—I even had some fans. When I set up the equipment, I
heard shouted greetings of "Amp Boy!" I felt like the guy on Cheers
when everyone called his name as he walked through the door. It was
all good.

One time while in Tucson I tried an experiment. I was taking all
these psych classes in college, and I was going to see, even with my
minimal fame, if I could influence how people dressed. My usual
attire was nothing exciting: jeans, shirt or turtleneck, and a leather
jacket in cold weather. This night Glen had loaned me his blue corduroy cape with a black velvet collar. It was one of the band's outfits.
I wore black shoes that were called Beatle boots. I put a chrome chain
dog collar around one of the boots, and for no reason I put an orange
corduroy neck pillow on my left shoulder.

When we returned in two weeks, sure enough there were kids
in the audience with capes, dog chains fastened around their ankles,
and a few even had different variations of a pillow on their shoulder.
Even though I was only a few years older, at that moment I feared
for our youth.

I went back to my jeans and turtlenecks. Over the next few
months, I found the kids had given up wearing capes and neck pillows, but the dog chains around the boot seemed to have caught on.

One night at a club when the band was between sets, I was sitting
on the stage because it was very close in the small room where the
band was relaxing. Dennis's girlfriend came running up to me.

"Some guys are going to beat up Dennis. Hurry!" she cried.

I was thinking maybe I should get help but decided against it,
and instead told her to go. Outside, I found Dennis preparing to

fight six mean-looking guys. I hurried over to Dennis and said some-one inside needed to talk to him, then I herded him in the direction of the door.

I turned back to look at the would-be attackers. They seemed very confused. You could see them thinking: *well, if he had to go talk to somebody, I guess we can't fight him. Maybe he'll come back.* What to do. What to do. I guess the fog finally lifted. *He may not be coming back. We don't know how long that guy's conversation is going to last, but this guy's here now. Let's get him!* It appeared to be a unanimous decision.

I didn't think they would fall for the "I have to go talk to some-body" excuse again. Sizing up the odds realistically, things did not look good. Suddenly, they started punching me, but only my back and my shoulders were taking the hits. They weren't really doing any damage. I managed to take out the guy I was facing with a quick uppercut to the jaw and a left to his face. I guess I forgot to mention my dad enrolled me in Marine Corps combat training courses as a preteen with an emphasis on hand-to-hand combat. Thankfully, I wasn't being held so they could gang up on me. More blows settled on my upper body. I kicked at one guy, and he yelped in pain as my foot made contact with his shin. Unfortunately, I then tripped over the first guy I had punched, who had started to get up. As I landed, I instinctively tucked into a fetal position with my hands covering my face and head as punches and kicks rained down on me.

I saw the bright light I didn't want to walk toward. I was still in a fetal position when a couple of angels picked me up and.........threw me onto the hood ornament of a '56 Pontiac. It made a great impression on my spleen. I believe it was the first and only time my belt buckle met my spine. In reality they weren't angels at all. They were the Tucson police. One of them must have thought I was dirty, because he dusted me off by standing me upright and roughly shaking me.

Behind the police, I saw Mike Bruce run through the door and swing on an overhead bar that was attached to the building. He kicked out with his feet to move the people back, and let go, sticking the landing. I would have given him an 8.5 on the dismount. It wasn't that clean.

"I want to press charges!" Mike Bruce shouted.

This caught the police officer's attention.

"You want to press charges against this guy here?" one officer asked, pointing to me.

At the same time the rest of the band showed up, piling out of the rear door of the club. I might have gotten kicked in the head once or twice, but to this day I swear Vince came out ready to do battle with a pair of maracas in his hands. John Speer held a Roger cymbal stand over his head and was prepared to use it like a bat. The police looked at him, and John Speer looked at the police. He decided, rightfully so, to make a very quick U-turn and head back into the club.

Dennis and his girlfriend hurried over and explained what happened. The police said nobody was going to be arrested, and no one was hurt. The guy I hit whined that he was. The police looked at him and turned away. By this time a sizable crowd had assembled, all interested in what was going on.

One officer said, "Everybody back in the club, and if we have to come back here again somebody is going to get arrested."

Once back inside the club, something amazing was about to happen. I had heard the term "mothering instinct," but I thought it applied to mothers and their children. I was wrong. Three girls came up to me and started to mother or smother me.

"Amp Boy, look what they did to you!" one said sympathetically.

"Yes, I know. I was there. But did you see what I did to the other guys?" I quipped.

The girls were just being kind. Someone asked if I'd like a Coke. I said, "That would be great."

48

"You need to clean up," another chimed in.

I thought for a moment that she was going to spit in a handkerchief and wipe my face with it, but luckily she produced a wet paper towel from the bathroom. I thanked her.

One of the girls said, "I was out there and saw everything."

"You should have jumped in to help me," I joked.

"We know some of the boys who beat you up." Boys? How young were these kids? Was I attacked by a bunch of fourth graders?

"Did anybody see the two guys I took out?" I asked humorlessly.

"I could have some friends beat them up," she offered.

"No friends, and no beating up anybody okay?" I replied. *Unless you want to*, I thought.

"I have some medicine in my bag," said a girl helpfully. "Aspirin and Tylenol."

I took the Tylenol, thanked them, and said I was feeling better. And I was. Every once in a while, something good happens out of something bad.

Yes, the Spiders and Amp Boy were doing alright, and more changes were just ahead. John Speer and Dennis Dunaway bought cars. John purchased a 1958 Chevy Corvette with blue and silver paint. Not very practical, especially if you're a drummer. He might have been able to carry his drumsticks in it. But it was a Corvette, it was beautiful, and he would look really good carrying those drumsticks. Dennis bought a white 1964 Ford Falcon with chrome rims and big tires on the back. It was a very good-looking car with an aggressive stance to it.

I can remember one incident with that car. The Ford Falcon engine must have had really good compression, because it blew a spark plug right out of the block. The ride got just a little rough after that. And by a little, I mean a lot. The Falcon had turned into a Bronco—a bucking bronco, to be precise. He drove it for a long time after the spark plug left the engine. I was thankful that I hadn't eaten anything before the trip. After literally rockin' n rollin', he finally stopped at a gas station, got a new plug, installed it, and away we went. Later on, Dennis's car was to play a major role in the very existence of the band.

An Accident, a Drunk, and a Rancher

I had many unusual experiences while I was with the group. One of the first occurred after playing at a venue in Prescott, Arizona. It was well after midnight when we started for home. Part of the group rode with me, and we took an alternate route back to Phoenix. The others left taking the normal route. It was the same mileage on both, but my route was more scenic, winding through hills and tall timber.

We had driven about four miles out of town when we noticed a pair of lights shining straight up through the trees. Slowing down, we saw that a pickup truck had driven off the road and traveled backward down an embankment, then fifty feet down a ravine, and had finally come to a stop after hitting a tree—a rather large pine tree. This was actually very fortunate for the driver, because this was the only barrier between him and the bottom of the ravine. It was also fortunate that the truck hit the tree with its back-end, which caused the headlights to shine upward into the night sky.

We pulled over and hiked downhill to the truck, the hazardous trek made easier by the headlights lighting our way. The driver, still in the truck, was alive and appeared to be in good health, but he wasn't making much sense. We soon realized he was drunk. As we helped him out of the wrecked truck and climbed back up to the road, he repeatedly asked, "How did I get down there?"

We took turns saying, "We don't know. We weren't driving with you."

I asked him, "Do you need to go to the hospital?" I didn't really know if there was a hospital in Prescott, and I was hoping that he knew whether there was, and if he needed to go there.

"No, I'm fine. I would just like to know how the truck got stuck in that tree."

I asked him where he lived. He said he had a ranch about six miles away.

"Okay. We'll take you home."

When we got to the ranch, he asked what the time was. Vince told him it was 2:30 a.m.

"Why don't you stay here, and you can head out in the morning?" he offered.

We agreed to stay because all of us were dead tired, and the thought of driving a hundred miles more didn't appeal to me. He took the key down from over the door, unlocked it, and led us into the family room. It was quite a large room comfortably furnished with plenty of couches and chairs for us to sleep on. We settled in for the night with plans to get up in a few hours and leave for home. Around 5:30 a.m. I heard, as I'm sure everyone else had, muffled voices behind the door.

"There are strangers sleeping in the family room, and they have long hair!"

This didn't sound good. Maybe the owner hadn't told anyone we were here? By this time, we were all wide awake, but pretended to be asleep. Don't ask me why, just the paralysis of fear, I guess. The door opened. The biggest human being I ever saw filled the doorway, and I don't mean he was fat. Fat wouldn't stick to this guy. Cowboy boots, jeans, denim work shirt. He was the real McCoy. He didn't have to sound tough; you immediately knew that he was.

He stood for a moment in the doorway observing us then said in a calm, but intimidating, voice, "What are you doing here?"

I knew instantly that the first and last words out of my mouth were going to be "Sir." We took turns explaining, since our voices faded and throats started to close from fear after just a few words. We talked, and he listened.

By this time, several other people had come into the room and were staring at us. He, meaning the really big man, spoke, and we snapped to attention.

"Describe him and his truck."

He sounded perturbed. It might have been time to invoke the unwritten law of every man for himself. We did as he asked, and in great detail.

He said, "I fired him two days ago. He was a drunk. He was drunk most of the time."

We nodded our heads vigorously in complete and total agreement.

"Find him," he ordered, and the assembled ranch hands immediately moved out to search. He was located sleeping in the barn, and he collaborated our story—what he could remember of it. That was the last time we saw him. I would like to think that he was driven back to his truck where the ranch hands helped extract it from the ravine and the pine tree, and he went on his way. At least that's what I forced myself to believe.

The rancher's wife, who had been listening intently throughout our ordeal, spoke firmly to her husband.

"Quit, now. You scared these boys enough. They were trying to help a stranger in trouble. Let's all go in and have some breakfast."

Yes, dear. I think I love you, I thought. We sat down at the large kitchen table and waited quietly while she cooked breakfast. Her husband joined us. She asked if I wanted a cup of coffee.

"Yes, thanks."

"How do you like it?" she asked.

"Plain is fine." Truth be told, I'd never had a cup of coffee in my life before. Or after that, for that matter.

I drank some and said, "This is good."

Actually, I was looking for a place to spit it out, but I didn't want to offend her. She set plates of eggs, bacon and toast on the table, which were hungrily devoured. After a while, I began to relax and tried to start a conversation with the rancher.

"We have something in common."

He looked skeptically at me and said, "What exactly would that be?"

"Farming." I told him a little bit about myself and living in North Dakota. He seemed interested, so I continued.

"What do you run on your ranch?" I asked.

"Mostly Herefords."

So far so good. He said he also raised Guernsey's for milk. Another excellent choice. I preferred Holsteins, but I wasn't going to say that.

"And chickens," he continued. He was beginning to loosen up.

"What breed of chickens do you raise?" I asked.

"Plymouth Rocks."

I could have said I agree to disagree, but I didn't. I'm not a complete idiot.

"They do well in cold weather, don't they?"

He nodded in agreement.

After finishing breakfast, we thanked them for their hospitality and understanding, got into the Plymouth and headed home to Phoenix with stories to tell.

Courtesy Paul Brenton

4

The Family Gets Bigger

The Spiders made the decision to take the group to the next level and agreed that changes were needed to get there. They needed lighting, someone to take care of bookings, new places to play, and a record. With the addition of Dick Phillips, who later became Dick Christian, and Charlie Carnal, these goals were met. Dick was hired to take care of the band in town, on the road, and procure bookings, and whatever else the band needed him to do. I thought that was why they had me, but I was very happy to share that responsibility with Dick. At first, he was mostly involved with picking up girlfriends and retrieving things that had been left at home and were needed for the shows… like guitars. And Charlie would take care of the lighting.

Charlie and Dick were very amiable guys, liked and trusted by everyone. Dick would be in and out of the lives of the Spiders and The Nazz, and later Alice Cooper. He was capable, charming, witty, and a smooth talker.

Charlie was a character and also a very nice guy. I have to admit The Spiders had a knack for picking good people to be around them. I always considered myself very laid-back, but compared with Charlie I was the life of the party. He was soft-spoken and polite. He brought his pet rabbit along when the group moved back and forth between

L.A. and Phoenix. Once, I accidentally sat on the rabbit when it was hiding behind a couch cushion. I said, "I'm sorry." Typically, Charlie replied, "No problem."

On the other hand, the rabbit might have had something else entirely to say once it regained its senses. Charlie was fond of wearing an orange-colored hat with a wide round brim, a 6-inch or 8-inch crown, and an orange and black hat band. It resembled an oversized bowler hat.

As the lighting guy, Charlie built two light boxes, each about five to six feet long. Each box had six white flood lights that could be changed to colored lights by closing the lid, which had pieces of color film attached to it. He had a couple of black lights, ones that were four feet long. They were always a crowd pleaser. He also constructed a homemade strobe light from a metal ammunition box. It had two flood lights and a fan motor with a metal disc with two slots cut in it. Everything was wired to another metal box where he operated micro switches for the lights and regular switches for the black lights and strobe. He played it like a piano.

Charlie also fabricated a light wheel—on steroids. He got the idea from the colored light wheels that shined on chrome-foil Christmas trees in the '60s. He could light up the whole stage in red, blue or gold with just the turn of a dial. To shake things up he would increase the speed which created an effect of spinning lights. It was dazzling and a little nauseating at the same time.

One of my favorite pieces from the light show was the Electro Lucent Mind Machine, also known as "Big Joe." It was a giant color wheel, not to be confused with the earlier color wheel on steroids which used colored film for the effects. This bad boy was an 8-foot round plywood disc mounted on a motorized windmill type structure. The motor wasn't powerful enough to turn the disc without first getting it going by hand. The wheel was the brainchild of Glen, Dennis, and Charlie. Jack Curtis, owner of the VIP Club, probably funded the project because he got to name it. Jack had posters printed that sometimes gave the wheel top billing over The Spiders, and sometimes it was the other way around.

"Big Joe" was painted in a way that I can best describe as a photograph the Hubble telescope might have taken: bright reds, blues and blacks, with touches of photoluminescent paint, and Visine eye drops splashed around. Dennis and Glen had discovered that, under a black light, Visine turned the whites of eyes a bright yellow. This was an accidental finding, along with the intriguing discovery that, when girls passed in front of the black light at the door to show their hand stamp, their white bras would be revealed under their blouses. The band sometimes used the Visine to draw "secret" pictures and sayings on their clothes. Secret because they could only be seen under the black light. Dennis and Glen often confiscated Jack's front door black light for the show, which upset him no end.

The Electro Lucent Mind Machine was set up at the back of the stage behind John Speer. Sometimes, when it was really spinning, it wobbled because the stage was not level or the wheel was out of balance. We were afraid the disc might come loose and separate John's head from his body. Any ensuing decapitation publicity would, of course, get the band noticed, but that grisly trick could only be done once. I crawled behind the machine to hold it down. With the device spinning behind John, the crowd became hypnotically mesmerized. Dancing stopped and the patrons stared blankly, their heads slightly tilted, repeating "John, John, John."

Unfortunately, due to its size and weight, the wheel had limited use and was rarely used anywhere but the VIP Club. Dick Phillips tells a story that we hauled the Mind Machine up to Winslow, Arizona, before the Eagles made the town famous, and used it for a show. This was just after the group changed its name to The Nazz. After the show, two cowboys came up to Charlie Carnal and asked him, "Is that what LSD is like?" Charlie, with a wide grin replied, "Yes, and so much more."

When the group became Alice Cooper, Charlie's light shows sometimes received better reviews than the band. Actually, you can change sometimes to most times. The guy was good. I wish I had known as much as Charlie did about wiring and electricity. He was humble about it and carefully designed everything to fit in the Plymouth without taking up too much room, which was good because the Plymouth was starting to run out of space.

A road manager and booking agent: check. A great light show: double check. Now to make a record.

Charlie Carnal
Courtesy Toodie Mueller

Dropping Out

By 1966, the band had begun to write their own music and played an original song or two each set to see if any garnered interest. The one showing the most promise was a little ditty called, "Don't Blow Your Mind." Later on, it was informally changed to: "Don't Blow Your Mind Like You Did Last Summer." They agreed the song would be the one to record. All they had to do was get it made. Copper State Recording Studios was chosen, and it was back down to Tucson for us.

But that posed a bit of a problem—we were all still in school. It wasn't that we couldn't just get out of Junior College, on most days we spent hours in the Student Union hanging out and playing a game called spoons. To play spoons, a plastic spoon handle was placed under a second spoon's bowl. Points were made by hitting the first spoon, which knocked the second spoon into a cup two feet away. It was sort of like Tiddlywinks, only much, much cooler.

At Glendale Community College, Dennis and I took an art class together. He was good, but I took it for an easy grade. Every attempted art project I created was called "Madonna with Child." There were other classes, too, but we could easily give them up for the fame and fortune that awaited us.

5

The Band Makes a Record

We drove to Tucson and, after first checking into our favorite motel loaded with a brand-new batch of porno magazines, arrived at Copper State Recording Studio to work on "Don't Blow Your Mind." Dick had lined up a couple of jobs at the Monterey Club in Tucson to help offset our expenses. He was doing a great job.

It was during this trip that some members of the band asked to borrow the Plymouth Fury to run a few errands. I tossed them the keys, jokingly telling them to bring it back in one piece, and off they went.

A few hours had gone by before I saw the vehicle pulling into the motel parking lot. The first thing I noticed was the front tire on the passenger side was not going in the same direction as the other front tire. When I mentioned it, they innocently claimed they had just been driving around when they heard a loud noise from underneath the car and steering became a major problem: the car kept wanting to turn left. They said they'd wrestled the car all the way back to the motel.

A quick look underneath revealed a tie rod had broken, which was not an easy feat. Bending a tie rod was more common, but breaking it was something very different. That took some doing. I was extremely skeptical of their story, but it was more important at that point to get the car fixed. There was a garage down the street, and I got the car there with considerable effort and perseverance. It seemed the car really had a preference for the buildings on the opposite side of the road.

The mechanic came out and asked, "What's the problem?"

"Broken tie rod."

"How did you manage to do that?"

"I was told it just broke."

"Really?" He sounded surprised.

He said he could get it done in a few hours, and that the car would need a wheel alignment which he didn't do. I thanked him for trying to get the repair done so quickly and said I would take care of the alignment. I always intended to have it done but never got around to it. I also never got around to hearing the real story about what had happened on that fateful day. I bet it was a doozy.

On the day to record, we arrived at the studio at the scheduled time. Sound baffles were set up, microphones were in place, and the equipment was hauled in and put where it needed to be. Everybody met with the sound engineer/producer. Cayce was an interesting person and a whiz with the mixing board. Making a record was both tedious and exciting at the same time. I guess it was tediously exciting.

The sessions would always start with: "What if we…" fill in the blank: Change this. Do this. Do that part here, turn this part up or down, hold this guitar chord out. When it came together and everybody said, "That's it," *that* was the exciting part.

I remember at one point Cayce stopped and said, "John, you need to fill in a gap here, maybe with a cymbal crash."

John said he couldn't do it because of what he was playing at the point Cayce asked for the change. Casey looked around the room.

"You," meaning me, "hit the cymbal when John tells you to," he said.

We worked on the drum and the cymbal part. When John nodded his head, I was supposed to hit the cymbal, so I did—I thought I actually hit the cymbal a little late, but Cayce said, "Great."

There was smiling and nodding going on in the booth. Who was I to disagree?

Cayce tried to explain to the band what constituted a perfect song. The song he used as an example was the Fortune's "You've Got Your Troubles, I've Got Mine." He was always saying, "Listen to the horns. Listen to the voices, to the harmonies."

I just didn't get it. I was hoping that the band did, but it was over my head. It was a good song, but there were greater songs out there that better fit The Spiders' style and sound. It took fifty years to understand what he had been talking about. I had just left a grocery store in Prescott, Arizona, and the Fortune's song "You've Got Your Troubles" came on the radio. I pulled into a parking space, turned the sound up and listened. Cayce was right. The song was perfect. Again, there were better songs, but Cayce had tried to tell us that, structurally, the song was perfect. It's the vocal phrasing, the harmonies, the horns, everything flowing beautifully. It was an example of a very well-produced and arranged song.

You're never too old to learn.

The Spiders' song "Don't Blow Your Mind" and the B side "No Price Tag" was finally finished. It was in the can, as they say. The song was recorded on tape and would be put on 45 vinyl records under the Santa Cruz label. We hoped the record would do well locally in Phoenix and Tucson, which it did, then make its way to California, the rest of the country, and then the world!

62

New Sounds, New Ideas

The Spiders, complete with a rope spider web, props, and go-go girls, were now the house band at Jack Curtis's VIP Club. They were still playing clubs and schools in Tucson, and in smaller towns around Arizona and New Mexico, too. The smaller towns were kind of interesting, but dangerous for young men with long hair.

In one small Arizona town, a person dressed like a cowboy waived a knife menacingly in front of Vince in an attempt to scare him and probably impress his girl, but it did neither. Vince kept on singing, not even giving the pretend cowboy a second look. Finally, the cowboy's girl and some friends dragged him away from the stage. It wasn't usually that bad at the shows, but you had to be on your guard, just in case.

Most of the time the crowd would congregate in front of the stage not to listen to the music, but to stand in the black lights. The kids were drawn to the lights like moths to a flame. They would pose and show off in the light. Their skin turned purple, their teeth brilliant white, and if anybody was wearing a white shirt, the shirt would glow, and girls' bras were scandalously exposed under their clothes. If Charlie turned the black lights off and switched to other lights, the crowd chanted, "Turn the lights back on. Turn the lights back on!" Charlie obliged rather than face their wrath. The whole performance would be done with the black light on.

After a show, I would pack up the equipment. Charlie handled the lights so they wouldn't be damaged, and he'd leave with someone else in the group. Usually, Glen would ride with me back to Phoenix. It was quite normal for the town folks to escort us out of town. Some threw empty bottles of beer at the car, or hurled insults, or both. Often the police would follow us for a couple of miles then turn around, or sometimes they just wanted to talk.

"What were you doing in town?" they would ask.

"Playing at a local dance."

"Where are you going?"

"Back to Phoenix."

They would walk around the Plymouth looking at the car, probably wishing they had one. The officer would ask for my license and registration, then sit in the patrol car until another police car arrived. After a short discussion, they'd come over and hand me my ID and say, "You can go."

To which I would politely say, "Thank you, officer."

All the while Glen fumed. He knew better than to say anything.

Dick worked on getting more bookings and trying to schedule interviews with record and talent agencies in Los Angeles. He was able to book some jobs for the band in Albuquerque, New Mexico. On one trip to Albuquerque, I remember two incidents. The band was scheduled for an interview at a local radio station. The group was escorted into the radio booth, and I followed behind. They all sat in chairs while I stood in a corner.

The DJ began the interview. "The Spiders are playing in Albuquerque for the first time, and everyone is looking forward to hearing them play." He went around to each member of the group with a microphone asking what they did in the band. Vince said vocals and harmonica, Glen lead guitar, Mike rhythm guitar and vocals, Dennis bass guitar and vocals, John drums.

"And you?" He was looking at me.

Dead silence. *Say something you idiot*, I thought. He was probably thinking the same thing.

I blurted out, "I turn up the volume."

I vowed to never again go into a radio booth. There were exceptions to every rule, and I went once more with that same DJ. He did the interview, this time leaving me out.

The second incident was that Dick, to save money, had booked all eight of us into one single room at a motel. Two would check in, six would sneak in. Oh, this wasn't even the strange thing. That was the norm. There were no porno magazines in the drawers. That wasn't the strange thing either, though it was a bit of a letdown. I guess Tucson was just more advanced in hospitality services than Albuquerque. The strange thing was at about 1:00 a.m. there was a loud knock on the door. I thought it was the police coming to inquire what time we wanted to be followed out of town. I got up and opened the door. People were much more trusting back then. There stood a man in uniform.

He said, "Are you the people looking for an Air Force officer?"

I thought about asking the group, but I didn't.

I responded, "No," closed the door, locked it, and put the chain on.

I asked everyone if I had heard what I thought I heard. They all said, "Yes." I nodded, and said, "Okay," and we went back to bed. Before drifting off to sleep I thought about the group playing the next night. *That's* when the police will show up to find out when we're leaving so we can be escorted out of town.

Dick wanted to send tapes of the band's music to talent agencies, clubs, and record companies in Los Angeles. In those days there was no such thing as a CD, or flash drive, or streaming. Cassettes wouldn't even be invented until the next year. There were 4 track tapes and 8 track tapes, and reel-to-reel tapes, and record players. That was about it. Dick had the band record five songs on a reel-to-reel, had them duplicated and sent out to people who we hoped were eager to discover exciting new talent.

In the meantime, everybody got down to the task of creating a look that might produce a big, new buzz. John Speer said he would wear a top hat. It wasn't exactly a top hat. It was a hat though, and it was tall. He also said he would get a new set of drums, ones that had just come out, and they would look different than any others. They were called pancake drums. The drums were the same diameter as a regular drum, but they were not the same depth. The depth was only about three inches, and the drums, except for the snare drum, broke down to sit inside a case even with the cymbals. I appreciated this because it would take a lot less time setting the drums up, less time taking down the drums, and best of all, they took up less room in the Plymouth.

Dennis changed the look of his Airline bass. He'd found exactly what he wanted at a local hobby store or possibly a Woolworth's. He purchased a sheet of plastic imprinted with what can be best described as a colorful three-dimensional overlay of red and blue pinwheels. Once applied, they covered the whole front of his bass. The pinwheels gave the illusion of getting larger or smaller as the guitar moved. I doubt there was anything like it before, or after. In 1967, this was mind blowing, and it looked good in Charlie's lights.

Dennis also started to develop his patented stage moves: the deep bow and swaying of his bass guitar, often followed by the "crouch" with knees bent and the guitar pointed outward like a rifle. And of course there was his signature prance, his body bent back, his weight transferred to his left leg with the right leg bent at the knee, toes pointed downward his foot almost leaving the floor, finished with his world-famous kick, spin and walk, or kick and walk, but never kick and fall over backward.

For his new look, Glen got a box. It was a tape machine called the Echoplex Maestro. He recorded his guitar on a piece of tape and then played it in a continuous loop. The Echoplex could turn normal guitar sounds into very strange sounds. He was able to play this loop either fast or slow, and he could control it with a lever and a foot pedal.

I liked it a lot, but it was how he used it that had me in constant state of anxiety. The Echoplex was connected to his guitar and his amplifier but sometimes he forgot and would drag the box across the stage. I had to find a way to secure the Echoplex and figure out something so he could turn it on with the foot pedal and control the speed with the lever. I finally settled on attaching the Echoplex to the seat of a wooden folding chair and taping the foot pedal securely to the floor where he could easily reach it with his foot to turn it on or off. And he could reach the lever to adjust the speed. I lived in constant fear that just hours before a show it would break and he would want it fixed in someplace like Eloy, Arizona, or some other small town.

Glen also played his guitar with a tablespoon. Not just any old spoon—a spoon with good weight, balance, and a wide handle. When eating at a restaurant, he was excited if he found the perfect spoon. Plus, they were good for eating cereal in the morning. He would use the spoon as a slide, moving up and down the guitar strings, and he'd also bounce it on the strings. He could produce some very unique sounds with that spoon.

Mike Bruce said he could play the piano on stage which would add an extra element to the music. I was not as enthusiastic about this idea as I was with the pancake drum set. There went that extra space I had with the new drums—taken up by an electric piano.

Someone suggested they all get matching jackets. They would be black with gold buttons and black epaulettes. The band members' mothers made them, bless their hearts. They even made one for me. I told them that I wasn't in the band, but they said, "You need to look nice, too." I didn't wear the jacket very often, afraid of getting it dirty.

Yes, things were looking up. New sounds, new clothes, new ideas, and new places to practice.

Dennis Dunaway Bass
©Len DeLessio

Toodie

Toodie Mueller was a huge part of our life. Toodie is immortalized in an Alice Cooper song, "Today Mueller," from their first album, *Pretties for You*. She made us brownies, cakes, pies, and cookies and bought food for the band. She drove us around in her blue 1967 Mustang. She was unfailingly upbeat, never a bad word. She came to every gig that she could. She was just a great friend and still is. Even with her baking and driving us around, she had time to introduce me to my girlfriend of the future, but not the present because I was too stupid to act in the present. Toodie reminded me quite often of this failing.

"What's wrong with you?" she'd ask, and she wasn't the only one.

Toodie came from a very large family…maybe twenty or thirty kids. I couldn't keep them all straight. Some of the gang at her parent's, I'm sure, were kids from the neighborhood. Toodie lived in a huge low-slung brick ranch-style house with a tiled roof that sat on two acres and had a pool and a stable with horses and chickens and dogs and hamsters and assorted cats, and a basement, which was a novelty in Phoenix.

When the band practiced there, it was like a mini concert because kids and adults would pour out of everywhere to listen, and at the end of the practice there would be food. They would actually feed us! Win-win. Topping it all off for me were the horses. Toodie invited me over to ride once in a while. After we moved to California, Toodie would still visit bringing baked goods and groceries, and sometimes my future, but not in the present girlfriend.

When we were back in Phoenix, my future girlfriend's parents let the band practice at their house. From then on, her parents, Don and Barbara Mitchell, blamed the band for the cracks in the plaster on the living room ceiling. Once again, more children. There were nine kids in her family, three girls and six boys. I was beginning to think that married people in Phoenix didn't have much to do in the '40s and '50s. I was an only child, and it never occurred to me that people would want more.

1966 Me   Mike Bruce

Courtesy Toodie Mueller

Even my dad let us practice at his house, which was pretty amazing considering my dad was an ex-Marine and, just for your information, there is no such thing as an ex-Marine. They wear the uniform on the inside as well as the outside. He did get on me about my hair from time to time, but eventually we came to a truce, or rather we chose to ignore it. I wouldn't mention it, and he wouldn't bring it up.

One day I went to dad's house when he was having a cookout with some of his retired Marine Corps buddies. I knew when I walked in that I was going to be in for a boatload of grief. It started out with the classic, "Is that a boy or a girl?" followed with a whistle or two, and "He looks like a hippie." I tried to ignore them and shake it off. I took as much as I could then I started answering back.

"So, you think I'm a hippie just because of my hair?"

"Yes, we do," was the immediate reply.

"You guys know me. I've hunted and fished with you. I even cut your lawns when I was younger," I retorted. "I don't smoke, drink, or do drugs, which I can't say for most of you. I can't even breathe in here for all the smoke, and I doubt if that's iced tea you're drinking,"

"It's what your hair represents," one said.

"My hair is a style change, not a lifestyle change. If I cut my hair tomorrow, would I suddenly morph back into my old self?"

Then I said the unforgivable thing, which I regret to this day.

"If I'm a hippie because of my hair, are all Marines like Lee Harvey Oswald because he was a Marine?"

Everyone in the room immediately stopped talking and the silence was truly deafening. I knew I had crossed the line and quickly left. The following day I went back to the house to apologize for what I had said in anger. My dad told me I was right.

"They shouldn't have said those things to you. The way you wear your hair shouldn't define who you are. It shouldn't, but it probably does to most people. You can't judge a book by its cover."

Can't judge a book by its cover. I thought about it, again. Can't judge a book by its cover. Why hadn't I said that instead of criticizing the Marine Corps?

"Why don't you bring the band over to the house to practice?"

"Really?"

"Sure, let's hear what they sound like."

The band practiced at my dad's house two times. For years the back corner of the family room had a black smudge on the white shag carpeting from John's drum foot pedal.

"No problem," dad shrugged. "We'll just put a rug down over it."

The band was on its best behavior, and my dad liked the music. He said the guys were all gentlemen. He didn't know them like I did. They bestowed the title of Daddy Spider on him, which he really enjoyed.

I Fought the Law and the Law May Have Won, or It Could Have Been a Tie

Neal Smith, aka the world's tallest drummer, hung out with The Spiders and The Nazz. He'd practice with them on occasion and would sometimes meet up with the group in Tucson.

One time in Tucson, The Spiders were playing at a club when Neal came down from Phoenix. The club was stifling hot and Neal and I went outside to get some air. We were joined by three girls for conversation, and that was about it. Most of the girls who went to these clubs were between the age of sixteen and seventeen years old. I knew them from other trips to Tucson and had talked with them before at other shows. We sat inside the Plymouth because it was a sweltering summer night, and the car had air conditioning. Air conditioning is a wonderful thing. Suddenly, a whole lot of flashlights were shinning in our faces through the windows. We were ordered to get out of the car. It was the Liquor Patrol, a group from Tucson with badges who went to clubs in town looking for underage drinkers.

"Have you been drinking?" an officer asked.

I said, "No," which was true. "I don't drink and nobody else has been drinking."

They searched us and found nothing. Then, they searched the vehicle and found an unopened pint of vodka under the front seat. I was about to say, "You guys planted that," then I thought about who had been my traveling companion on the drive to Tucson—Glen!

"That's not ours," I said.

They weren't buying it. They let the girls go, but arrested Neal and me. We posted bail. It was one hundred dollars. Neal and I had a little over twenty dollars between us, but thanks to the girls who had followed us, the rest was covered, with the stipulation that they were to be paid back, which they were. You would have thought the pleasure of our company would be enough. We were ordered to appear before a judge in three weeks for trial and possible sentencing. Just great. Note to self: search car after traveling with Glen.

By the time I got back to Phoenix, I was really angry. We were innocent. We were totally unaware that the vodka was in the car. Glen apologetically said he'd forgotten it under the seat. He claimed he had put it there three trips ago. Note to self: clean out the car more often.

I went to the library to read a book on Arizona law. I was going to go full on Perry Mason with these guys. I thought I had them. No breathalyzer or blood tests were given to anybody. Not to the girls or us. The girls weren't arrested. We were all underage. If the girls had been let go, Neal should have been, since he hadn't been drinking. I owned the car so I guess I may have had culpability because the bottle was in my car, but I was totally unaware that it was there. Illegal search and seizure, nobody had been drinking or caught drinking. So why were we and the car searched? Where was the probable cause?

We were just two boys sitting in a car with young girls. Okay, when you say it like that it does sound bad.

But I had the smoking gun for our defense, a signed notarized letter from Glen saying he was the one who had put the liquor under my seat more than a month ago and he had never told me. Plus, two of the girls in the car would testify on our behalf that no one had mentioned there was liquor in the car. Case closed. Found not guilty on all charges. The day of the trial I was loaded for bear. Justice would be served! Neal and I sat in the courtroom ready to go. The girls were there to give their statements.

The judge asked, "Are you Michael Allen and Neal Smith?"

"Yes, Your Honor."

"Mr. Prosecutor, are you ready?"

"Your Honor, may I approach the bench?" Mr. Prosecutor asked.

After a few minutes of consulting, the judge said, "The arresting officers can't be present for today's hearing, so it has been requested we reschedule for a month from now."

I protested, "Your Honor, we live in Phoenix and we are here ready to proceed. And I have witnesses who skipped school to be here." I should have left the skipped school part out. "May I speak to you for a few minutes?"

"Yes, but be brief."

I went through everything in about thirty seconds, finishing with Glen's letter. I thought he was impressed, but he was probably just amused.

He said, "Plead guilty to the charges and I will suspend the sentence and place you both on probation for one year. If it's agreeable to the prosecution."

"That's fine, Your Honor," Mr. Prosecutor said.

"And you?" the judge asked, looking at me.

"Okay, but let me talk it over with Neal."

We quickly agreed, but it's not what I had wanted. I wanted to have the arresting officers break down on the stand and admit they had arrested us because they were biased and prejudiced by the way we looked. Just like Perry Mason would have done.

But this deal worked, too. I would just have to search the car more often after Glen rode with me.

Back to Albuquerque

After a job at a club in Albuquerque, a group of teenage girls invited us to come over and watch TV.

"Are you sure your parents won't mind?" Dennis asked.

They said their parents wouldn't be there. Underage girls and no parents—what could possibly go wrong?

Vince asked, "What's on TV?"

"*The Taming of the Shrew*," one of the girls said.

I wondered why anybody would want to watch a movie based on a Shakespearean play about a guy who makes a bet that he can make this girl subservient to him.

Another girl quickly spoke up. "It's not *The Taming of the Shrew*, dummy, it's *The Attack of the Killer Shrews*."

Suddenly, Shakespeare sounded better. *The Attack of the Killer Shrews* was a Grade Z movie with dogs dressed up in fake fur running around eating people.

Before anyone could say, "Thanks, but no thanks." Vince piped up, "That's one of my favorite movies!"

It would have to be Vince. Nobody else would have said that. We really were boring people. It was pouring down rain, so what else could we do other than sleep? What could possibly go wrong? I would say that phrase a lot with the band, but I had a really, really bad feeling about this. At the house, the girls made popcorn and brought us cokes and we settled in for a little late-night TV. Everything was going fine—for about 45 minutes. Even I was surprised and relieved.

Then one of the girls exclaimed, "Look at all those police cars!"

That was our cue to leave, even though we were just eating popcorn, drinking cokes and watching *The Attack of the Killer Shrews* on TV.

We ran outside into the pouring rain. John Speer attempted to jump the fence into the neighbor's back yard, but an angry Doberman on the other side was having none of that. Meanwhile, police, who were now soaking wet, swarmed the backyard with guns drawn searching for us. I believe the expression "they were madder than a wet hen" applied to this situation.

After running around looking for a way out we were discovered, soaked, shaking, and huddled together under the eaves of the house. Paranoia can sometimes be your worst enemy. The neighbors must have called the police when they saw us get out of the cars and go into the house, "*Drugs and orgy and we weren't invited!*" Inside the house, the police were interrogating the girls. They would have some serious explaining to do when their parents got home. I could just hear one of the girls: "*They just came over to watch Taming of the Shrew.*" What kind of deviants were they?

We were herded into the back of a police wagon, where at least it was dry. Officers had us empty our pockets and took down our names and addresses for the record. John Speer thought he'd play a prank on the police. It seemed to me that they were not the type of people you wanted to play a joke on while sitting in the back of a police wagon, but what did I know? John said he would tell them that there were drugs hidden inside the Plymouth. The police would have to tear the car apart in the rain trying to find the drugs.

"Let's just say you did, but you don't," I said. None of us were amused.

We were detained for a couple of hours and given a lecture about watching bad movies where decent people live. We never saw the end of the movie. I didn't care. I had seen it before.

Toodie Saves My Life

The Spiders decided they should move to Los Angeles, but still had a few contracts to honor. It was at one of those events that Toodie saved my life, not with a homemade pie or brownies, but from actual bodily harm. The Spiders were playing at a local junior college in Phoenix where a sizable crowd kept yelling at them to turn the music down—which was improper attendee etiquette. The message it sent to a band was, "we don't like your music, or you." They did turn the music down, but apparently not down enough. The crowd continued to harass them. Annoyed, Vince, for the last fifteen minutes of the show, whispered the words to the songs, and the band followed suit by playing very, very softly. Not surprisingly, the crowd reacted unfavorably.

When the show was mercifully over, the band high-tailed it out of there, leaving me on my own to pack up. I backed the Plymouth down a road that was basically a wide sidewalk bordered by a grass lawn, found a large furniture dolly, and began breaking down the equipment. A security guard approached and said he would only be there for fifteen minutes more, and I needed to look outside. What I saw was like a scene from Alfred Hitchcock's movie *The Birds*. Specifically, the last scene where frightened people walk quietly to a small car while thousands of birds watch them from trees, fences, and rooftops. Now, replace the birds with junior college students and you've got the picture. They were lined up on both sides of the Plymouth and standing on the grass lawn or leaning against the building staring silently at me. *This is not going to be a good end to the night*, I thought. There was just one nervous guard who obviously wanted to be somewhere else. I wished he would take me with him.

Between the auditorium and the Plymouth was twenty feet of open ground. I saw two individuals sitting on the open tailgate. It was considerate of them to put it down for me. I thought about my situation for a moment, then decided to go out there and load up the equipment as if nothing was wrong. What else could I do? If I hid in the building, the crowd would just get angrier. Also, I knew that the security guard wasn't going to let me stay. I was hoping some girls would come to my rescue, but I didn't see much mothering instinct out there.

I finished loading the rest of the equipment on the dolly and went through the doors and down the sidewalk toward the car. There was a disheartening click of the door locking behind me. There went any option for a safe retreat. I rolled the furniture dolly up to the tailgate. The two young men silently stood up and moved away from the Plymouth. As quickly as I could, I loaded the equipment into the back of the vehicle. I was as grimly silent as the crowd.

When I finished, I pushed the dolly up against the building's locked door. As I walked to the driver's side, I gestured for the people in front of the car to move back a little. To my surprise, they complied, and when I slowly drove off nobody tried to block the car. Instead, they fell in line and walked behind and alongside the vehicle. Maybe they had read an article about how hippies were dangerous when provoked, or maybe the school had a policy against destroying lowly Amp Boys on school property.

I was still in the parking lot when I noticed everyone running back to their cars. It looked like they intended to follow me. I guess nobody had anything better to do on a Friday night. I was almost at the street, still trying to decide which way I should go to escape. Go right, I thought, and cleverly put my left turn signal on and drove straight out into the street.

Suddenly, a blue streak of a car came up behind me with lights flashing and horn honking. It was Toodie in her 1967 baby-blue Mustang, blocking the students following behind me! I floored it. Right turn, right turn, and left turn onto a long street. I turned my lights off. After a couple of miles, I turned them back on but stayed on the side streets until I got home.

I don't know what would have happened to me that night, but I don't think the mob wanted me to go with them to an after-hours party. Thanks to Toodie and her Mustang, I never had to find out.

Courtesy Toodie Mueller

Another Fight. I Don't Understand What Makes People Want to Hit Me.

The Spiders played at a dance at the Community Center in Scottsdale. The hall was rather large and filled with an appreciative crowd. It was winter and actually cold outside, but inside it was hot and steamy. I was wearing a Navy peacoat purchased at a favorite Goodwill store we all frequented. The coat was heavy and warm but fit almost too snugly. I walked outside to cool off. I was talking to some people who wanted to know if I was in the band and why I wasn't inside playing. I explained I worked for the band. I hauled their equipment. They said, "Cool." I swear to God one of them said, "You're Amp Boy!"

I was about to ask him how he knew my nickname when somebody tapped me on the shoulder. I turned to see who it was, and a fist met my eye. I was momentarily stunned from the blow, and saw beautiful, shining stars. Surprisingly, a second punch didn't follow. Instinctively, I locked my hands behind my assailant's head and swiftly brought it down to my rising knee. Luckily, he was shorter than my six-foot five-inch height—most people were. That blow loosened him up a little, but I noticed that something was wrong. I was having trouble seeing out of my right eye, and the peacoat now felt very warm and very heavy, and also very restrictive. I couldn't really move my arms all that well.

One of his buddies jumped on my back and simply rolled off, falling to the sidewalk before running away. With my right hand, I grabbed the guy who had hit me and tucked his head neatly against my hip. Because the coat was bulky, I couldn't tell if I had him by his neck or his head. I walked him around with his body bent over at the waist and his head resting on my hip. Every once in a while, he would squawk, and I would hit him on the top of his head with my left fist, probably ineffectively due to the coat's restriction. I considered running him into a wall or lamppost or rock, anything to end this. I could tell he was also losing interest.

After a few minutes, I told him, "I'm tired of this. I'm going to let you go, and if you try to hit me I will send you home in an ambulance." Or something to that effect.

He didn't answer, but I released him. I noticed that his neck was bright red. It may have been a reaction to my wool coat, or the grip I had around his neck. He and his friends left quickly. I was drenched in sweat and removed my peacoat. I sat down on a nearby step to cool off. People who had seen the fight were gathering around me to discuss it. I think the popular consensus was that the fight was "strange," as in not enough action. They seemed genuinely disappointed. Then a girl came up to me.

"Look at your face. It's awful."

I was thinking, *I know I'm no Robert Redford, but come on!*

She grabbed my hand and said, "You come with me."

She and two other teenage girls led me away…mothering instinct. You gotta love it. They took me straight to the girl's bathroom.

"I can't go in there," I protested.

"Well, we're not going to the boy's bathroom," one of the girls replied firmly.

Yes, I thought that would be much worse.

She stuck her head into the girl's bathroom and yelled, "I've got a boy out here who got beat up. I'm going to bring him in."

Wait a minute. I didn't get beat up. He got in one punch, I thought, but I didn't say it. The girl's bathroom was neat and orderly—a real change from the boy's restroom. The three girls gathered together around me.

"You poor thing. Does it hurt?"

I looked in the mirror. I could see why they thought I got beat up. My eye was swollen and becoming a beautiful shade of purple and blue, and my eye had a little blood in it. One girl gave me a cold compress for it. Another washed my face and hands with a wet paper towel. After cleaning me up, we left the girl's bathroom, and they sat me in a chair inside the club. They asked if they could bring me something to eat or drink. One guarded me while the others got the food. This sure was a strange way to meet girls, but I was starting to appreciate them more and more. The band was informed, probably by one of the girls, about what happened to me. They all came over to assess the damage.

"You got beat up pretty good," Glen said.

"I didn't get beat up. You should see the other guy," I objected.

"Yep, you sure like to get into fights," Dennis commented.

"No, no I don't!"

Never did, never will.

The Spiders had been the opening act for a lot of big-name groups: The Yardbirds, The Byrds, Lovin' Spoonful, The Animals, The Youngbloods, and The Blues Magoos with their song, "We Ain't Got Nothing Yet," even The Swingin' Medallions with their big hit, "Double Shot of My Baby's Love," The Swingin' Medallions were a unique band. For one thing, there were eight members. They had guitars, drums and a horn section and resembled a bunch of frat-boys from South Carolina. They were clean cut but with a striking characteristic—they wore matching multi-colored plaid pants, though no swinging medallions could be seen. Along with coordinated pants, they had coordinated dance moves. During the song "Double Shot of My Baby's Love," they broke off into pairs and faced each other with a microphone stand between them and proceeded to do some pelvic thrusting with their arms extended over their partner's shoulders while swaying back-and-forth.

This proved to be very entertaining and provided the teenaged audience something to hoop-and-holler about.

After the show, some of us went back to their hotel room, which was much nicer than anyplace we stayed. The band wanted to ask if there was anywhere that they could play besides Phoenix or Tucson, but the Medallions were more focused on dividing up the large pile of cash sitting on the bed than chatting about gigs, so we left.

We always hoped that somebody from one of these groups would say something to somebody such as, "You got to see these guys. They're great."

Unfortunately, that never happened.

We're Going to Disneyland!
Not Really, It's Just Los Angeles

A wise man once said, "California is the place you should be," and so we followed the oracle's advice. We packed up the Plymouth, and I believe Dennis's car, and headed out. Dick had gotten new mug shots—I mean headshots—made of The Spiders and had the tapes of songs to give to record companies, club owners, and management companies, plus a thousand Spiders business cards to hand out in L.A. Dick had set up a few auditions that would pan out, but at a much later date.

I remember that we didn't have a place to stay the first night or the second. Dick—I don't know how he did it—talked a stranger into letting us stay at his apartment. I guess people back then weren't concerned about being murdered by seven long-haired strangers. As we sprawled out in his living room I imagined how the conversation had gone: *You seven want to stay at my place? No problem. What time do you want breakfast?* Dick really must have the gift of charm, and in abundance.

Somehow, our new friend spent the remainder of the first night being interviewed on a late-night call-in talk radio show about a group called The Spiders, who were staying at his house. The D.J. quipped about getting some bug spray to take care of the spider infestation.

Dick now had gotten free publicity for the group! How does he do it?

Our stay came to an abrupt end, however, when the bananas our host had bought to feed his pet Iguana were consumed by some of the band members. I don't remember our benefactor's name, but he took a chance, letting seven total strangers from Arizona into his apartment. I would have never done that, even if Dick asked me. Thank you for your hospitality, bravery, and foolhardy generosity.

We spent our last night in Los Angeles sleeping outdoors in a park, convinced how nice it would be if we never had to sleep in a park again.

We headed back to Phoenix to work out a plan for the next trip to L.A. Our first foray to Los Angeles wasn't bad. We might even have said it was a success. Dick had passed around some photos and lots of business cards, handed out several demos, and a few auditions seemed promising. No recording contract or management company surfaced, but it was just the first trip. We hoped good things were right on the horizon.

Ahead of our next trip to L.A., we had a promise of work. I remember one job: it was opening for Strawberry Alarm Clock. Their hit was "Incense and Peppermint." Before the performance, John was in a panic because he couldn't locate the special wrench to adjust his pancake drums, but I had one. I gave it to John and they played to an appreciative crowd.

During Strawberry Alarm Clock's show, they set their electric keyboard on fire by using a propane tank with some gas jets attached to it. The burning instrument was a nice effect in the subdued stage lighting, and you could cook on it if you had to. My concern was that the fire marshal would charge in and hose down the stage. He would have responded unfavorably to a piano being set on fire in an old building without sprinklers.

However, setting the piano on fire had a profound effect on Vince. He wanted something like that, only bigger and better. Note to self: Vince liked theatrical effects. And just how will that affect me? Mike mentioned he'd like his piano to be set on fire. I was more than happy to comply with his request, but could we wait until we got home?

Things started to improve, as in more jobs, during this trip. The Spiders were beginning to gain some ground in the L.A. market. Amazingly, Dick found us somewhere else to live and, again, I don't know how he did it. This place was between Sunset and Hollywood Boulevards right in the center of the club scene: The Whisky a Go-Go, the Galaxy Club, and others. It was the Holy Grail of locations. Our kind benefactor's name was Doak Roberts, and he worked for Tony Curtis. He had a small two-bedroom, one bathroom California bungalow, painted white inside and out, with oak floors and vintage furniture. He welcomed eight people, plus Charlie's rabbit, into his home, and the odd assortment of girlfriends, friends, and people we had just met who came over and sometimes stayed a night or two.

Even my hope-to-be girlfriend Ellen came one time with Bonnie, Dick's sister. She was wonderful, but I just didn't know it then. Late one night, or actually early one morning because Vince was a night owl, he and Ellen decided to go to an all-night coffee shop on Sunset Blvd. Everyone else, including me, went to bed. They came home after 3:00 a.m. Vince went to his bed, but because the house was basically wall to wall sleeping people, the best place Ellen could find to sleep was on the floor underneath the dining room table. I guess I wasn't much of a gentleman back then, but to be honest I was sound asleep.

When I saw Vince the next morning, the first words out of his mouth were, "What's wrong with you? She likes you." I know. I was an idiot but wouldn't be for much longer.

Ellen was well liked by everyone in the band. The next night she and Vince talked for a long time. He told her how much I liked her, and that she should tell me she liked me, too. She didn't, of course. Later, out of the blue, Vince said, "Ellen, if you'd marry me, I'd be the happiest man in the world." It wasn't a proposal or anything like that. Vince was just being a nice guy. I hoped.

Ellen

My girlfriend of the future and I did have one intimate moment at Doak's. The bathroom was constantly in use—there were eight of us, nine if you counted Doak and ten if counted Charlie's rabbit. I would usually shave in the living room using a mirror hung over a chair. As I was preparing for my morning ritual, Ellen came over and asked if she could shave me. At first, I thought she wanted to borrow my razor, but I quickly realized she was actually asking to shave me. I said, "Sure," handing her my Gillette Blue Blade razor. She had six brothers, and I figured, wrongly, that she had seen it done numerous times. I lathered up with my can of Foamy and sat on a stool.

She began, her hand resting on my shoulder, and brushed my hair back from my face. Her long hair touched the back of my neck as she leaned toward me. *I really could get used to this*, I thought. All was going well until she drew the razor sideways across my neck. Alarmed, I grabbed her hand. I was expecting to find blood squirting from my neck at any second, but all was well—no harm done. The Foamy saved my life. I explained how shaving was supposed to go. She did a great job in the end, but the magical moment vanished. On the bright side, it was the first time I'd held her hand, even though to her it must have seemed that I was fending off an armed assault.

One day, feeling bored, I decided to take a walk down to nearby Hollywood Blvd. Doak's tiny bungalow could be a little close with all of us, plus the rabbit, crammed into it. It was good, even necessary, to get out on my own every once in a while. I had just made the turn onto Hollywood Blvd. when I was stopped by a man who claimed to be an L.A. detective. He showed me no ID, so I had to take his word for it. However, he was quite insistent that I show him mine. Naturally, I complied. After the usual questions that I had answered many times before, he threw me a curve ball.

"I know what you're doing. You are looking to buy drugs."

I told him that I really wasn't.

"We know what it's all about." He elaborated. "You give someone a peace sign. He gives you one back. Then you give him another peace sign, this time it's with the back of your hand toward him and not the palm. This means 'I'm looking for drugs.' If he returns the peace sign in the same way, it means 'I have drugs for sale.' You didn't think we knew that, did you?"

This was all news to me. I felt I should thank him for the information, but I decided not to. All I knew about the reverse hand peace sign was that in Europe it was the equivalent of giving somebody the finger. I guess you would need to check one's nationality before conducting a drug transaction.

He concluded his conversation by saying, "We will be watching you."

As he walked away, I wondered who this "we" was.

Despite the confrontation, it was a good day for a walk, and to top it off I saw Little Richard handing out small bibles from the back seat of a limousine. I also saw Troy Donahue, but someone had to tell me who he was.

Anyway, back to Doak and not my failure to commit. It was at Doak's house that I truly fell in love. Not with Ellen, but with *Her. She* was Doak's car—a white 1955 Jaguar XK140 convertible.

It was singularly the most beautiful car I had ever seen. It was totally impractical, but who cared? When a car looked that good, it didn't need to be practical. I gazed mournfully at my faithful old friend, my Plymouth Fury station wagon. Maybe a little soap and water and wax, perhaps a black racing stripe on the hood over the top and down the back would take away the lust for Doak's Jaguar. Nope.

At this point, I'm going to skip ahead a few years to tell you a story about after I had left the band. The very first car I bought when I moved back to Phoenix was a red 1955 Jaguar XK140 convertible with chrome wire wheels. It was the Sterling Moss Edition. It even had a small plaque on the inside saying that. Was it practical? I didn't care. It didn't have air-conditioning. I didn't care about that, either. I would care a whole lot that summer, though. It didn't come with windows. I would have to find those. They weren't the roll up kind, they were bolted inside the car. It didn't have a convertible top, which I would have to buy, but it had the frame and thirty rolls of three-inch medical adhesive tape could work, somewhat, until I could afford to buy a top for it. It came with a twenty-page owner's manual. There were letters that people had written to the Jaguar Company regarding their cars. My favorite was from an owner complaining that the car would stall every time he drove his Jaguar in the rain. The response from Jaguar was: *A gentleman does not drive his Jaguar in the rain.* Classic.

A while ago, I saw a photograph of Neal posing with some of his automobiles. In one, he was sitting on the hood, or bonnet for you Brits, of a Bentley, his long legs sticking out over the grill. He also owned a Mercedes convertible, and a Jaguar XKE. Had Neal lusted after Doak's Jaguar as I had? I wondered if he ever drove his Jaguar in the rain. I never did with mine, although I once tried to cross a stream. I was surprised when, because of the wake I had created, it stalled out halfway across. My side-mounted carburetors had flooded.

The book only said don't drive in the rain. There was nothing about crossing a swollen stream! Thirty minutes later it started up, but the gas tank was losing gas. I had inadvertently put a hole in it. A little J B Weld and a metal patch fixed it right up.

Back to my story. We were all living at Doak's house and life was good, except maybe not for Doak. Most of us stowed away neatly in one of the bedrooms—mattresses wall-to-wall. Charlie's rabbit reluctantly shared the couch with me. We had come to an understanding since I'd accidentally sat on him. Most of the time he avoided me like the plague after what came to be known as "the incident," and I was just fine with that. We let Doak have the other bedroom where he could find solitude and probably cry himself to sleep every night. We came out of hibernation around noon and took over the place.

Nazz Drumhead
Courtesy Jeanne Carney

6

The Nazz

Rumors of there being another band called The Spiders were apparently true. The main Spider-name competition was a group from Japan. There were six or seven members. They sang, danced and played their own instruments, already had a couple of albums, and were touring in Europe. You could easily tell one Spider group from the other: one Spider group wore gold jackets, the other wore new black jackets. To the band, gold jackets were so last year, so "Earwigs." But in the end, there could only be one Spider group. In actuality though, there were six other Spider groups running around. However, one of them wasn't going to be The Spiders I worked for.

The band had new photos taken. Gone now were the black jackets. The new look was going to be more hip: jeans, t-shirt or long-sleeve shirt, and pullover sweater, but this new look would disappear soon enough for an even newer look, something with a little more pizazz. Something with a little more sparkle. Something with a little more…Cindy.

A new name was needed, one to go with their new image. Everyone had an idea what it should be. Even I brought up a name, half in jest. The name I offered was Colonial Aggressions, I was a big fan of Paul Revere and the Raiders. Anyway, the name Colonial Aggressions was roundly rejected.

I honestly don't remember how the name The Nazz came about. They were looking for something that nobody else would ever think of. I've heard several theories about the origin of the name. One was that it rhymed with jazz. It had Arizona's initials in the name, and it was another name for Jesus, The Man from Nazareth—Vince's father was a minister. I don't think Vince wanted to bring religion into the band's name. I still remember John Lennon saying the Beatles were more popular than God. Lesson learned.

Toodie told me The Nazz was thought up in the back of her blue Mustang on the way back to Arizona from Albuquerque. She said Vince was rhyming words together, and nazz popped up after he said jazz. If Toodie says that was how it happened, that's good enough for me.

The Nazz was chosen. It was easy to say and easy to remember. In Arizona, they were promoted as The Nazz, formerly known as The Spiders, formerly known as The Earwigs.

That name that will last forever, they thought. Yeah right. Colonial Aggressions would look pretty good in six months.

The Madhouse on McDowell

The Phoenix Coliseum: home of the Phoenix Suns for twenty-four years. The Sun's announcer called it the Madhouse on McDowell. Along with basketball games, the Coliseum was host to livestock shows, horse auctions, the state fair, the traveling circus, and occasionally concerts. It held 15,000 people and was a concrete building inside and out. It was a large venue for Phoenix at the time it was built.

One year during the reign of The Spiders, there was an event billed as "The Battle of the Bands." It was really just a show with local bands playing. There was no actual competition to it, no trophies or cash prize. The Spiders, being one of the top Phoenix bands, wanted a good showing at the event. Even though bands weren't fighting for supremacy, John Speer took "The Battle of the Bands" quite seriously. Must have been that competitive streak fostered by track and field events at Cortez High School.

During the performance of one of our perceived band enemies, the drummer wore a wig that made him look a little like Brian Jones of the Rolling Stones. John repeatedly reached in from behind the curtain and tried to remove the drummer's wig by poking at it with a drumstick. John's antics annoyed the drummer—a lot. Trying to see who was messing with him, the drummer was constantly looking around and adjusting his wig, which made him lose concentration. After the show, the furious drummer ran off the stage searching for his tormenter. What he saw backstage was a group of people trying to look innocent. Which we were. John was nowhere to be found.

Glen had been delegated added responsibility by the other members of the band. The Nazz were busy writing new songs and, to protect their new material, they copied the lyrics onto a piece of paper and dated and signed it.

In addition to copying the lyrics, they needed to document the music in musical note form, similar to sheet music. Glen was the only one who knew how to do that. At least that's what the others told him. This was painstaking work, especially if there was more than one song to get down on paper.

Once completed, they put their transcribed music, dated and signed, along with a recent front page of the local newspaper, into a manila envelope. The envelope was sealed and taken to the Post Office and mailed back to themselves. To make it official they needed the date stamp from the Post Office. The unopened envelope, along with any reel-to-reel tapes of their songs, was placed in a box for safe keeping and delivered to one of the parents in Phoenix for secure storage. This was how you protected your music from being stolen in the sixties.

Opportunity Knocks and You Better
Answer When It Does

Our fortunes greatly improved with the jobs at the Cheetah Club, formerly the Aragon Ballroom, home of Lawrence Welk and his band and the lovely Lennon sisters. This may have been where Alice Cooper got the idea to use a bubble machine in their show. Lawrence Welk used them for years, in fact bubbles, as in Champagne, were his signature thing. The times they were a changing.

The Cheetah Club was a very large building, and it sat right on Ocean Park pier. It doesn't exist anymore—in 1970 a fire burnt it to the ground and, just in case something hadn't been destroyed in the fire, a huge storm or hurricane removed any remains, along with the pier, in 1983.

The Cheetah Club was square shaped and the stage sat five or six feet off the ground. There were long sheets of stainless-steel hanging in a circle from floor to ceiling surrounding the dance floor. There were openings between the panels so people could move around the floor, find the restrooms or visit the poster shop. The panels brought to mind curtains of death, because they swung wildly whenever someone bumped into them. I imagined arms and legs being lopped off.

One night, a more than slightly inebriated Jim Morrison jumped-up and, getting a hand hold, hoisted himself onto the stage, shocking the band, The Yellow Pages. Jim could have just as easily walked around back and climbed the stairs to the stage. But if you wanted to make a grand entrance, and if you wanted to sing and dance when you got on the stage and, if you were THE Jim Morrison of The Doors, you just climbed up and sang and danced. The Yellow Pages watched him and kept the music going.

The crowd had long since stopped dancing to focus on Jim, but things really got interesting when he began to feel overheated and became extremely interested in removing his clothes! Seeing this, the

Cheetah's employees raced up the stairs gesturing frantically for him to come their way. Several times he started toward them then, suddenly, he'd spin around and swagger back on the stage. When he began his provocative striptease, the crowd, especially the women, were delighted and enthusiastically encouraged him by whistling and cheering. Finally, the employees, and others, convinced him to come off the stage. It was rumored that they enticed him by pointing to a lovely young woman holding a bottle of something. And that was the last we saw of Jim Morrison that night. He certainly gave me, and the crowd, something to talk about.

During their first performance at The Cheetah, The Nazz received a very favorable reception from the crowd, and most importantly, from the manager, Sherry Cottle. Dick quickly moved in with some new negotiating skills to procure more bookings.

Shortly after, we were invited to move into Sherry's house. How does Dick do this? Not only does he finagle a place for the band to stay, even if temporarily, but the band played more dates at the Cheetah Club. What's more, Sherry said she could find them jobs at other places.

When we told Doak that we were moving out, he looked like he was going to cry—tears of joy, without a doubt! I don't know how this good man put up with us. Thank you, Doak, for what you did. I'm pretty sure I could not have done that. No, I'm *positive* I couldn't. I'm just glad there are people like you to make up for people like me.

We were now safely tucked away in Sherry's house, but we would move into a rented house in Venice Beach soon. In the meantime, this house was larger than Doak's and was closer to the Cheetah Club. We were moving on up.

Sherry was a divorced mother of three little boys, therefore when we were around the children, we all had to be on our best behavior. I believe it was Dick who discovered one of the children needed glasses because he had trouble reading, not because he couldn't understand the words. He just couldn't see the words. Plus, he was bumping into things and couldn't catch a ball tossed directly to him. Once he got his glasses, everything was fine.

Hanging Around the Santa Monica Pier

Three of our favorite things to do were to hang out at the Ocean Park or Santa Monica pier, go to the Farmer's Market on Melrose, and listen to music outside the Whisky a Go Go. Yes, we truly had exciting lives. These really weren't three of our very favorite things by choice. They were due to our circumstances. Poverty had a great bearing on what our favorite things could possibly be.

Outside the Whisky a Go Go at night, we'd stand around listening to the music telling ourselves that someday we'd be on the *inside* playing, while other bands would be hanging outside listening to us, The Nazz. Not now, but soon, very soon.

Late one night we went the Santa Monica Pier to witness something called the green tide. This was where ocean water becomes phosphorescent green from a certain algae microorganism. Quite pretty. As we gazed down at the water, a car drove onto the pier. Usually, at that time of night, it was the police wondering why we were there. But it wasn't the police. It was somebody in a Ferrari, a bright red Ferrari hardtop. I commented that I thought it was a 275 GT but wasn't sure.

When the owner got out, I asked him.

"Yes, it is. I just got it," he said.

I was right. The man seemed a little surprised that I knew. I appreciate American muscle cars, their aggressiveness and style, but I always seem to be drawn to European cars because of their maneuverability and style, despite having electrical problems and undersized radiators. Yes, they were impractical, but who cares?

He asked if I wanted to see it. Without hesitation I said, "Yes, please," and approached slowly—after all, people with long hair and people with short hair were not supposed to get along. As I came closer, I recognized the man. He was James Garner! He was proud of his new car and wanted to show it off. He walked with me all around the Ferrari pointing out its special features. It was red and shiny. What other color would a Ferrari be? I peered inside—just beautiful, all leather and gauges. I gushed at least a dozen times how much I liked his car. Especially after he said it was a v12 with a top speed over 160 MPH.

Thanking him for the tour, our attention turned to the glowing green tide. I told him that I worked for a band called The Nazz and they played quite often at the Cheetah Club. Without turning his gaze from the green water, he said he would have to stop by and listen to them.

"If you have any trouble getting in, have somebody come find me," I stupidly said.

His face showed his amusement. Upon immediate reflection I thought, *Idiot. He is James Garner. He won't need my help to get into the Cheetah Club.*

Then, he casually asked me, "Who is your favorite actor?"

"John Wayne," I blurted out without thinking.

Realizing who I was talking to, I quickly added, "You're right up there, too, Mr. Garner."

God, how much more stupid could I possibly be? Don't answer that.

"John Wayne is a good choice. Unfortunately, he wouldn't like *you*," he replied, grinning.

He said he had to go, that he had to get up early the next morning. As he drove away, I could hear that car's finely tuned exhaust roaring. One afternoon not long after that, according to Dennis, James Garner came by and listened to the band practice.

PACIFIC OCEAN PAR
POST OFFICE BOX 224
SANTA MONICA CALIFORN
TELEPHONE 213-392-45:
CABLE CHEETAH-LOS ANGEL:

CHEETAH

Dec 1 1967 1:00 a.m.

Dear Ellen,

Yes, it's me, fresh on my trip of fame and fortune in California, Changing people and their ways. Change for change. People will have to come up to my standards. I will never go down to theirs.
Toodie was mistaken. I didn't eat her brownies. I used them to brick over a hole in the fireplace.

Since we're talking about me, I did a neat John Wayne thing last night. Sherry locked her keys in the office at the Cheetah Club. So, with one mighty blast I kicked the door in. Not only kicked it in, I put a hole through it and split it into two pieces. Broke the lock and removed half the plaster on the door wall. It was great needless to say. I was quite pleased with my destruction.

I hear Jack Curtis has opened up a new club. Good for him. I hope it does well.

I spent a quiet birthday at home with my friends around me: Pink Floyd, The Animals. You know, just the usual gang.

Tell Toodie just to send the tape by mail and tell her I just acquired the new Jimi Hendrix and the brand-new Cream tapes. I hope the poor girl doesn't cry too much, not that I can blame her.

So, if I don't see you around, I guess I won't see you.

Mike

It's a John Wayne Sort of Thing

Late one night, Sherry had to go to her office at the Cheetah Club. Everyone decided to go with her, and we piled in the Fury. Did I mention we lived exciting lives? Once at the club, she discovered she didn't have her door keys. Each of us took a turn trying the knob, and each having the same lack of success told Sherry the door was indeed locked. Sherry didn't want to go home to retrieve the keys, so she came up with a plan.

She said, "Mike, kick the door in."

"Okay," I agreed, uncertainly.

The door was solid wood, and I had no idea if I could. I hadn't had much experience kicking in doors, but I considered that it might look good on a resume. Chants of "*Kick that door. Kick that door*" echoed down the hall. I eyed the lock location, stood back, and assaulted the door with my foot. There was a loud crack—thank goodness it wasn't my leg. The sound was the door shattering into several pieces. Parts of the door, frame, molding, and bits of plaster flew across the room and hit the wall behind her desk.

"You can go in now. The door appears to be open," I said, nonchalantly.

"I said kick the door in, not destroy my office!" She was laughing, as were the others.

"Sorry." But I was actually quite pleased with myself.

We moved into a new place in Venice Beach. It wasn't much, but then we didn't really need much, basically a place to sleep and practice, which this place provided. As often as possible we took advantage of Sherry and went to her house to hang out.

Neal Smith, who was a drummer from a group in Phoenix called the Holy Grail would, from time to time, come to L.A. to visit, and sometimes he would bring his sister, Cindy. Neal, along with Cindy, would soon play a big part in the band.

The More the Merrier

One group we were all looking forward to seeing at The Cheetah was Pink Floyd on their first U.S. tour. I watched the show from the overhead room where the light shows were run. The light show for Pink Floyd was done by one guy, Mike Leonard, who was literally amazing, and I wanted to know more about what he was doing.

The stage and the amps were draped in white, loose-fitting sheets with small fans positioned under them. When the time came, Mike pushed a button, turning the multi-colored strobe lights on. The bright lights reflected off the white sheets. And when he activated the fans, the sheets lifted and flowed with movement as the lights pulsed through and onto them. It took the old white strobe lights to a whole new dimension.

Strobes make everything look like an old-time movie, where movement appears jerky and chaotic. But these color-strobes hitting the slowly undulating sheets created an entirely different illusion. It felt like the entire room was moving, flowing back and forth. The stainless-steel sheets hanging from the ceiling reflected the colors which heightened the effect. Sometimes colored cellophane, or oil on an overhead projector for the liquid part of the light show were used, the light again focused on the white sheets. And he was able to use lenses and prisms to create a kaleidoscope effect, enveloping the entire stage in endlessly changing multicolor light patterns.

He told me to watch carefully for the next effect; he would only produce it for a short time. He switched on two strobe lights, a green and a red strobe. Pulsating colors flooded the room. Even from my lofty perch the effect was disorienting. Below, people on the dance floor stumbled into each other, clinging to the nearest person for support. Just when I thought they were going to start toppling over, he turned it off and everything quickly returned to normal.

It was only then that everyone noticed the band, Pink Floyd, had disappeared.

The light show was great, and Pink Floyd was great. They played songs from their first album, *The Piper at the Gates of Dawn*. The night was a huge success.

Shortly after that Pink Floyd show our group grew by one more person. That person was Les Braden, one of the Pink Floyd road crew. We suddenly had a new traveling companion and housemate. Syd Barrett's declining physical and mental health may have had something to do with it. Les was an amiable British bloke who could tell a good story. He was also a skilled carpenter, and he liked American girls. Actually, he liked all girls.

One day he casually mentioned he had Ringo Starr's drumhead, the one that said "The Beatles" on it. We all thought, *Sure you do*. He went to his room and when he came back it was in his hands. He had The Beatles' drumhead! He said he had gotten it at a studio where The Beatles were recording and he'd removed it from Ringo's drum.

> *"The road from legitimate suspicion to rampant paranoia is much shorter than we think."*
> Captain Jean Luc Picard

We were at Sherry's house one night when around ten o'clock a car pulled up in front and stopped.

I spotted the car through the living room window. The driver turned off the headlights, but turned on the car's interior lights.

"Is anyone expecting company?" I asked. "There's a car out front."

Everyone shook their heads or said no.

Dennis asked, "What are they doing?"

"Nothing. Just sitting in the car," I said. This brought everyone to the window to see for themselves.

"Do you think they are cops?" Alice asked.

"It's just two people sitting in a car," I answered.

The thought that they might be undercover cops getting ready to raid the place crossed several minds.

"Is anybody holding?" Sherry asked nervously. A couple of hands went up followed by a few choice expletives.

"The cops will turn the water off before they raid the house. Turn off the lights, even the porch light. Flush everything you have on you," Glen said.

I started to say, "I think it's just.........", but the chaotic sounds of people scrambling in the dark and bumping into things, in what sounded like—and was—a frantic attempt to find the bathroom drowned out my words. After rounds of flushes, their mission was accomplished and everyone joined me back at the window.

"Why are they still there?" Glen asked anxiously. "They must be waiting for the rest of the police to show up."

Les Braden spoke up, "I'm going out there."

Multiple alarmed voices exclaimed, "Don't do it! They will shoot you. This isn't England!"

Bravely—or foolishly, we all thought—Les opened the front door and went out.

Everyone else took cover behind the furniture. We expected gunfire any second. I thought about having to send his body back to England with a note attached to it: "*Sorry. We told him not to go out there.*"

What seemed like hours passed, but it was only a few nerve-wracking minutes. Some of us emerged from behind the barricades and peeked out the window to see what was going on. Les wasn't dead yet, but it couldn't be very much longer, we all thought. He was speaking to a person in the car, raising his hands, gesturing, and pointing in different directions. When he bent over and stuck his head and an arm through the passenger window, everyone let out an audible gasp, even me. I was starting to buy into the paranoia, imagining guns drawn and shots fired.

At last, Les straightened up, backed slowly away from the car, turned and walked toward the house. The car started up and drove away down the street. Les came inside through the front door and switched on the lights. A lot of adrenaline was pounding through our veins. With one voice, everyone yelled, "What did the cops want?"

"Oh, they weren't cops. It was just an older couple who got lost, and I showed them on a map how to get to the freeway. They were very nice."

Les Braden
Courtesy Toodie Mueller

7

Lose One, Gain One

When not playing in Los Angeles, The Nazz sometimes headed back to Phoenix or Tucson, but not as often as before, to play gigs, and to visit family and friends. During one trip to Phoenix, The Nazz managed to put out a 45 record, "Wonder Who's Loving Her Now" and "Lay Down and Die," which were produced by Dick Phillips on the *Very Record* label. Dick, being the producer, wanted to punch up the line "I wonder who's loving her now" with background singers to make it stand out from the rest of the song. He looked at me, and I clearly conveyed a message. I just haul, I don't sing.

After thinking for a few minutes, he came up with an idea. I don't know if a light bulb turned on over his head or his fingers snapped as he blurted out, "I've got it!"

This stopped me from suggesting that maybe The Shirelles would do it. They were a pretty good girl group. My almost suggestion wasn't too far off, though. His idea was to find two girls to sing in the background, and he just happened to know two young ladies for the job.

He contacted Toodie Mueller and Jacque Memmott, another friend of the band. He'd heard them singing and harmonizing to tunes on the radio as Toodie drove them around in her blue Mustang. Problem solved. They were both excited to help out, and at rehearsals they sounded good. Dick's first foray into being a music producer might pay off.

The big day came at the Phoenix studio. Everything and everyone was ready. Except for one problem, no Toodie, and we were unable to get hold of her. If they waited much longer, they'd lose their studio time. Forced to go ahead without her, the song was recorded with Jacque singing in the background along with the other band members. The song sounded great. To this day it's one of my favorites. If you just happen to have an original 1967 copy or find one hold on to it. It's probably worth some money.

Hours later, Toodie got in touch with Dick and explained that her parents had insisted she go to church with them. Her parents likely hoped God would intervene and keep her from hanging out with us.

This was the last time John Speer would ever play on a Nazz record. John may have felt something was about to happen. He wasn't communicating with the band very much by this point. Instead of staying with us at Doak's, he would stay at his girlfriend's house. Of course, if it meant that I wouldn't have to share a bathroom with seven other guys, I would probably have done the same thing. Even when we stayed at Sherry's house, he didn't hang out much with the group.

What caused the break-up with the group in November 1967, or even who initiated it, I don't know. It may have been John's own idea, or the group's decision. It was rumored he didn't like the direction the group was headed, but I do not know if this was true. Years later, John came to visit Ellen and me but he really didn't want to talk about the band. I didn't press the subject.

At any rate, he left the band. It wasn't until the following day that I heard what had happened. Even Charlie didn't have any inkling of it, and if the rabbit knew, he wasn't talking. But, by the time I got up the next morning, John was gone, and Neal was in.

John Speer
Courtesy Toodie Mueller

Very soon after, we headed back to Phoenix so Neal could practice with the band and learn all the songs. I was left with a problem. Neal had a double set of drums, which would take up a lot more room in the Plymouth than John's pancake drums. John's drums could be broken down and put into two cases. Neal had regular drums that did not break down.

I had a choice to make, get a humongous roof rack or buy a trailer. As it turned out, I did neither. Eventually, I chose to trade the Plymouth in for a green 1964 Dodge A100 van with both side and back doors. I went from the Plymouth's pushbutton transmission on the left side of the steering column to a shifter located on the dash on the right side of a steering wheel. It looked very space-age, like it belonged on a jet fighter. The van had air conditioning that definitely was not as good as the Plymouth's. This was most likely because the engine was located between the two front seats. We were protected from the engine's heat by a cover. Excuse me, *insulated* engine cover. Right, insulated. You could roast a turkey on that engine cover. To reduce the heat radiating from it, I wrapped the cover in quilted moving blankets. That helped some. At least I could rest my arm on it without burning myself.

The van had enough storage for all the equipment and people, provided they sat on the floor and didn't mind sliding around. It had seat belts, which weren't even required in 1968. Concerned for my safety, my dad had supplied a pair of seat belts for the van. He told me to install and wear them. I thanked him and said that I would. Installation proved to be a problem, since the belts were too short for the van's seats. Actually, the seats weren't the problem. They were roughly the thickness of a stadium seat brought to football games to keep from having to sit on concrete. The problem was that the van's seats sat on top of, and were bolted to, metal risers. I solved the problem by attaching the belts directly to the seats, sliding the webbing underneath the frame and securing the webbing with a couple of bolts and washers to the frame. As long as the seats remained fastened to the metal riser, we'd be safe and secure. It was probably the only van in the country that had them. Who knows? They might come in handy, someday.

Furnazios

The band worked constantly while in L.A. writing and practicing their new songs, but when they returned to Arizona, they searched for a place to relax. Enter the Weeds of Idleness. The Weeds were a group of three young ladies who worked at Mountain Bell Telephone in the daytime and practiced being a band at night. They kept a set of drums and two amplifiers in the living room of their small house. The Weeds did a pretty good rendition of Jefferson Airplane's "Somebody to Love." Their house, along with Bonnie's, was one of our go-to places. We usually went over in the evening to hang out or practice right about the time the girls were thinking about going to bed. We hoped they, and the neighbors, didn't mind. The Weeds never complained.

Because they had actual paying jobs, they also had money to feed us almost every evening we were there. They would make Furnazios. Never heard of Furnazios? It was a snack of Doritos smothered in cheddar cheese, broiled in the oven a few minutes and served hot and gooey. These were scarfed up, literally, in seconds. I'm not totally sure, but the Weeds may have invented nachos with cheese. I believe Mexican restaurants might have actually stolen the Weeds's recipe!

The Weeds called them Furnazios because of Vince's last name, Furnier. It has a certain ring to it, yes? With any other of the band members' names, it doesn't sound as good—Buxnazios, Smithnazios, Brunazios, and Dunnazios just aren't as appealing.

The group practiced at their house, sometimes until two in the morning. They fed us and generally put up with us instead of going to bed, and not once did they ever say, "Can you guys just leave already? We have to get up in the morning." Sorry, once you fed us, we were like stray cats, we kept coming back.

Besides all that, in their spare time, whenever that was, the Weeds concocted stories about us and our exploits. They weren't just a few pages long; they wrote full-on stories complete with illustrations and front and back covers. The stories were fun and gratefully appreciated by all of us. I wish I had kept at least one of them. I'd like to read the tales of Alice and his merry band of men, along with Amp Boy, their faithful driver, again. I naturally liked the stories about me. They were the best. The Weeds wrote a chronicle of humorous stories about all of us before the name The Nazz or Alice Cooper meant anything to anybody. Thank you for everything you did for us, Lorena, Julee, and Linda, or if you prefer, Weed 1, Weed 2, and Weed 3.

Below is an excerpt from one of the storybooks when the band was called The Nazz. It was given to me by Dennis Dunaway. The man saves everything.

L.A. NIGHTS AND DAYS

TO BE SUNG TO THE TUNE OF CALIFORNIA NIGHTS BY THE ANIMALS

INTRODUCTION:

THIS PROGRAM IS DEDICATED TO THE PEOPLE AND RESIDENTS OF 2129 SOUTH CRENSHAW--WHO MAY NOT KNOW IT BUT THEY'RE BEAUTIFUL? (THAT WASN'T OUR IDEA, THAT'S HOW THE SONG GOES) IF ANY OF YOUSE GUYS OUT THERE DON'T GET THIS SONG, SAVE UP ALL YOUR MONEYS AND FLY TRANSFREAK AIRLINES (ON MIKE ALLEN'S HALF-FARE TICKET WHICH HAS EXPIRED ALREADY) TO CRENSHAW. IT WILL BE WORTH IT, IF NOT FOR THE SAKE OF THIS SONG, BUT CAUSE YOU'LL GET TO SEE THE NAZZ AT CHEETAH.

> Piercing screams--forget your dreams
> Doors move--Cher's kids all over you
> On a street in LA called Crenshaw
>
> Long Gone Miles, broadcasting now
> His voice sounds like a dying cow
> On a street in LA called Crenshaw
>
> NAZZ weren't born there
> Perhaps they'll die there
> We here the food ain't so hot down there
>
> (Pause)   Oh-hh South Crenshaw
>
> (Here insert Mike Allen's beautiful guitar-
> picking version of Secret Agent)
>
> But soon the Weeds will be there too
> Crenshaw ain't nothing to what we do
> On a street in LA called Crenshaw
>
> (Fade out)

Toodie often drove one or more of us to the Weeds's house. Some-times, Ellen came along. Toodie knew Ellen liked me, and I liked her, and she did her best to get us together. One night at the end of an evening of TV and Furnazios, Toodie said, "Mike, you drive Ellen home. You live closer than I do."

Ellen was shy, and there was not much conversation during the ride, but I was happy to be alone with her. I think that night could have been a beginning for us, but I just said goodnight and dropped her off at the curb. I know, I'm an idiot.

The Weeds of Idleness made rock and roll history by opening for The Nazz at a high school dance. Everyone, including Les, was at the Weeds's house when Vince suggested they open for the group. At first, they were hesitant but were finally convinced. They decided on two songs. I offered to pick up their equipment, set it up, and return it the next day. It would be their first time playing in front of people other than us. One song they chose was Jefferson Airplane's, "Some-body to Love." I don't recall the other. They received quite a good response from the audience. It was novel then to see girls playing their own instruments and singing. After I moved their equipment off to the side, I went over to them.

"How was it?" I asked.

"We were so nervous. I'm still shaking," said Julee.

"Yes, but how was it?" I prompted.

"It was great!" Lorena said. "Lights in our faces, compliments from Charlie, the applause and people cheering. It was great!" All three of them hugged me.

"I didn't do anything," I protested. "I just hauled your equip-ment over here."

"You were the closest one we could hug!"

They chose to hug me over Les.

Neal Shot Film at 11:00. Alcohol and Guns Truly Do Not Mix.

It was a warm spring night in March 1968 in Phoenix. But of course in Phoenix every night was a warm night. We were bored, tired of practicing, having fittings for the new clothes Cindy was making, and working on new songs.

"You want to go to Bonnie's?" That was Dick's sister's house.

"No, done that," Neal said.

"How about the Weeds of Idleness's house?"

"No, did that yesterday," Vince replied.

"Let's go kill something," someone suggested. "Anybody have a gun?" All eyes turned to me.

Yes, I had several, but which one would fit the low skill level of this group? I thought of my Browning 12-gauge A5 shotgun. I knew the recoil would knock any one of them down. Plus, it was a semi-automatic shotgun. If you kept pressing the trigger, the gun would keep firing. So, no. A lever action Marlin 30-30 rifle? I had visions of them imitating Lucas McCain from *The Rifleman* TV show—walking down a street firing from the hip. That would hurt. So, again, no. A 1911 model 45 Colt Automatic? Oh, God no. Rounds would be fired off in all directions. The gun will be in control of them and not the other way around. Realistic chance of survival, zero at best.

I settled on a single shot Winchester 22 rifle with two built-in safety switches. I made each of them promise to stand behind the shooter at all times. With that precaution I figured we all had a chance to make it out alive. A slim chance, but a chance, nevertheless.

I went home to retrieve the rifle and a box of ammo. They went home to retrieve some doctor feel-good tonic. It's good for what ails you. It must have worked, because by the time I came back they were feeling no pain. Vince, Neal, Vince's sister Nicki, and I drove out to the desert where I gave them a crash course on how to safely operate the weapon.

While the boys peed on every cactus they saw, which in their condition in the desert at night might not have been the best thing one should do, I set up tin cans at various distances, taking the rifle with me just for safety's sake. After finishing the setup, I walked back to the van and put the headlights on the targets. They took turns firing, trying to get as close to any can as possible. At first, they had little success, but after some practice they hit several cans. I can positively state that no animals were injured during our marksmanship contest, unless they died from laughter.

After about an hour and a half of this fun, we decided we'd had enough. We stood in a group to brag about who was the best shot, ridicule the worst, and make plans for what we'd do the next day. Suddenly, a shot rang out. There was a moment when we looked at each other not comprehending what we'd heard.

The confusion cleared when Neal exclaimed, "I've been shot! Vince, you shot me!"

Vince had been holding the weapon and had forgotten to clear the chamber or put the safety on. What made it worse was I had lost sight of the weapon and hadn't cleared the chamber myself. I was supposed to be the responsible one.

Neal hopped around on one foot swearing like a sailor. Shock was wearing off as pain set in. We quickly loaded him into the van and drove to the nearest hospital emergency room. Because he knew the police would be called, Neal said he would say he had accidentally shot himself. He didn't want Vince to get in trouble. The police arrived in short order and questioned Neal privately.

He thought they seemed satisfied with his answers. However, when they came out to the waiting room, they found us and the grilling commenced. Since we hadn't had the forethought to formulate a solid story about Neal shooting himself, our story was deliberately lacking in detail. I don't think they really believed what Neal or the rest of us had to say, but they reported it as an accident, and that was that.

Neal was released from the treatment room with a below-the-knee cast on his leg and instructions to leave it on for six to eight weeks. A drummer with a cast on his leg—how was that going to work? According to Neal, Vince's father paid the bill that night through his insurance company, and Neal kept the bill as a souvenir. I guess the police kept the bullet as a souvenir. I can almost hear Vince's father talking to him about the shooting. *"Son, you are not going to shoot any more people, are you? Isn't that right, son?"*

"Oh, dad…"

We never again went shooting. I'm pretty sure my rifle was never fired after that night. I still own it. I had the idea I should put it in a display case with a plaque: Rifle Alice Cooper Used to Shoot Neal Smith. That was such a good idea I recently did just that. It's now in a case on the mantle over our fireplace.

While the band was in Phoenix, something significant happened. The Nazz, seemingly the safest name in the world, was already being used by Todd Rundgren's band, wait for it…The Nazz. Once again it was back to the drawing board for a new name.

A name that would prove to have a monumental impact on the group.

Poster by Alice Cooper
Courtesy Paul Brenton

8

The Birth of Alice Cooper

Alice Cooper, Inc.

8914 SUNSET BLVD.
LOS ANGELES, CALIFORNIA 90069
PHONE (213) 657-8890

3 22 1968 3:00 p.m.

Well Ellen, certainly took you long enough to answer my letter. Shame, Shame.

Mike Bruce, Glen, and Neal are back in Phoenix to take care of Mike's draft status and Neal's foot. The new name of the group is Alice Cooper. It became official at the Blue Cheer show. Blue Cheer plays through a lot of amplifiers and are very loud. If you like a lot of amplifiers and loud music, they are definitely the group for you.

Vince's parents will be here Friday and Saturday. So, we'll have to be on our best behavior. Anyway, how has your busy life been? Staying out of trouble, aren't you? If you send me Toodie's address, I would like to write to her. Say hi to anybody you see. That line sure is stupid. I would hate people who would ask me to say hello for them. Oh well.

Mike

In Phoenix, we often hung out at Bonnie's house. She was Dick's sister and had a small apartment where we were always welcomed, day or night. She would sit on her sofa with a large bowl of sunflower seeds next to her on the table, smoking cigarettes and drinking coffee while we watched TV and talked and laughed well into the wee hours.

Me, Bonnie Phillips
Courtesy Toodie Mueller

Brainstorming for a new name happened there. Suggestions were tossed around and graded on their merit. Glen threw out the name Husky Baby Sandwiches. It received a lot of comments and laughs, but no. I even proposed Colonial Aggressions one more time. I pointed out that if they'd used it the last time, they wouldn't be looking for a new one now! I thought I had them for a minute, but once again there was little interest, and it was voted down. If any new band out there wants to use that name, feel free.

The name Alice Cooper was pitched by Vince, because no other band, especially not an all-male band, would ever have used that name. There was a very good chance no female group would choose it either. Most of the female groups at the time were singing groups: The Supremes, Dixie Cups, Shirelles, The Ronettes, Martha and the Vandellas. There was a blues player by the name of Al Kooper, though. He tells a story that after the Alice Cooper group became popular some mighty weird people started showing up at his concerts. The Al Kooper name was close, but not that close. There actually was an Alice Cooper character, though. She was the housekeeper on *Mayberry R.F.D.* Her appearance on the show didn't take place until later that year.

As a bonus, there could be backstories surrounding the name. One was that when five guys walked out on stage everyone would ask, *"Where is Alice Cooper?" "Who's Alice?" "Did she show up? Did they break up before the show?"* There were all sorts of possibilities. It was both shocking and thought-provoking that they'd have a female name for the group without a female singer. The audience would be confused, expecting a girl singer, but there wouldn't be one, and they would tell their friends and then they would all be confused. It sounded good, really good. I mean, it was no Colonial Aggressions, but then again it wasn't bad.

That was the birth of Alice Cooper, formerly The Nazz, formerly The Spiders, and formerly The Earwigs. They made a quick visit to the Ouija board for validation. This thing spit out volumes, like it was being controlled by unseen hands. Probably Vince's. It said Alice Cooper was unfairly convicted for being a witch and was put to death. She had cursed the people who killed her and would come back to torment them, and all their descendants, and blah blah blah. This was good stuff. Who owns the rights to the material? It had "blockbuster" written all over it. The Ouija board needs to get an agent.

At last, they had a new name, and I had a new van. Well, more precisely a used green Dodge van. One of the first things the newly formed Alice Cooper group did was to order Alice Cooper Inc. stationary and Alice Cooper Inc. envelopes and Alice Cooper Inc. letterhead. The "Inc." added that touch of class.

In the beginning, the intention was that the band was Alice Cooper. But the bio they presented in interviews included the detail that she was a person and a witch. The conundrum was the whole band couldn't be a witch named Alice. The transition was inevitable. Almost immediately, Vince was cast in the roll of the fictional Alice. Newspaper articles referred to Vince as Alice after first mentioning the band, Alice Cooper. Fans asked Vince for Alice's autograph and, the more famous the band got, the more they evolved from the group named Alice Cooper to a single person. It took a little longer for those of us who knew him as Vince to make the change.

> Sargent, Jon. "A well rounded evening of rock." *Arizona Republic,* Phoenix, Arizona, May 24, 1969

> *Appearing on stage entirely decked in sequins, glitter, and long hair—very, very long hair—the group tended to look much like refugees from a Ziegfeld Follies chorus line.*

> *As for their music, it was about as logical. A perfect example could be "Meet Me on Mars" (sic)*

An event at the Phoenix Coliseum was a show advertised as "The triumphant return of Alice Cooper back to Phoenix." Iron Butterfly was also on the playbill. Getting as much hype as Alice Cooper was the large round rotating stage the groups would perform on. A stage that came with a very unique set of problems, not the least of which was what to do between acts with all the amplifiers, drum cases and extra supplies for the bands—things that were usually stored behind the stage and out of sight. Now, they would be on the rotating stage in the middle of the Coliseum floor and visible to everybody. If exposed equipment proved to be a distraction, what about me? I usually spent my time sitting on those cases behind the stage ready to swing into action if I was needed, or waiting for the group to finish performing. Exposure was also a problem for Charlie, who liked to be out of sight but on stage left or right. He had to sit on the revolving stage flipping his switches in full view of the crowd or settle for the next best thing, which was to walk with the slowly spinning stage while flipping his switches.

Some of the props wouldn't be a problem even though they would be visible during the entire show. They could still be stored behind the amplifiers. Alice just needed a path to get to them. The door that Alice sang through for the song "Nobody Likes Me," however, was a big problem. It was too heavy and awkward for Alice to carry very far by himself. When the time for the door came, I was forced to hoist the door over my head and run alongside the rotating stage, timing my speed so I could hand the door off to Alice wherever the stage came to a stop.

The stage itself was more than a little unstable; just walking on it was a wobbly adventure. If you suffered from motion sickness, you wouldn't want to ride that thing. It also audibly groaned, squeaked, and creaked. A revolving stage was a relatively new idea, and the crowd didn't quite understand the concept.

During the show the audience walked along with it, following the band around and around not comprehending that, if you sat in one place long enough, the band would come back to where you were. They were continuously getting up, walking and changing their seats to stay in front of the band, and were not quiet about it. They may have thought that their constant movement was part of the experience. At times, the stage would suddenly jolt to a stop and then restart with a jerk, causing the band and the audience as well to lose their balance.

The sound system for the show was the actual P.A. system used for the Sun's games. It was perfect for announcing scores but not so great for music, which ricocheted off the hard surface walls and echoed through the concrete canyon. Just as annoying was the lighting system, which had two positions: on or off, daylight bright, or pitch dark. All this led to Shep pulling his hair out, which wasn't good because he didn't have all that much to begin with. The show was not quite the triumphal return Alice Cooper had hoped for.

JD's

JD's in Scottsdale, Arizona was a very interesting club. They advertised on the radio that they were at the river bottom, and everybody in town knew where that was: on the border between the cities of Scottsdale, which called itself "The West's Most Western Town," and Tempe, which at the time was home to Arizona State University and 20,000 college students. How was JD's going to tap into both the Country Western and the rock and roll markets? Easy, they had two clubs, one above the other. The upper club hosted Country Western music, and the lower club was for the cave-dwellers. That club was all about rock and roll. Upstairs you might listen to Marty Robbins singing "Streets of Laredo," and in the basement you could hear Vanilla Fudge singing "You Keep Me Hangin' On." We preferred the cave dwellers. Nothing against Marty Robbins. He was great, and I still listen to him on my 8-track tape player. Ask your parents, they'll tell you what an 8-track tape player is, or if they don't know, ask your grandparents. They for sure will know. I think 8-track tapes were responsible for fifty percent of all the litter along streets and highways, fluttering spools of broken recording tape on the ground all the way across America.

There was one major hazard at JD's: leaving the club and walking to the parking lot. The parking lot was where rednecks and cowboys came in contact with hippies and long-hairs at the end of the night. The problem was solved with police, security, and staggered show hours.

Alice Cooper at JD's Scottsdale, AZ.
Photos Courtesy Toodie Mueller

Crazy Larry

As I mentioned, we frequented the Farmer's Market down on Melrose. It was open 24 hours a day. At midnight they brought out freshly baked loaves, including mini loaves, of bread. With the little money we had we would each buy a mini-loaf and share one stick of butter, eating our bread while sitting on the curb watching the world go by. This world was still quite busy and interesting at midnight.

Many rock personalities shopped at the Farmer's Market: The Mamas and the Papas, The Doors, The Turtles, Judy Collins, Three Dog Night, and others. At the market, rock stars could come and buy their food and not be bothered by anybody. It was like a shopping sanctuary to them.

However, the most interesting scene wasn't of rock stars pushing shopping carts. The most interesting was one that played out one night between Crazy Larry, AKA Wild Man Fischer, and Phil Spector, the music producer. I did not give Crazy Larry his name. Around Hollywood he was well known as being a little eccentric. He was a singer and writer of songs. His thing was, if the people wouldn't come to him, he would go to the people. That was exactly what occurred the night Crazy Larry saw Phil Spector.

Crazy Larry spotted Phil as he was leaving the Farmer's Market and made a beeline toward him. Catching up, Crazy Larry began singing the only song I ever heard him sing. It was called "Merry Go Round." Let's see if I can remember the words. It went something like, "Merry go, Merry go, Merry go round. Merry go, Merry go round." It helped if you shouted the words, as Larry did. You could sing as many choruses, all the same, as you wanted, and Larry liked to sing a lot of choruses.

This particular night, unfortunately for Phil Spector, his arms were loaded with groceries. As Larry sang, Phil walked briskly around and around his car trying to get in, while Larry followed in hot pursuit singing, "Merry go, Merry go, Merry go round." It's sort of ironic, isn't it? Larry chases Phil Spector around and around his car while singing, "Merry go, Merry go, Merry go round." Eventually, Phil Spector got in his car, thanked Larry for the serenade, and said he would think about it.

I don't think Larry was dangerous. He was just driven to succeed. The funny thing about all this was that six months later I saw an album titled *An Evening With Wild Man Fischer* featuring "Merry Go Round" See, perseverance does pay off! The album was produced by Frank Zappa for his new label, Bizarre Records. In the very near future Bizarre would become extremely important to the band.

It occurred to me that the next time the group was at the Farmer's Market and Phil Specter showed up, the band should chase him around his car singing some of their songs. It might pay off for them, too.

Sherry was now booking us at the Cheetah, and other clubs. One night the group opened for Three Dog Night, and Deep Purple. The concert went fine, but because something was wrong with the Dodge I had to rent a truck on short notice.

The rented truck was a flatbed with wooden stakes around it. After they finished playing, Charlie helped with loading up and putting tarps over the equipment. We secured the load with ropes and headed out to our Venice Beach pad. Charlie liked to smoke cigarettes and he was inhaling in the cab, blowing the smoke and flicking cigarette ashes out the window. My lungs and I appreciated the gesture. We had driven several miles when people started driving up beside us honking their horns, shouting, and wildly waving their arms. By now, I was used to this behavior, but not in L.A. I glanced in the rearview mirror and was surprised and alarmed to see smoke and flames coming from the back of the truck. The packing tarps were on fire!

I pulled over as quickly as I could, and Charlie and I shot out of the truck. We threw the burning tarps to the ground and tossed the non-burning tarps over the ones that were on fire and proceeded to jump up and down on the tarps. I kicked dirt on the fire and that, along with Charlie's frantic jumping, extinguished the flames. It must have been quite a sight to see two long-haired men dancing around on burning tarps. Thankfully, the equipment was fine—the only damage was to a couple of the tarps. Note to self: buy more packing tarps.

Working for Sherry had its perks; we could get into the Cheetah Club to see the headliners for free. One time we were behind the stage talking to someone about something, when Sherry in a state of excitement ran up and said, "The announcer hasn't shown up yet. Go up on stage and announce the group. They're already up there!"

"Are you talking to me?" I asked.

"Yes. Get up there!"

Halfway up the stairs I turned. "Who are they anyway?"

"The Watts Hundred and Third Street Rhythm Band," she said.

"Who?" I asked.

Why couldn't it just be a simple name? The Doors, The Who, The Kinks?

I got to the stage and spoke into the microphone—and said *almost* the same thing the announcer would have said: "Ladies and gentlemen, the Cheetah Club is proud to present, The Rhythm Band from Watts 103rd Street."

I had butchered their name. They glared at me, it wasn't love in their eyes. It gave me the feeling that I should apply to the witness protection program. I was never asked to do any announcing again.

9

New Managers

Sherry, I believe, wanted to manage Alice Cooper. However, the group was hedging its bets. They had arranged an interview with a couple of guys, Joey Greenberg and Shep Gordon, who were from New York and already managed some musical groups. One, they said, was The Left Banke who had hit records, "Walk Away Renee" and "Tiny Ballerina." Many years later we learned maybe they didn't have that much to do with The Left Banke.

Joey and Shep were "discovered" by Cindy Smith, Neal's sister. How did all this come about? Well, I will tell you what I know, and what I surmise.

Cindy had a friend from Phoenix named Linda Leis. A brief side note about Linda. She married a fellow named Bill Chadwick, who worked for The Monkees. He even tried out for the TV show along with Steven Stills, but wasn't chosen. He became a singer and song writer for the Monkees and other bands, an extra on the show, and a good friend to the group.

Cindy and the future Mrs. Chadwick had moved from Phoenix and were working at a Hollywood boutique called Inside Outside. It was a place where groovy people shopped to get even groovier, buying hip clothing and trinkets. One day, fate walked through the door in the form of Joey Greenberg and Shep Gordon, and the rest, as they say, is history.

I don't actually know what was said, but I must set the scene. It probably went something along these lines: low lighting, sitar music playing softly in the background, the scent of sandalwood incense wafting through the air. Joey and Shep stroll through a curtain of sparkling colored glass beads and…cue Cindy.

"Peace to you, my brothers. May I help you?" Cindy asked, pleasantly.

"And to you, my sister. Just looking, thanks. You have some really groovy threads and for not too much bread," answered Shep.

"Right on! If you need to see anything, just ask. By the way, do you happen to be band managers?"

"Why do you ask?"

"I was picking up a vibe from you. My righteous brother Neal and an equally righteous and dreamy bass player named Dennis are in a band. Dennis doesn't know it yet, but he will become my boyfriend. He's going to marry me and we will have a great life. The Tarot cards said so."

It could have happened that way, and why do bass players get all the girls?

"Far out! What's the name of the band?" Joey inquired.

"Alice Cooper."

"Is she pretty like you, foxy lady?" Shep asked, coyly.

"She's a he."

At this point Joey and Shep, bummed out by this information, start backpedaling toward the front door.

"The whole band is named Alice Cooper," Cindy explained.

Joey and Shep pick up the pace heading to the exit, as images of a band in drag crowd into their brains. This was some sort of bad trip they were on, they thought.

"Frank Zappa is interested in them. He wants to do an album and go on tour with them," Cindy said, smiling prettily as she followed them.

They stop mid-stride.

"Why...yes. We are managers of musical talent. Let's talk. The Alice Cooper Band you say? The whole band is named Alice Cooper and no women? This could be outta sight. We can dig it."

Over the next few years and beyond, Cindy would become invaluable to the group and especially to one special person.

Joey and Shep agreed they would see the group at the Cheetah Club, and if interested they would be in contact. They came, they saw, and they were interested in Alice Cooper. Maybe.

The band had a meeting to discuss what new managers from New York could do for them. Bookings back east and in Canada had been promised. This was something the group wanted: greater national exposure. Joey said they were in contact with several record companies. He also told them that the lead singer from The Left Banke could join the group. This suggestion was immediately rejected. Their future was starting to look very good, thanks to Cindy Smith.

Shep Gordon   Joey Greenberg
Courtesy Toodie Mueller

Fate and The GTOs Intervened

Frank Zappa stopped by the Cheetah Club one night to see Alice
Cooper. This was brought about by Miss Christine, a girl Vince was
seeing. She had told Frank about the band and said, "You need to go
check these guys out." She was responsible for giving Alice a very dis-
tinctive frizzy perm. Miss Christine told him she wanted his hair to
look just like hers, but Alice's hair looked like he had stuck his finger
in a light socket. Miss Christine left this Earth way too early, dying at
the young age of twenty-two in 1972.

She worked for Frank Zappa. She was also in a band called The
GTO's, which stood for Girls Together Outrageously. They certainly
lived up to the outrageously part in dress, appearance, and attitude.
To this country boy, they seemed like the type of women your mother
warned you about. But, when you got to know them, they were really
quite nice. Strange but nice. Once they became aware someone was
nervous around them, that person became the focus of their atten-

tion. After they finished with the torment, they would give him or her a hug and say they were just teasing and it was all in fun. I know from first-hand experience.

The group consisted of Miss Christine, who was nanny to Frank Zappa's children. This connection was of paramount importance to the success of Alice Cooper. Other members were: Miss Pamela—who in the 1980s wrote a bestselling book, *We're with the Band*—Miss Mercy, Miss Sandra, Miss Sparky, and Miss Cinderella. One of The GTOs main things was to dress in oddly assembled outfits, sometimes pants and skirts together, sometimes extremely short skirts, paired with pieces of vintage clothing, and they'd wear heavy eye makeup.

They often visited us at the Landmark Hotel. One day Miss Mercy cajoled me into putting on her skirt. I wore it around the apartment until, quite unexpectedly, a couple of the Chambers Brothers showed up. I made haste to get back into my Levis, struggling to look cool after that.

The GTOs liked to hang out at clubs and on Hollywood Blvd, attracting a lot of attention from tourists interested in having their photos taken with the girls. In 1969 they released an album titled *Permanent Damage* on Frank Zappa's Straight Records. If you can find the album, you will have a nice and rare item. Jeff Beck, Rod Stewart, and other notables performed on it. I can only remember a few song titles: "Who is Jim Soxs," "TV Lives," and "The Eureka Springs Garbage Lady." Whenever The GTOs came to a show, they'd take over the dance floor. Always strange but always entertaining.

The night Frank came to the Cheetah to see the group we were told he might have left before they performed. Taking no chances, a few days later the band arrived at his house at 7:00 a.m. somehow believing they had an appointment to play for Frank. *Who has an appointment to hear a band at 7:00 in the morning?* I kept thinking on the drive over. Our normal schedule was going to bed between 2:00 and 4:00 in the morning, sleeping through breakfast and lunch, rising from our hibernation and proceeding to eat our weight in groceries, if there were any in the house. I had seen 7:00 a.m. only rarely since moving to L.A. It has never been my favorite time of day. If any of the band had ever seen that hour it would've been a surprise and quite a shock. *What are all these people doing on the road at this time of day?* they'd wonder. *Right, they're all going to work.*

Pulling up to the house, we stormed the front door. Frank's wife Gail, with Moon Unit in arms and looking like she just stepped out of a *Leave it to Beaver* episode, let us in. Before she could protest, "there must be some kind of mistake," we had set the equipment up in a room off a hallway that led to Frank's bedroom. The audition began, and loudly.

Miss Christine rushed up and exclaimed, "What are you doing?" She was quite distraught.

Needless to say, Frank and no one else in the household for that matter had expected to be roused at that early un-godly-for-a-musician hour. Looking disheveled and very surprised, Frank emerged from his bedroom wearing a bathrobe. He did not appear to be a happy man and pointedly remarked that the appointment was for 7:00 p.m.

"But you're here now, so let me try and wake up while I drink a pot of coffee," he said.

I wanted to tell Frank that I knew 7:00 was the wrong time, but reconsidered.

After hearing them play, he said he liked them, but for all the wrong reasons. The reason, he explained, was because he'd seen the audience at the Cheetah Club walk away from the band when they started playing. He thought that any energy, even negative energy, was positive. Joey and Shep had also picked up on that.

Frank Zappa had started a record label called Bizarre Records, and thought that Alice Cooper could be a perfectly bizarre fit. He wanted to sign them, but none of them were twenty one. The parents signed the contract for them. It was all starting to come together. In the group's mind, all they needed now were new songs, new clothes, and stage props.

Everyone headed back to Phoenix. Even Les came along. The group got busy writing new songs. Cindy went to work on new clothes. She was a talented designer and worked continuously sewing for the group. She even designed clothes for me. I don't know why, but she did.

Jack Curtis, the owner of the VIP Club who gave The Spiders their first big break, had opened a new club called Alice Cooper attempting to capitalize on the group's fame, or it would seem by the limited success of the club, the lack of. The interior walls were painted bright pink. That might have been a recommendation from the band or Dick. The space was quite large, which made the dismal attendance even more noticeable. Les thought he'd entertain the few there by attempting to light his farts on fire. Everyone thought the act stunk.

The club would only last a couple of months before it folded. Its poor location might have contributed to the failure. When the wind was right, it was just a few deep breaths from the stockyards.

The Cage of Death

Kirby, Fred. "Alice Cooper Drives Its Message Home." *Billboard Magazine,* June 28, 1969

It's difficult to tell how much of Alice Cooper is put-on, although in "Nobody Likes Me," the put-on was obvious. Here, the lead singer, who also calls himself Alice Cooper, bemoaned his fate while singing through the grill of a door, while guitarist Mike Bruce and bass guitarist Dennis Dunaway argued to the contrary.

Alice had some new props in mind for the show. One was a car horn that actually honked. I made a trip to a junkyard and located a steering wheel, a horn and a car battery—I didn't know anything about transformers back then. They would have made my life easier. I fastened the battery to the steering wheel and the steering wheel to the horn wiring. Forty feet of cable was then connected to the steering wheel so Alice could "drive" the imaginary car around the stage.

The second prop was a door, which was used specifically for the song "Nobody likes Me." We went through several door incarnations before settling on The One. To be completely honest, of all the props they used, I hated the door the most. The first door I found in someone's garbage. It was solid wood, two inches thick, and weighed a ton. I nailed a couple pieces of 2x4 lumber to the sides for stability, but they provided very little of that because of the door's weight. The door didn't have a window in it, so when Alice used door number one he had to stand to one side holding the door upright with one hand and the microphone with his other. One night it nearly toppled into the audience taking Alice with it. Luckily, a couple of people in the first row stopped the door and Alice from crashing into the crowd. We left it behind after the show.

Door number two, again, was found in someone's trash pile. This one was a kitchen-door, solid on the bottom with individual small glass window panes on the top. Some of the panes had broken out, and I removed the rest of the glass leaving just the wood frames. This made the door minimally lighter, it was still heavy and awkward. I constructed two removable braces to hold the door upright and steady. With the new braces, Alice could sit down to sing.

However, before he could start, I had to walk out on the stage, which I never liked to do, carrying the braces then go back for the door. The tricky part was not knocking the the braces over while setting the door into them. When I did occasionally knock one over, howls of laughter and cat-calls erupted from the audience as I struggled to hold the door and at the same time stand the brace upright. The band watched me, enjoying my exertions as much as the crowd.

After I had the door positioned and fixed in place, I still needed to bring a chair or stool out for Alice and place it behind the door. Every once in a while, after setting the chair down and leaving the stage, Alice kept the crowd and himself amused by signaling me to come back and pointing to a different location for the chair. He pretended to assess the new location and again, not liking where the chair was, would shake his head and point to a new place. When he finally gave me an approving thumbs-up, I slinked off the stage greatly embarrassed, while the crowd cheered and applauded.

Once the door was set up, my only real concern was Alice might get his head stuck in one of the empty frames and the fire department would have to extricate him by whatever means necessary: saws, axes, jaws of life. It would have made for a very interesting show. Anyway, door number two was used for a few of months, but in the end it proved to be a back-breaker for one guy, me. I *accidentally* forgot to load it after a show one night. How dumb was that.

I happened upon the third door in a hardware store while looking for something else, probably solder for one of Dennis's broken guitar cords. It was a damaged aluminum screen door. The screen part was ripped. I picked the door up. It was so light that I think I started to cry. A couple of metal L-brackets and it was good to go. It was perfect, light and sturdy, and Alice could drag it all over the stage without any problems, plus it fit easily in the Dodge van. Everybody in the group liked it, and my back thanked me time and time again.

Over the next few months the door went through a change. It became more versatile: one side was the white screen door, then someone applied a thin layer of wood and brick wallpaper on the other side leaving the window part exposed—just in case Alice wanted to do the balcony scene from *Romeo and Juliet*.

"Nobody Likes Me," the song the door was specially built and used for, was one of the band's most popular songs, yet it was never recorded on any Alice Cooper studio album. It was, however, recorded from live performances on *Live At the Whisky*, and *Toronto*, and was just plain bootlegged.

The band came up with two versions of the song. In one version toward the end, they sang about liking him and his dog Spot. In a darker version they hated him, all his family and his dog.

I can offer one insight, perhaps, into why the song was never officially recorded. They could never rehearse it without breaking down in fits of laughter. After a few minutes, they calmed themselves, and someone would say, "OK, Ok, we got this." The band began the song again, but one person would look at another person and grin. That started the laughing all over again. This was when the swearing commenced, followed immediately by more laughter. They would eventually finish rehearsing the song, but not without a lot of effort. On stage, the song went off without any problem at all. Maybe the door fell over taking Alice with it, or I tripped trying to lug it off stage after the song was over, but the song was perfect.

The last but certainly not least prop was the Cage of Death, or Fire. It was known under both names. Either name meant something bad was bound to happen if you stepped inside. I believe Dick or Les came up with the idea. Thank God it only lasted for one performance, though we tried to use it at another, because it surely would have earned its name.

The Cage consisted of six-foot long strips of plastic bags knotted every four inches and hung about three inches apart inside a three-sided wooden frame. The concept was to light the plastic strips on fire, which was a nice effect. The flames would burn the strips up to the knots, which would then burst into flames. The burning knots fell to the floor while the fire climbed to the next knot, etc.

The first time we used it was at an outdoor concert in the daytime. I believe The Grassroots were headlining. In daylight the effect was totally lost, and the wind made the chances of Alice's survival remote at best. He was game to try it anyway. This was a nearly disastrous decision as flaming balls of fire and death buffeted by the wind flew at him from all directions. He looked like he was swatting at a swarm of bees.

The second time we planned to use the Cage was inside a building at night, but that was put to a stop by either a skeptical fire marshal or stage manager.

"What does this thing do?" he asked.

I explained it to him.

"You do what?" He seemed genuinely perturbed.

"You light these things on fire and flaming plastic balls explode and drop to the ground," I repeated. Saying it out loud does make it sound bad.

He said, "Take this thing off the stage right now! In fact, take it out of the building!"

A sad end to the Flaming Cage of Death, but on the other hand think of how many lives were saved. Another plus was that it gave Alice's singed hair a chance to grow back.

There were a few more miscellaneous props: crutches saved from our numerous accidents and body parts saved from our numerous accidents. No, wait. That's not right. They were parts from mannequins we acquired on our journeys. There was also an assortment of swords Alice employed to maim and injure poor defenseless Amp Boy, and an old tire Alice rolled into the audience during the show. I guess that was considered performance art. Then there was the bull whip, which was taken away from Alice after multiple concerns for personal safety were voiced. And justifiably so.

10

Les Comes Through

Jimi Hendrix was performing in Phoenix and we wanted to see him. However, we didn't want to pay for that privilege. A scheme was devised: I would borrow my dad's land yacht—a Cadillac Coupe Deville—fill the car with the band members dressed as if for a performance, and drive to the back gates of the concert venue. Les, in his best British accent, which came easy for him being that he was British, would lie to the gate guard telling him, "This is the Soft-Machine," which was the band playing ahead of Hendrix. We hoped this would get us past the police and security teams. What could possibly go wrong? Incredibly, that was exactly what happened, and nothing did go wrong. Believing our story, Security escorted us to the backstage dressing rooms, where we hung out for ten minutes or so with Jimi Hendrix and his band. I doubted they would remember us being there because they looked pretty stoned. My memory is of them just staring at us, or maybe it was at the wall behind us.

We left to situate ourselves out front for the show, but Jimi Hendrix and The Experience was late coming to the stage. They were perhaps still staring at the wall. Neal began yelling, "Let's get it on! Let's get it on!" I moved away from him. As we had gotten in under false pretenses, I thought it best to keep a lower profile. After a long delay,

Jimi and his band found their way to the stage—perhaps responding to Neal's yelling and curious to see what all the ruckus was about.

We enjoyed the concert. It was great and very loud. There was no encore despite the crowd's insistence. We left immediately after the concert, afraid security would wonder why the group they'd ushered in hadn't performed. We should do this more often!

Les's performance at the Hendrix concert almost made up for him trying to hit on my future girlfriend every time he saw her. It was time I made my move.

By this point The Spiders, The Nazz and Alice Cooper had played a lot in Tucson. Tonight's show was a return to a high school for a dance on the basketball court. The band had almost finished for the night when I made my move. Ellen had been sitting on the bleachers with Les. It was cold in the auditorium, and Les had been holding Ellen's hands, under his armpit no less, to warm them. Just to warm them. Like I believed that. When he wandered off, I sprung my trap. That doesn't sound right…I put my plan in motion. My scheme was to appeal to her mothering instinct. That she was a nursing student was a bonus and worked to my advantage. I would claim to be sick. It needed to be a simple illness, nothing contagious. I didn't want to scare her off, so I faked a migraine headache. Brilliant! I'd never had a migraine, but I felt I could pull it off. Just look miserable. I could easily pull that off. I sent someone to find her, say I was sick and could she come look at me. When she arrived backstage, I was lying on a bench with my forearm across my eyes. I told her about my fake headache and waited for some sympathy. No sympathy. I got the serious clinical future nurse instead.

"Where's the pain? Is it throbbing? Are you nauseated?" she queried as she laid a cool hand on my forehead.

"No, but I'm starting to feel sick." I said, trying to look miserable. I was afraid my plan was falling apart.

"Are you sensitive to light or sound? Are you starting to break into a cold sweat?" she probed.

Oh yes. I'm definitely starting to break into a cold sweat, only for real now. By this time everyone knows I'm an idiot when it comes to girls. I was afraid to say anything more to her for fear she would send me to the hospital emergency room.

"It's probably just a simple headache," I mumbled, trying not to meet her eyes.

She agreed, "Yes, probably just had a headache." Ellen produced two Tylenol tablets from her purse. "I'll get you some water, drink lots of water. I'll ride with you in the van back to Phoenix. You're not driving. I'll ask Dick to drive."

I was a genius! Everything had worked like a charm. I made myself a bed in the van by spreading a quilted packing blanket on top of Dennis's amplifier. Ellen perched on Glen's amp applying cold compresses to my forehead. We talked for two hours. I promised I would call her the next day to tell how I was doing. I did and asked her out for lunch. She accepted.

"I thought you had a brain tumor by the way you were acting!" she teased.

What! Oh, who cares, I had a girlfriend, in the present. She told me much later she had waited three long years for me to ask her out. What can I say? I like to take things slow. I know, you don't have to say it.

The band should have moved to Tucson since they played there all the time. When she could, Ellen came down to Tucson for a show. Sometimes she rode with Toodie, other times she would ride with me and Glen.

Once while the band was playing, we were sitting in the band's dressing room. I asked Ellen what she was learning in nursing school.

"Cardiac compressions. We practice on dummies."

"Well," I said, "I'm here."

"Are you sure you want me to practice on you?" she asked.

I had no idea what a cardiac compression was, but if I could score some points by taking an interest in her studies, so much the better for me.

"Sure, go ahead," I replied.

"Just lie down on the table, with your arms at your side."

She positioned her hands over my sternum and proceeded to introduce it to my backbone. Luckily, my heart was in the way to keep them from meeting. I bolted up.

"Are you trying to kill me?" I exclaimed.

"No, quite the opposite. CPR saves you from dying. It keeps your heart beating," she explained with an amused smile.

"I can see why you practice on dummies!"

"Like you?" she laughed.

Yeah, like me.

We Loaded Up the Van and Headed to Beverly Hills. Well, Actually It Was South L.A.

We were ready to head back to Los Angeles, bringing our partially incapacitated drummer along. We had let our Venice place go and were moving into the Hollywood Landmark Hotel, which was close to the Sunset Strip and Hollywood Blvd. This was the first of several stays. It was an easy walk to The Supply Sargent, one of my favorite stores, and Fredrick's of Hollywood. Across the street you could catch a movie at Grauman's Chinese Theater. The plaza in front of the theater was where movie stars left their hand and foot prints pressed into the cement.

Our room at the Landmark was in the rear on the second level overlooking the pool. It was three bedrooms with lots of rollaway beds and a living room, and we all called it home. Despite the multitude of beds, I chose to sleep on the floor of the closet. It was kind of stuffy in there at night, but at least it was private, unless someone needed a jacket. The best part was that with the door closed it was nighttime all day long. Every once in a while, I slept in a bed when Glen or Mike stayed overnight at their girlfriend's. It didn't always work out though, because sometimes they'd come back sooner than expected. Dick would wake me and I'd have to relinquish the bed and return to my home-away-from-home, the closet.

The hotel was famous among rock personalities. Janis Joplin frequently stayed there and died in room 105 in 1970. It's a tourist attraction now. I stayed up all night once, watching with rapt attention as a porno movie was filmed inside a first-floor room and in the swimming pool. Noticing my keen interest in the proceedings, a man inquired if I wanted to be in the movie. Feeling somewhat embarrassed, I politely declined and told him I just wanted to watch. Afterward, I wondered if maybe I had been a little hasty in refusing his offer. This could have been my big break in case hauling musical equipment around didn't pan out. I might have become a porn star. I needed a catchy name, though. I came up with Steve Stunning. Oh well, an opportunity squandered.

The hotel was OK, but we had a lead on a new house. The Chambers Brothers had leased a place, but they were going on tour to promote their hit record "Time." They asked if we were interested in using their house. It sounded perfect. There was even a small basement to practice in they said. We got the address and said we would come check it out. They directed us to take the freeway and get off at the Crenshaw exit.

With high expectations, we hopped in the van and headed to 2129 S. Crenshaw Boulevard, found the address, and got out of the van. We stood on the curb and studied the house. It was old, built in the early 1900's, had a Victorian feel to it and in its day was probably quite the showplace. Unfortunately, this wasn't that day. The house had three stories and needed a fresh coat of paint—the white paint was cracked and peeling. To be honest, the inside could have used some sprucing up, too. The Chambers Brothers waited inside to show us around.

The tour was interesting. The bare wood floors needed refinishing and creaked with every step. The wallpaper was old and faded and peeling. Large sections had been torn from the walls. The windows could not be opened. Not by us anyway. They were either painted, glued, or nailed shut. Wooden stairs leading up to the second floor groaned and popped with every step, like they were warning us not to go up there. Upstairs were three bedrooms and a bathroom, all in the same condition as the downstairs. The bathroom had a vintage claw foot tub with a shower arm attached to the wall, a white porcelain pedestal sink, and a functioning toilet. This bathroom was shared by five or six guys. Need I say more?

The whole place needed a lot of work, but we weren't that particular. We just needed a place to sleep and practice. The basement practice room we'd been promised was not just small—it was tiny. Basically, it was a hand-dug hole under the house that you got to via steps carved into the dirt. They kept a set of drums down there and that was it, because there wasn't room for anything else. I suppose we could have grabbed some shovels and removed more dirt to make the hole larger, but I think that might have compromised the already compromised foundation.

As a bonus though, the house came with a few pieces of furniture that were actually comfortable. I spent some quality time sleeping on the couch instead of climbing the creaking stairs to sleep on a mattress on the floor. The Chambers Brothers said there was a guy who lived upstairs on the third floor. His name was Long Gone Miles. What should we call him, we wondered. Mr. Miles, or Long Gone?

I don't know who made the final decision, I just know it wasn't me, but the Watts area of Los Angeles would be our new home.

The Chambers Brothers told us to enjoy our stay, but added a cautionary note. "It's best that you don't go out in the neighborhood at night."

That was okay, because when we went out, we usually went to Sunset or Hollywood Boulevard to listen to music or go to the Farmer's Market for bread. They also said that people in the neighborhood *shouldn't* bother us. This was somewhat less than reassuring. Disclaimer: we were all babes in the woods. We were just out of our teens and knew nothing about Watts, Compton, or Crenshaw Boulevard. When we did occasionally walk around the neighborhood, the locals stared at us, but we got stares wherever we walked. There were no 24-hour cable news programs at that time to inform us—the news, which we rarely watched, was on at five o'clock in the evening and 10 p.m., and that was it. We hadn't been there for more than a week when someone commented, "Sure are a lot of black people in this area."

It was no more than an observation. This was still the era of peace and love. But that was going to change.

Long Gone Miles was heard but seldom ever seen. He was out all day, and we were only aware of him late at night. He had wired the entire house with speakers and broadcasted music from his room in the coveted midnight to 4:00 a.m. slot. It was just like listening to the radio, except better, no commercials. He played his mostly vintage records, announcing the artists and giving commentary on the music and performers. He had vast professorial knowledge of the music, and we were his students, eager to learn about the beginnings of the Blues. He played artists like Lead Belly and Robert Johnson. Long Gone commented he, Johnson, was the person who made a deal with the Devil to play the blues. Long Gone was quite an educator, and I should have been taking notes.

One night Dennis, who was a regular listener, and Glen went upstairs to visit him. Glen told me he'd brought a bottle of something, and they passed it around and listened attentively as Long Gone talked. I was content hearing his gravelly voice coming from the house speakers every night at midnight. Up in my bedroom or on the couch, I enjoyed his music until I fell asleep.

One of my greatest finds at the Crenshaw house was in the backyard, which was nothing but weeds and tall grass. Walking around back there one day I literally tripped over a 1958 Jaguar XK 150. Though it had seen better days before being left to rot in the elements—the top was ripped to shreds, the leather seats had disintegrated, and the wood trim had cracked—it was still beautiful. It even had roll-up windows, not the bolt in kind. I thought it might have belonged to one of the Chambers Brothers, but I was unsure who actually did own it. I cleared the overgrown grass and weeds from around and even inside the car to get a better look at it. Though it was in an advanced state of decay, it was still classic looking. I briefly thought about taking it back to Phoenix and restoring it, but I figured it really wasn't mine to take. Too bad.

We met some of the neighbors of the Crenshaw house, teenagers mostly, who would come over to visit and were curious about what we were doing there. We explained we were living in the Chambers Brothers house until they got back from touring. That seemed to raise our stock a little higher.

One of our visitor's mothers came over, probably to check up on who her son was talking to, and invited us to dinner. Dennis said we would do that if we could play for her and her family. The family set up tables on the lawn for themselves, us and a few other neighbors. She had prepared an authentic Italian dinner, which was excellent. The band played, and everyone seemed to appreciate the music. The band even returned to their Spider days and covered some blues songs. We talked and laughed, and everyone enjoyed themselves. We walked home with the thought that we knew just a little bit more about our new neighbors, and them us. We truly are more alike than different. Along with that knowledge, we also got a ton of leftovers. The mothers at the party adopted us and wanted to make sure we were well fed, and we really appreciated that.

As the Summer of Love ended, "The Winter of Our Discontent" arrived. Our neighbor-friends came to see us. They were concerned and warned us that "something" was about to happen. For our safety, they said, we may want to consider moving. That got my attention. In the summer of 1965, the Watts riots had taken place. We didn't know if the "something" they were warning us about might be another incident. We had been hearing a lot more gunshots and police sirens in the area, and witnessed protest marches for civil rights. On their advice, we decided it was time to pack up and leave. The neighbors concurred.

On April 4th 1968 at the Lorraine Motel in Memphis, Tennessee, the world was going to change.

11

Topanga Canyon

Topanga Canyon house
Courtesy Toodie Mueller

Excerpt from letter to Ellen dated 3-22-68:

I am dying of a cold at the present time. I got it dragging lumber 2 miles up the hill in the rain at 3 in the morning because Les "procured" it and it took two trips to get it up the hill.

I searched for a house in the for-rent ads and thought I might have found something.

The ad read, "House for rent in Topanga Canyon. Remote, yet close to L.A. Furniture included." The keywords were remote, Topanga Canyon, and furniture. I made the call to set up an appointment to see the house.

At that time, Topanga Canyon was a sparsely populated rural area south of Malibu with tall trees, hills, streams, and wildlife. It had a post office, country store, and gas station all rolled into one old cabin-looking building. Topanga was an up-and-coming location for hippies and an up-and-coming neighborhood for musicians. If you made it big, you moved to Laurel Canyon. But, if you hadn't, you lived in Topanga Canyon. The Canyon had a wild feel to it. Along with deer, there were squirrels, rabbits, and wild peacocks sounding off with a noise only they could make. How could such a beautiful bird produce such a hideous sound?

The house in the ad was for a two-bedroom, wood-framed white cottage. It had a small stone patio with a fence around it, and there was a walkout basement with a room perfect for practice. The only visible neighbor was down the hill below us. We hoped having a relatively close-by neighbor wouldn't be a problem. The decision was made in minutes.

"We'll take it," someone said.

We said the same thing about every house we ever rented. We were one-stop shoppers. We moved in a few days later. For now, the band was neatly tucked away in a house in the woods, with great views, no traffic noise, no gunshots or sirens. It was just us and the sounds of the forest. In other words, it was very peaceful. What the house lacked in size was made up for by the serenity of its location. I felt I could happily live there forever.

One bedroom had a triple bunk bed set. Neal, Cindy, who had agreed to move in, and I commandeered those beds. Alice also shared our room, and Les handily built a box-bed for him. It resembled a coffin. No matter, Alice was content to sleep in it. I had difficulty sleeping in the Topanga house; it was too quiet at night. I had grown used to Long Gone Miles's raspy voice and the nighttime music, along with the occasional-to-frequent gunshots and sirens that lulled me to sleep. I solved that issue by putting a small speaker in my pillow connected to a little radio with its speakers turned off. I slept great after that.

Cindy and I were bunkmates. Actually, she occupied the middle bunk of our triple-bunk-bed set up. Neal overseeing everything, slept in the top bunk. He managed to climb up there even with his leg in a cast. I installed a small speaker in Cindy's pillow so she could drift off to sleep to music. I controlled the radio station we listened to, but I do believe she changed stations from time to time. The best thing about sharing a room with Cindy was she didn't snore, unlike the rest of my roommates. I actually wished Alice was sleeping in a coffin, so I could close the lid to muffle his snoring.

In the other bedroom, Les built another bunk bed wide enough for two full-size mattresses. Mike Bruce and Les moved into that room. The basement contained several small rooms as well as a practice room, and the rest of the band, Dennis and Glen and Charlie and Dick, slept down there. It looked like everything and everybody was going to be okay. Not exactly rooms of our own, but we never had that in the past, so why start now? The small but adequate practice area in the basement had a bank of windows that opened to let air out, as well as let fresh air in—a plus as it could get pretty ripe down there. Everything worked out furniture wise, too. There was a couch and a kitchen table with chairs. We even had a TV, so we were all set.

To make it feel more like home we practiced our decorating skills by tacking posters up in the living room. Les built a coffee table "house" for lizards and bugs, and the occasional snake. I had no idea where Les got the lumber for his projects—one day the pieces were just there. I brought a set of deer horns and an old key-wind pendulum clock from Phoenix. Dennis proceeded to paint the clock dial white. Dennis and Alice started painting the kitchen. Well, actually, not the kitchen, just the cabinets—they painted faces on the cabinet doors.

One of the most unusual things we installed was a trap door from our bedroom closet to the basement. Landlords gotta love us! I guess someone was a little paranoid that we needed an escape hatch in case the police showed up. We could jump down from the first floor to the basement and escape out the basement door, which was on the same side of the house as the front door. I think the police would have noticed.

We even had a dog. Well, it was somebody's dog. We heard it belonged to Billy Grey who, as a young boy, played Bobby Benson in the 1951 movie, *The Day the Earth Stood Still* and played Bud on the TV show, *Father Knows Best*. The dog liked to spend time with us, coming over in the morning and staying until afternoon, then he'd leave presumably to go back to his owner's house or perhaps another house he had on his schedule. Les named him Dag. I don't know if the name meant anything or if it was just a British name.

Neal whiled away the time trying to remove his leg from the cast with a hammer and screwdriver. With an assist from Mike Bruce, they took turns whacking away at it. I saw no danger there. Perseverance was its own reward, however, and eventually they were successful, but there was a lot of yelling and complaining before that, which I'm sure had an effect on the peace and tranquility of our Topanga Canyon neighbors and the surrounding area.

Along the driveway leading to the road above the house was a long, steep bank covered with a thick blanket of ivy. One day when I was bored, I dug into the ivy to discover that it was being supported by a block wall and a hidden set of concrete steps topped with a stone statue of a lion head. The steps led to the road above. The only thing I could figure out was the now-overgrown property must have once been part of a large long-gone estate.

One weekend Toodie and Ellen drove to Topanga from Phoenix. To celebrate our visitors' arrival, Les cooked an English favorite, roast beef and Yorkshire pudding for dinner. The groceries for our feast were likely provided by Toodie, who always bought food. After dinner we sat around the kitchen table being entertained by the sociable Alice, who told story after hilarious story. Ellen said she laughed so much that her face hurt afterward. She remembers Les, the Yorkshire pudding, and Alice making her laugh till she hurt, but she doesn't remember if I was there. Boy, the bloom was coming off this relationship in a hurry. To be honest, Alice was always very funny and, Les's Yorkshire pudding wasn't bad either.

The neighbor down the hill was Bob Denver's ex-wife, Maggie. Bob was a TV star. He played Gilligan on *Gilligan's Island* and Maynard G. Krebs on *The Many Loves of Dobie Gillis*. Maggie fed us sometimes, which made us like her even more. Even if she hadn't fed us, she was still a very nice person to be around. She was into a "New Earth" type of spiritualism. On occasion, she would offer to "read" our auras and try to help us realign our chakras to be in a better place. I was really enjoying living in Topanga, so I believed my chakra was just fine. To perform the aura reading Maggie stood us in front of her white refrigerator. Mine, I was told, was white with streaks of blue. Maggie said that it was a good aura. She told me what it meant, but

I really don't remember. I think it had something to do with being a good person. Who knew?

Once practice was over, the house emptied out pretty fast. In their free time, most of the group headed for the bright lights and big city, and they had girlfriends. Vince had Miss Christine. Later that year he would meet his long-time girlfriend Cindy Lang. Glen also had a girlfriend. Her name was Djinn, and she was every inch his equal in all things, especially personality wise. Mike Bruce and Neal had girlfriends. Even I had a girlfriend. She lived in Phoenix, but that still counted. So on occasion the house would be empty. Well, relatively empty.

I spent my time sitting out on the front patio, feet propped on the wall watching the world go by—as much of the world as one could see. Life was good in Topanga.

One day a couple walking by on the road above the house called out, "Nice evening."

I turned to say, "Yes, it is," but stopped mid-sentence. The couple holding hands on the road were stark naked. The girl wore only a pair of sandals and carried a leather bag with beaded fringe slung over her shoulder. I was hoping she carried sunscreen in it. The guy wore a pair of white Chuck Taylor Converse All Stars high-tops. Not to be snippy, but just about everyone preferred them in black.

I don't understand why people in California wanted to walk around naked all the time. Especially the men. Who wants to see that? No one would ever do that in Arizona, unless they wanted to burst into flames.

I concentrated on not looking where I wasn't supposed to be looking. We carried on a brief but seemingly never-ending conversation. She said her name was Skye. The guy's name I don't remember. It could have been Earth, Wind, or Fire. For some reason I found it quite difficult to converse with naked people. What do you say? Nice outfit you're not wearing. Dig the shoes.

I invited them to come back later to listen to the band practice. They accepted. I hoped they would be wearing some clothes or else there would not be much practicing going on. They did. And they did.

We had a lot of company at the Topanga House. L.A. friends dropped by. Family and Phoenix friends drove in to visit—we were always on our best behavior for those who would bring or buy us food. Along with the family and friends, rock stars, future rock stars, neighbors, and complete strangers came over to hang out. This was the culture in Topanga in the '60s.

Late one night there was a knock on the door. Three long-haired strangers stood outside on the patio. We assumed they were neighbors, and without hesitation invited them inside. They could have been part of the Manson Family for all we knew. Actually, Charles Manson and followers lived in Topanga for a time when we were there. Fortunately, our paths never crossed. Our visitors brought beer as an introduction, so......welcome to our humble abode. They dined on beer and Furnazios. I had a coke.

After an hour or so chatting about what I don't remember, one of our guests began acting strangely. For long periods, he stared and smiled at one or the other of us, or at no one. Just stared and smiled—mostly at Glen, who didn't see the humor in it. After a while he started reaching up in the air picking and grabbing at things that weren't there, just like you would at a 3-D movie. The band, and myself included, grew uneasy and concerned about our guest. At one point he got up and proceeded to have an intense conversation with the drapes. The conversation must have gotten heated because he, or the drapes, decided he should remove his pants. Underwear was not optional, since he wasn't wearing any.

Surprised and definitely not amused, we simultaneously and silently agreed the party was over. I was quite prepared to grab Alice's bullwhip, which we had hung on the wall for safety reasons—our safety after the band refused to let him use it on stage—tie our guest to a chair with it and stuff a rag in his mouth. Finally, one of the strangers spoke.

"He's on an acid trip," he said, explaining his friend's behavior.

OK, so no rag in his mouth? In 1968 I was as naive as it came to such things as drug-trips, and I believed the band wasn't that far ahead of me. I had never experienced anything like this before.

Twice in five minutes, the acid-addled stranger got up from his chair and exited the house. His friends brought him back and sat him down again. The third time he walked outside, his friends calmly went to their car and drove away. We looked at one another and wondered what do we do now? We were left with a hallucinating naked person, and we didn't even know if he was housebroken.

I was in favor of tying him up and tossing him on the couch so he would be comfortable. I wasn't totally unsympathetic. It wasn't his fault he was stupid. Oh wait, yes, it was.

By now, it was close to three o'clock in the morning. Everyone was tired and wanted this night to be over. Charlie, bless his kind heart, offered to stay up with our new-found unwanted friend and try to keep him calm. The rest of us went to bed.

Hours later we woke to find Charlie asleep on the couch and the drugged-out stranger nowhere to be found. Genuinely concerned, we searched the property to see if he had fallen into a hole, down the hillside, or worse. Our efforts revealed nothing, so "out of sight, out of mind." Seeing that we were awake, the neighbors came by to ask if we had heard or seen the crazy naked guy last night. They said he had been yelling and breaking into houses and chasing the wild peacocks telling them to "be free," which, of course, they were. They were wild. We looked at one another.

"No, we didn't hear or see anything," Alice chirped. The rest of us nodded in agreement.

"You got off lucky. He was totally high. This morning he got into a neighbor's house down the road. They found him in the living room, naked and confused. They gave him some orange juice and a caftan to wear, and after a while he went on his way."

Well, that was a bit of good news, and just maybe his pants would fit someone in the band.

The ex-Mrs. Bob Denver still stopped by periodically with food, checking that our chakras and auras were aligned. Dag visited and assumed his position, usually under somebody's feet in front of the couch, and hoped for a big meal. We all were hoping for the same thing. He'd stay until something or somebody told him he had to go, which was welcomed because he suffered from severe flatulence. At least I think it was the dog. Anyway, he took the blame even when he wasn't there. On the road above our house, Billy Gray occasionally rode by on his motorcycle. Once in a while we caught a glimpse of Steve McQueen riding his Triumph motorcycle or driving a Ferrari on the main Topanga Road. Our lives were simple.

If there was nothing on TV we could go outside, grab a chair, put our feet up, and listen to bands or music playing from all over the canyon. I heard a voice I recognized as Neil Young's singing with different musicians. We might hear Canned Heat or Spirit practicing.

Spirit had a guitarist named Randy California. Jimi Hendrix gave him the name when Randy played in Jimi's band at the age of fifteen. The band was called Jimmy Jones and the Blue Flames. Randy's real name was Rudolf Wolfe. He died in 1997 saving his son from drowning when a riptide carried him out to sea. Great musician and a great father.

If this wasn't enough entertainment for us, we could drive to the Topanga Corral. From the outside it wasn't much to look at, and truthfully it wasn't much on the inside either, but if you understood what it was you wanted to be there. Any number of famous artists came to listen or play. I believe Taj Mahal regularly performed on the weekends. You might see Jim Morrison come by to listen to music or recite poetry. Canned Heat and Spirit dropped in to play, and Linda Ronstadt was frequently there. Neil Young, David Crosby, and Steven Stills were regulars. The list was extensive. There's a legend that Janis Joplin got into a fight while playing pool and swung a broken whiskey bottle while taunting her adversaries, "Nobody better mess with me." I firmly believe nobody did.

It was just a great place to hang out and see the famous and not-yet-famous play. It was a Topanga treasure. Unfortunately, the Topanga Corral burned down in 1970. It was rebuilt and burned down again in the 1980's. This time for good.

Photos by Toodie Mueller at Topanga Canyon

Dennis, Alice with perm

Alice with his lightened hair and Mike Bruce

Alice, Neal in window

Neal, Alice and Dennis

Alice, Neal, Dennis, Dick, Me partially hidden

Alice with perm. Photo taken through Dick's hair

Charlie Carnal

Cindy and Neal Smith

Alice (kneeling), Dennis

Dennis with perm

Jacque Memmott and Toodie Mueller

Les Braden, Me, Alice, Cindy, Dag

Ellen Mitchell and Me

Me, Toodie

Michael Bruce

Neal with Dag, Les Braden   Me, Glen

Me, Cindy, Mike Bruce, Neal, Glen

Neal with cast

Neal and Mike Bruce trying to remove cast

Dennis with perm

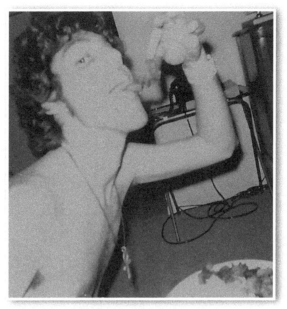

Dick eating pizza

Glen and Dick

Charlie and Dennis

The Séance

It was Halloween in May in Topanga. What would be better than to hold a séance? We were not gifted in the occult, though we had used the Ouija board a few times. Norma Greene, a friend of ours, said that she could do it and volunteered to be the witch. I didn't even know you needed a witch or a mistress of ceremonies at a séance. She said she knew everything about being a witch. We thought that was strange, because we always thought of her as being normal and nice and pleasant to be around. Or was that part of a spell she cast over us? Anyway, no other witches stepped forward. We gave her the job of setting up for the séance. Not to put any pressure on her, but we invited some friends.

Jim Morrison and Robby Krieger from The Doors, David Crosby from The Byrds, and Paul Rothchild from Elektra Records were there. Jim Morrison said he was looking forward to the event.

A few weeks earlier, it was rumored, Jim had gone to the former Houdini estate in Laurel Canyon. Sometime after midnight, he sneaked onto the grounds and, in an attempt to summon the spirit of the dead magician, danced naked in the pond/fountain. He didn't have much luck summoning Houdini but had great success in summoning the owner, who shouted that he had called the police. Jim grabbed his clothes and streaked back to his place a short distance away on Laurel Canyon Blvd.

The big night came. The séance was held in the basement directly under the trap door so some of us could watch from above. Norma drew a pentagram in blood on the floor. Just kidding, it was white chalk. She placed a metal dish filled with a dark liquid in the center of the pentagram. I hoped it wasn't blood. A black candle sat in the middle of the dish. More black candles were placed around the room, along with some sort of flowers or weeds. Norma must have researched the hell out of this project, because the scene looked creepily authentic.

Our guests, along with some of the band members, moved downstairs and sat on the floor in a circle around the pentagram. Norma appeared dressed in a black-hooded robe. She looked and acted the part, not seeming to notice the rock royalty assembled in the basement. Charlie and I were observing all this from above through the trapdoor. Others would periodically join us. Norma began with an incantation to see "who" was out there and who wanted to talk. She was staring at those in the room, mainly at an uneasy Jim Morrison, while high-pitched shrieking and speaking in tongues came from her mouth. Norma asked for a sign. She was feeling a presence in the room.

At that very moment Glen walked into the closet above the séance room, either because he wanted to, or the spirit compelled him. In an instant he disappeared from sight as he dropped through the trapdoor and crashed to the floor below, right into the center of the pentagram. Glen, when perturbed, was a force to be reckoned with, and due to his unceremonious arrival in the basement, he was very perturbed.

Norma must have thought that she had summoned the Devil himself. The Devil was probably wondering, "What the hell was that!"

In the near-dark, screaming, yelling, and cursing, a lot of cursing, commenced. Glen, who had always been a prolific swearer, took his art to a whole new level. Disjointed sentence structure laced with profanity called on a higher deity to smite all his enemies. Norma, who had been speaking in tongues while sitting cross-legged on the floor was still cross-legged, but on her back shrieking in tongues.

Our terrified guests, doing some screaming and cursing of their own, scrambled over each other, knocking over the candles, and fled into the night. Most eventually returned, gripping crucifixes, I imagined. In the blacked-out basement, a lot of cursing, mainly from

Glen, was still going on. A few people had remained there, either passed out or paralyzed with fear, but nobody upstairs was going down to check on them. We had extra underwear should any require a fresh pair.

Charlie and I looked at each other across the trapdoor and wondered what Glen thought we had been doing there in the closet. Did he think we just wanted to lie on our stomachs on the floor and stare into the closet, or was Glen truly possessed by Norma's spirit? Had she somehow summoned Glen to join the séance by the quickest route possible, through the trap door? What on Earth would possess her to summon Glen? Charlie, I think, would have been a better choice. He would have made it a mellower séance.

On a happier note, Glen, calmer now, called out that he was okay. He had landed on the candle in the dish with the unknown liquid, which might have broken his fall, somewhat. There was also the strong probability that Jim Morrison had unwillingly helped Glen to a softer landing. Quite a night.

Even though the séance was pretty spectacular, another strange thing happened that night. Glen said he couldn't find his sweater. There was great sadness, not really. After all, Glen had just fallen on Jim Morrison! They later became good friends. We thought the sweater would turn up, and it did—about four months later. One day Glen excitedly announced that he'd found his sweater, and there was much rejoicing, and relief. Not really. The popular consensus was that Glen had loaned his sweater to someone after first borrowing it from someone else. Dick might have been the original owner, and Glen had simply forgotten.

Someone asked, "Where did you find it?"

Glen held up an album cover: The Doors, *Waiting for the Sun*.

"It's there. Jim Morrison is wearing my sweater!" he exclaimed, pointing to the cover photo.

Well, at least he'd found it.

One of the strangest concerts the band played was the 1968 Newport Pop Festival, which was held in Costa Mesa, California. That wasn't the strange part, in fact the concert wasn't strange at all. Tiny Tim and Sonny and Cher were the headliners, with Canned Heat, Country Joe and the Fish, and the Chambers Brothers, and others. The way the band came to play at the festival was the strange part.

Someone, probably Dick, received a phone call from Joey or Shep who were constantly hustling to get jobs for the band. He said the band would be playing at the Newport Pop Festival.

"Great! What day is that?"

The answer was, "Tomorrow."

That was unusual, but not strange. Bands would occasionally cancel due to sickness, another job, or because they didn't feel like playing. On this short notice the replacement band wouldn't be listed on the promotional poster. The poster just stated, "Groups to be added later."

"What time would we be going on?"

"Don't know yet, but you will be leaving early. Be ready before 8:00 a.m."

Is there such a time as before 8:00 a.m.? This was again uncharted territory. Joey and Shep picked the band up at a time before eight and headed out to Costa Mesa, a fifty-minute drive. I dutifully followed behind with the equipment, Charlie and any straggling band member who hadn't made it to the car. There wouldn't be a light show due to the sunshine, so Charlie came along just to help out.

We arrived at the band entrance gate and parked. Joey and Shep went to tell somebody that we'd made it. After a while they came back and said the band would be going on first, at 10:00. After they had a brief conversation with security, we drove to the stage area. There were two large stages set up opposite each other on either end of a field. I pulled up behind the nearest one and noticed a few things. The field where the concert-goers would be, and they were already starting to file in, was just dirt without a tree in sight. It had probably been used as an overflow parking lot. The crowd attending the event was expected to be enormous, and a large open space was needed. I have read the Newport Pop Festival was the first concert to have more than 100,000 people in attendance. The second thing I noticed was it was already getting warm. Not Arizona warm, but warm nonetheless and humid. Luckily for us, there was a tent set up for the bands to wait out of the sun and heat. Here was where it started to get strange.

Joey and Shep came up to me and said, "This stage will do," then rushed to help unload the van and set the equipment up. They had never before done that. An event staffer with a clipboard climbed on stage and asked what group this was.

Joey told them, "Alice Cooper."

He looked hard at his clipboard and asked, "Are you sure?"

As he was walking away, I heard him muttering to himself. "Nobody tells me anything."

I believe this man was Hugh Romney, one of the announcers for the show. In 1969 there was another festival in upstate New York, the legendary Woodstock. Hugh was there, but by then he was calling himself Wavy Gravy. One of Hugh's great quotes from Woodstock was, "Good morning! What we have in mind is breakfast in bed for 400,000." Unfortunately, he was only joking.

The Newport Festival crowd grew larger by the minute as more and more people streamed onto the dirt field. Close to being on time for their 10:00 a.m. appearance, Alice Cooper got on stage and started to play. Now, they were about three quarters done with their set and all was going well.

I was on the far side of the stage when I noticed that Joey and Shep were blocking the stairs on the opposite side and in a heated disagreement with a person. From his position on the stage, Dennis could overhear something of what was going on. It seemed that Alice Cooper was not actually scheduled to play at the concert!

Earlier, just after our arrival, Joey and Shep had attempted to convince the promoter of the concert to let Alice Cooper play. His answer had been an emphatic, "NO!" Undeterred by this rejection, Joey told security that we were a different band, The James Cotton Blues Band, who actually were scheduled to appear, and who were very talented black musicians who played the blues.

What the promoter heard that morning was not the blues, and when he came out of his office, he saw five pasty white guys playing not the blues.

The band finished their set, and Joey and Shep helped tear down and load up the equipment. I could get used to this. We caught some of Canned Heat's set, since they were the next act, but actually they were the first act scheduled to play before Alice Cooper beat them to it. And with that we headed home.

Alice Cooper, Inc.

8814 SUNSET BLVD.
LOS ANGELES, CALIFORNIA 90069
PHONE (213) 657-8890

October, 18, 1968 3:00 a.m.

Dear Ellen,

You sounded sort of weird in your last letter. It wasn't like your usual type, but depression has a way of coming out in a person's writing, and it showed in yours. Depression doesn't become you. Not at all. If all you had was a bad day, you're preaching to the choir. I understand completely. Besides, "things are getting better all the time." —Beatles. If you want to talk, I'm available most nights after midnight, but I have to be in bed by 4:00 a.m. I need to get my beauty sleep.

The band signed with G.A.C., so that's another big step out of the way. Also, Les Crane and his producer are interested in them for an early morning fifteen-minute television show before kids go to school. So, you might someday early in the morning see the Alice Cooper Show, but it's a long way off. But, so was the signing with a booking agent, and that's now a reality.
They start recording sometime in November… maybe. Zappa is getting back from Europe October 27th.

The band plays at The Bank (it's a new big club) the first and second. Everybody went to see Barbarella with Jane Fonda. It was alright but not that great. It had a lot of neat props and scenes, though. She wore some interesting outfits. It was good if you like a lot of sexy scenes. I was embarrassed, but I looked anyway.

So, I hope you feel better, because you really look good to me and other people when you're happy.

If you ever need or want anything you have only to write or call.

I love you,
Mike

12

New Music, New Look

The time had finally come for Alice Cooper to plan their first album. Most of the songs for the album were arranged in Topanga. They composed and practiced for hours in the serene, and peaceful house in the Canyon. During these sessions, most of the wildlife, including the wild peacocks, headed for the hills. Even Dag stopped coming by. The album was for Bizarre Records, Frank's record company, but ended up on the Straight Record label because of a record distribution problem. Unfortunately, the album would not be recorded until months later.

Frank Zappa was an interesting man. On the outside he looked like your typical hippie freak just waiting to get stoned and stare at fluffy clouds all day trying to make shapes into images. Nothing could be further from the truth. He looked the part, but he did not act the part. He was all business, and everything followed a schedule—his schedule. He did not do drugs or drink to excess. Anybody caught doing drugs or alcohol at practice or at a show was fired. His motto could have been, "Be on time and be prepared."

He had made it, we all knew, because he was living in a house in Laurel Canyon, not Topanga Canyon. I had seen the house before, but it didn't register on me because we were busy storming the castle with musical equipment in hand at an ungodly hour. I had thought that we would never be invited back after the previous 7:00 a.m. arrival and unscheduled audition.

The house didn't fit the image of what I thought was the sort of house Frank Zappa would live in. It was a large piece of property with an equally large split-timber house on it. The property had once belonged to Tom Mix, who was a huge western movie star in the 1920s. Tom Mix also had an Arizona connection, one he likely wished he never had. He died near Florence, Arizona when he rolled his car into a ditch. In 2016, many years after Frank's death, the former Zappa estate was purchased by Lady Gaga.

Frank's wife Gail was nice. She gave us cookies and was caring for Moon Unit, their first child. Not to be rude, we devoured them—the cookies, not Gail and the child. Frank, seeing the empty tray where cookies once resided, exclaimed, "Those must have been Alice's cookies!" This caused us to fear some sort of retribution for eating them. Honestly, there weren't that many.

Instead, he began talking about putting the album in a tin with assorted cookies. Unsure if he was serious or not, the group let it go. Upon reflection, it might not have been that bad of an idea. The album could be sold at both record and grocery stores and it would have been the only album ever with an expiration date.

We were given a tour before meeting with Frank to sort out a recording schedule. Some of the Mothers of Invention also lived on the estate and I hung out with the Mothers down in the basement while the band worked. The basement was quite large. On one wall there was a full-size bank vault. There were more rooms, presumably guest rooms, and a one-lane bowling alley. I couldn't begin to imagine Frank Zappa bowling. You can never tell. He might have been quite a good bowler with a high average. The Mothers advised me about Frank's work ethic and his drug and alcohol policies. I needed to remember to relay this information to the rest of the group. It was at Zappa's house that I met Suzy Cream Cheese. She was living in a small cabin on the property. She'd had a speaking part on Frank Zappa's *Freak Out* album, and Frank had given her the name. I guess several girls have used that name.

Alice Cooper, Inc.

8814 SUNSET BLVD,
LOS ANGELES, CALIFORNIA 90069
PHONE (213) 657-8890

Dec. 11, 1968 1:30 a.m.

Dear Ellen,

Well, it's all over, and I'm very glad to say it was all a great success. The guys got good reviews in all the newspapers. This is just an example. This was in The Herald Examiner: "Appearing with the Mothers was Alice Cooper. A new male quintet whose forceful sound concealed an often subtle and very funny combination of Science Fiction, Pulp, greeting cards sentimentality, and wide-eyed simplicity." There was more, and it was all positive.

They also got several jobs. They are playing at The Whisky January 2nd through the 6, and at the Fillmore in San Francisco January 15th and 16th, and then in Denver sometime after that. Then in February the album comes out, but it may be delayed. The album is supposed to have a Dali painting on it. Also the album is going to be put on display in a New York art gallery because of the Dali picture.

We'll be coming back to Phoenix around the 20th, or after, so I guess I'll see you in ten days, hopefully.

Love,
Mike

Outfits for the Band

PEOPLE—etc., Tropic Magazine, *The Miami Herald,* July 13, 1969

Q Who or what is Alice Cooper? My teenage son keeps telling me "he's" the greatest, but I can't understand what it's all about. *—E.L., Chicago.*

A Better watch your teenage son. Alice Cooper is a "sick" singer who claims to be half male, half female, and the reincarnation of a 17th Century witch. On stage, he wears dresses (or slacks), mascara, eye shadow and rouge, and claims he's the "end product of an affluent society." According to his critics, he's just the end.

After the group changed its name to Alice Cooper, a strange metamorphosis occurred. When we went into a thrift store to buy clothes, I would head over to the men's section shopping for jeans, turtle necks, and leather jackets. The band rushed to the women's section to paw through the racks searching for anything with sequins, bangles, beads, or fringe. I cringed when they began trying on, or excitedly discussing, what they had found. *That looks so good on you. You are so lucky—everything looks great on you.*

Their clothing choices, modeling, and remarks regularly caused a bit of a stir among the women, and certainly among the men in the store, but some of them would nod in agreement that the garment did look good on the person wearing it.

Neal was sort of left out, being vertically challenged. His height made him a striking figure, but understandably proved to be a disadvantage when shopping for women's clothing. Consequently, instead of finding sparkly outfits, he accessorized his look with long flowing scarves, rings, pins and bracelets. Even Glen embraced this new look. I expected to hear profanity-laced sarcasm ending sharply with "No!" followed immediately by more swearing. But Glen followed Neal's lead and wore scarves, lots of jewelry, and the occasional nail polish on just a few fingers.

I had a vision of the band conferring before a show to discuss who was wearing what so their outfits wouldn't clash. In the end I had to admit they looked pretty good. Oh God! Now I'm doing it. *Please God, make them wear this stuff on stage and not around the house,* I silently prayed. He complied. This fascination with woman's clothing dropped off dramatically when Cindy Smith joined our wandering group of minstrels. Her fashion sense and talent were considerable, and she began designing and sewing the band's stage clothing.

In addition to thrift store shopping and Cindy's designs, the band also delved into the world of used clothing sales held by the Ice Capades and the Ringling Brother's Circus, which had all the sparkly, dangly costumes one could ever dream of. Some of the outfits even lit up, but most pieces had frayed wiring and the working lights required a boatload of D cell batteries. We wondered if Cindy could fix them. She was a gifted designer and seamstress, but alas she was not an electrician.

Even though every member of the band liked the idea of being lit up, the realization that their pants or shirts might catch fire or they could be shocked by frayed wiring made them rethink the appeal of electric pizazz. However, they still managed to find several pieces which weren't likely to electrocute them. I even found a band uniform jacket with epaulets and a lot of braiding on the front for myself. I don't think I ever wore it.

Cindy kept busy designing and sewing clothes. She conceived a brand-new look for them: satin shirts with wide flowing sleeves, gold and silver lamé pants, scarves, and feather boas, and shirts that looked like short dresses. She made a pair of silver pants for Alice that looked like they were covered with short pieces of tinsel. Charlie's lights reflected beautifully off them in a dazzling display. One of the more interesting outfits was a collection with, vests, pants, and I believe a pair of chaps for Neal, all made out of clear plastic vinyl.

Mike Bruce usually wore the vinyl pants, foregoing the matching vest. Moisture built up inside the pants and sweat streamed down, making the outfit resemble a glass shower door after a hot shower. One time during a show at Thee Experience on Sunset Blvd so much water was pouring from his pants I thought he was going to pass out from dehydration. He sweated gallons of water every set. Thankfully, there may have been a blessing in disguise. He wore a long white satin shirt with the pants. Perspiration made it stick to his body, so there weren't any accidental nether-regions exposures. Unfortunately, the pants also caused a chaffing problem.

During a show at another club, the stage was set up against a large store-front glass window. While wearing his see-through pants, Mike gave passersby quite the show from behind. You might ask: did the band wear anything under their pants or not? The band was seeking maximum exposure—publicity wise of course—but the answer was yes.

Alice found a new prop. It was a sword. Actually, it was a French fencing saber. It had a shield that covered and protected his whole hand, but it didn't have a blunted tip. It had a broken-off tip. God help us all. When Alice had the sword in his hand, he *became* Errol Flynn.

The sword generated discussions about spicing up the show by having me jump on a springboard from behind the amplifiers, which would launch me onto the stage. Alice and I would then engage in a sword fight. I would lose, naturally. I was unenthusiastic about this new escapade. I had visions of two broken ankles from bad landings, of being propelled into the audience with a sword in my hand, or being hacked to death by Alice with the broken-off sword tip. Luckily for me, that part of the show never happened, although it was brought up from time to time. It always made me cringe.

What did happen one night during a concert was a chain on Neal's drums broke. Chains were attached to his bass drums and then to his stool to keep the drums from sliding away. Without the chain holding it, one drum traveled forward every time he used his foot pedal. I came out on stage, assessed the situation, and realized I couldn't fix it right then. Pressured to find an immediate solution, I pushed the drum back toward Neal and sat on the floor with my back against it to keep it from traveling.

Seeing my predicament, Alice realized he had a new stage prop: *Me*! He grabbed his trusty sword and began thrusting it in my direction. I thought it might add something to the show if I acted scared, except I wasn't acting. I crossed my arms in front of my face just as Alice slashed at me with the sword. The sword made contact, leaving a four-inch gash in my turtle neck sleeve and my arm. As blood flowed, the audience thought it was fake and howled. I thought it was real, and I was unfortunately correct. When the song ended, I fixed the chain, and wrapped a towel around my arm to stop the bleeding. From then on, I nailed the drums to the floor.

Anti-Drum Solo

In the sixties there was an event at almost every rock band's concert, and it could happen at any time during the set. The band would stop playing and step toward the back of the stage, the lights dimmed leaving a spotlight on the drummer. A time-honored tradition commenced. It was called the drum solo. It could go on for a few minutes, hours, or until the next day. When the solo ended, the audience would applaud, either because they loved it, or because they were thankful it was over.

Neal did what he called his "anti-drum solo." He set the mood by putting on a pair of safety goggles. It started out like a normal drum solo: the stage lights dimmed, and a spotlight hit him. The difference was that instead of the band stepping to the back of the stage, they took refuge behind their amplifiers. Neal's drum solo started out slow, sped up, and then proceeded directly to crazy. He stood up from his stool and moved around his drums as he hit them, kicked them, and tossed them around the stage. Cymbals crashed, literally, to the floor. He would pick up a cymbal stand and bang the other cymbals with it. He grabbed an armful of drumsticks and bombarded the drums and cymbals with them. When the drums were destroyed, and he'd run out of drumsticks, the solo was over and he'd collapse on the stage.

The audience emerged from behind the relative safety of their makeshift barricades and wildly applauded thankful to be alive and wondering how to get out of their promise to God to go back to church if they survived the drum solo. The band would hang back a little bit longer, sticking close by their amps just in case Neal found a few more drumsticks to throw.

An incident happened that didn't involve me, thankfully. During the show, Neal, like at so many others, put on his goggles, worked himself up, and sprang off his stool. The band, knowing what was coming, took cover as Neal, still playing the drums, circled. At one point he grabbed a handful of drumsticks, which he hurled forcefully at the drums and the cymbals. Usually, he would throw them so they landed backstage, where I retrieved them so they could be reused for the next show. This time however, one drumstick hit the drum and shot into the audience.

The show ended and we were backstage in the dressing room waiting for the crowd to leave. Everyone was talking and carrying on, allowing the adrenaline from the show to subside. Then, Dick Phillips walked in.

"Everyone on your best behavior." he said. "Clean yourselves up, and don't say anything about how bad she looks."

"What's wrong? What's going on?" Everyone spoke at the same time.

"One of Neal's drumsticks hit a girl in the face. This is serious," Dick explained. The realization that someone was injured took the air out of the room.

"I'm bringing her back in a few minutes. Lucky for us, she's a big fan."

Dick led her into the room. She appeared to be sixteen or seventeen. Her long hair was parted in the middle and hung down covering her forehead and part of her face. When she brushed her hair away, we were horrified to see a discolored lump the size of a hen's egg on her forehead just an inch above her eyebrow. If that drumstick had landed two inches lower it would have been disastrous. It looked very bad. I had visions of people running out of the room or throwing up in the nearest trash can.

Stunned, we stood motionless, the color draining from our faces. Her forehead looked like Neal had thrown a hammer at it. The young lady bravely said it didn't hurt much and lamented she hadn't even gotten the drumstick! Without hesitating Neal gave her two drumsticks. I would have given her a drum.

"Would you like some ice for your head?" Neal said. "It will help with the swelling."

"That would be nice," she replied. There was no ice.

"How about a wet towel?" I offered.

She nodded. A cold, wet towel was handed to her, and she pressed it to her forehead. A chorus of apologies followed. I even apologized to her. We sat and talked with her for about twenty minutes. Then, she said she had to go meet her friends who were waiting.

"Why don't your friends come back here?" Alice suggested.

"That's okay. I've got to be going home," she answered.

Another round of "We're sorry!" followed, and Dick escorted her back to her friends. Just another day at the office. In the future it might be a good idea to have the audience sign waivers warning of possible bodily harm and that the band will not be held responsible for injuries. Later on, at a different show, I was also victimized by of one of Neal's errant drumsticks. You would think I would have known better.

13

New Cities, Bigger Venues

The band began opening for Frank Zappa and The Mothers of Invention. The crowds were large and enthusiastic, sometimes too enthusiastic. It was during one of these shows that a guy hoisted himself up on the stage and managed to get to a microphone. He started playing his harmonica. In most cases, you let these guys play for thirty seconds or so, then you approach and tell them to go, and they exit to a round of applause, fist-pumping the air. They had their minute of fame, and that's it. This guy was different. He thought he belonged on the stage and would only get off when he was good and ready. The band looked at me, and I looked at them. It was time for him to leave.

I hurried up to him and screamed over the music into his ear, "The cops are coming. You need to get off the stage!"

I led him by the arm to the backstage stairs, and he started down but stopped when he was halfway to the bottom. Suddenly, he grabbed onto both handrails. I could feel every muscle in his arm tense up. He was not going to go quietly into that good night. He couldn't go back up the stairs because I was blocking him. I couldn't get him down because he was blocking me. I visualized the two of us tumbling down the stairs, each suffering a serious injury. Frankly, at that point I really didn't care about his being injured. I would ride him down the stairs like a sled if I had to.

We were at a stalemate when the cavalry arrived. A couple of Frank Zappa's roadies appeared, and the three of us forcibly pried his hands from the railing and carried him the rest of the way down. He kicked and yelled all the way. I seriously thought about dropping him on the hard stairs and letting the other guys drag him to the bottom by his feet, bouncing his head on every step—that might knock some sense into him—but I didn't. I wanted to, but I didn't.

He became more pliable as we neared the bottom, worn out from all the yelling and kicking.

The Zappa people said, "We got him. We'll take care of him."

I replied, "Thank you for the help. He was a handful."

I like to think that they escorted him to the back door and let him go. All I knew was I was going to be sore tomorrow.

We hit the road heading to new cities and venues: Seattle, Chicago, and Denver. The van was racking up quite the miles. The band performed with lots of popular groups: Chicago, Bob Seger, The Grassroots, The McCoys, The Nitty Dirt Band, The Doors, and on, and on, and on. The Alice Cooper group was playing at larger and larger venues, with six or seven big name groups headlining. These weren't just shows. They were events. I can't begin to describe every concert Alice Cooper ever played. There were dozens, if not hundreds of shows. My memory is not that good.

> MacCluskey, Thomas. "Alice Cooper Has a Baby
> Blast." Music Critic, *Rocky Mountain News*

> *Alice Cooper was pregnant—like pregnant with like
> heavy, heavy sounds!*

When she gave birth to those sounds in a concert at the University of Colorado Memorial Center Sunday night, she unloaded with such impact that it's difficult to believe the building is still standing.

It's also difficult to believe that one's ears and eyes and head could withstand the densities and amplitudes of the vibrations—sound and light waves— that crashed into them.

The band had been booked for a show at the University of Colorado in Boulder. I went to the cafeteria before the show and ordered an Alfred Packer Burger. While I waited for my food I asked the worker what an Alfred Packer Burger was. He brought over a laminated article that told the story. In 1870 he had eaten five of his friends when they were trapped for weeks in a blizzard. He was later arrested and convicted of cannibalism. At the sentencing, the judge remarked, "There were twelve good Democrats in this county, and you ate five of them!"

The show was held in the newly remodeled student union building. In the center of the room was a round, freestanding stone fireplace with a copper hood and stack. I set the equipment up in front of it. When the doors opened, the students filed in and sat on the floor in front of the makeshift stage.

During the show, a student prankster rolled a rather large rubber penis in front of the band where Alice caught sight of it. He grabbed his trusty sword with the broken tip. I thought, *Great, someone's going to lose an eye*. The band retreated behind their amps. Sensing danger, the crowd began scooting backward as Alice stabbed repeatedly at the penis, pretending it was a snake. After "killing" the snake/penis, Alice impaled it on the end of his sword and hoisted it into the air then proceeded to thrust it over the heads of the students. The guys all laughed, and the girls screamed. It was good that Alice had finally found a safety tip for his sword, but I doubted that it would go over big at a high school or church dance.

About this time, the band went into their planned food fight à la *Animal House*, even though the movie hadn't yet been made. Tomatoes began to fly. Some landed in the audience and were snatched up by the students and rapidly fired back at the band. Instead of their intended target, most hit the copper hood above the fireplace. By the end of the show, the crowd seemed to have had a great time and were in high spirits, all except the manager of the building. Who knew that tomatoes could take the finish off copper? We left Dick to clean up the mess, figuratively and literally.

It was also in Colorado that half the group wanted to drive back to Phoenix, and the other half wanted to go to L.A. I happened to be part of the gang that had their sights set on Phoenix—I had a reason to go back there now. On the road, we were caught in an early-season mountain snowstorm. I was unprepared, having neither chains nor four-wheel drive. We had come up to a high mountain pass on Pikes Peak Highway where the road went up the mountain then over and down.

Due to the ice buildup on the road, I tried several times without success to get to the top. I would nearly make it, but the wheels would lose traction and we'd slide down almost to the starting point. Never one to be discouraged by a challenge, I had Dick, Dennis, Glen, and Charlie get out of the van and try to stop it before it could slide further down the icy road. That proved to be a futile plan. It looked like the van was chasing them downhill, trying to put them "Under My Wheels." I've got to remember that line.

They were freezing standing by the van because no one was dressed for winter weather. One more try—almost to the top—but the van this time slid all the way back down the road, and again they had to jump out of the way to keep from being run over. I was getting further and further away from my goal.

On the next attempt, I gunned the engine, put the van into gear, and sped up the steep road, my rear tires slipping crazily on the icy surface. The extra speed, though, got me to the top. They climbed back in, half frozen now, but they warmed up quickly thanks to the engine being inside the van cabin.

It was only when I was safely at the top that I realized the road butted up against the mountain on one side, while on the other the road dropped sharply off into oblivion. And there were no guardrails! I had been so focused on getting up the mountain that I never even thought about sliding off straight down into nothingness. I guess young people really do think they're invincible.

We got to Phoenix in one piece after that.

Rickety Screech

We were on another one of our usual tours of Colorado in the winter. Why in the winter? I have no idea. I guess we're the only group crazy enough to drive in Colorado in the wintertime. We left Denver and proceeded to Aspen, which was next on our list of dates for the Alice Cooper group. There was plenty of snow, but the roads were clear. That was good, because I still traveled with neither four-wheel drive nor chains. It was a beautiful winter night, the mountain air was cold and crisp. The stars were amazing; the Milky Way cut a swath brighter than the moon across the night sky. All that was missing were the Northern Lights.

The club staff grumbled that it was going to get down to eight below zero. Complaining about minus eight? Why, we wouldn't even put on a sweater in North Dakota until it got down to twenty below! That's perfect ice fishing weather. I tried that once. Ice fishing was all the proof you needed to know that Hell really does freeze over. How could anyone possibly think ice fishing has any semblance of being fun? I think I may have lost a few toes because of the cold, but luckily they grew back. Thanks, perhaps, to playing in DDT as a child.

The band played, and everything was going great. The crowd was clapping and stomping their feet, probably attempting to restore circulation. After the first set, someone came up and said, "You should let my friend play his guitar and the group should back him up."

Usually, that would have been a nonstarter met with a polite, but firm, "Get Lost." But the guy was very persistent. He said his friend was a great guitar player. Better than Hendrix. Better than Chet Atkins. If Glen had heard that, there might have been a fight. In Glen's eyes nobody was better than Chet Atkins.

Alice shrugged and said, "Sure, why not." It was either the cold or the free drinks talking.

The band decided they would improvise something with a Paul Butterfield East-West feel. The guitar player could come on stage, and this "virtuoso" that nobody had ever heard of would plug his guitar into Glen's amp. The band began to play. After a bit Alice pointed his finger at the guy, which was his cue to come up. There was a smattering of applause as he climbed the steps. Did the audience know something we didn't?

He plugged into Glen's amplifier as per the plan, then proceeded to produce the most ear-piercing screeching sounds ever wrenched from a guitar. His instrument wailed like it was in agonizing pain and needed to be put out of its misery. I know that's what we hoped for. I think my ears might have been bleeding. The notes he played were something between a yowling cat with his tail caught in a door and someone straining to pass a kidney stone. I have personal experience on that one.

As he played, he was jumping, scooting across the floor on his back, leaping up and down, twirling, and windmilling. The band was taken aback by what they were seeing and hearing. He wasn't playing anything close to what the band was. After four minutes, an agonizing eternity, Alice signaled the band to stop in three, two, one, and end.

The guy must have thought the pause was for his guitar solo, and he took full advantage of his moment in the spotlight. He proceeded to step his act up a notch, if that was even possible. He ran back and forth across the stage, literally bouncing off the walls and doing leg kicks—now he thinks he's a Rockette—all the while continuing his musical assault, never missing a note. Actually, he could have missed quite a few, because nobody understood what he was playing. What came from his guitar actually made your teeth hurt. His performance looked like an exercise class with guitar, gone terribly wrong. Finally, drenched in sweat and looking like he was going to drop, he left the stage in triumph, in his own mind. There was another smattering of polite applause followed by stunned silence.

The band learned a lesson that night: when a guy comes up and says a friend is the greatest guitar player of all time and he should sit in with you, be afraid. Be very afraid. I remember for the next few days when anybody asked me a question, I would say, "What? Speak up. I can't hear you." After the show, the guys gave him an apt new name, and from then on referred to him as "Rickety Screech."

I'm Going to Stop by this Church First

We were back in Phoenix for a time. I planned to return to Topanga after a week or so. Glen and Dick decided to ride with me. The van was loaded down, crammed with musical equipment, a washing machine my dad had given me, a cake, and some homemade baked goods from Toodie. After picking Glen up, I stopped to collect Dick at his sister Bonnie's house. We hoped to leave by noon. However, Dick let us know that Alice and Dennis had decided to go. The more the merrier, I thought, but our departure time was getting pushed back.

I left to bring the two of them over to Bonnie's. By the time I returned, Mike Bruce had decided to come along, but he had someone to drop him off at Bonnie's apartment. Since everyone else was going, Neal said to count him in. Once we all were together, we would be heading out. This was really going to test out the shocks.

While we were waiting for the other two to show up, we passed the time playing with the Ouija board. It told us we weren't going to leave on time. I had already figured that one out. Tell me something I didn't know. It did. It predicted that we wouldn't reach the Topanga Canyon house, and we would stop by a church on the way.

At last, hours later than planned, we departed Bonnie's house at midnight and arrived on the outskirts of L.A. close to 6:30 a.m. Morning traffic was bad in L.A., but not as bad as it is now.

I should tell you I don't remember much about what happened next. I remember some of it, but not all. Most was filled in by band members, police, and witnesses.

I was driving in early morning rush-hour traffic. Why they call it rush hour, I don't know, because nobody really moves. I know, old joke. Suddenly, a gap in the traffic appeared both in front of and behind me. A rush-hour dream come true! *I'll ride this all the way to Topanga*, I thought. At the very moment I was rejoicing at the distance between me and the vehicles in front, a law of physics came into play—the law asserts two or more objects cannot occupy the same space, at the same time.

The driver of a yellow or tan station wagon with metal faux-wood siding wanted to be in the same space I was occupying. I have some memory of what happened next. I turned the wheel hard to the left and shot up the incline of the freeway's concrete wall. I thought I was doing quite well driving along the wall, because traffic had come to a halt in both directions to watch. A few seconds later gravity took over as I braked. Just what I needed, more physics. The van began to roll over, and over, and over finally coming to a stop, landing on its top. We literally felt what it was like to be inside a washing machine on spin, which was somewhat ironic because we were carrying a washing machine with us.

The number of times the van rolled was hotly contested. Dennis said five times. Mike thought four. Witnesses said three or four revolutions. The police didn't know. Anyway, at some point during all this tumbling, I decided, or it was decided for me, that I would be exiting the van by the most direct route possible: through the front windshield. Luckily, the front windshield had popped out seconds earlier with the force of a previous tumble and, luckily again, I flew through the opening created by the now-missing windshield, my seat belt still holding me fastened tightly in my seat. Witnesses said I skipped down the road for twenty or thirty feet, the back of the seat skidding along the pavement. Sparks flew, and my legs and arms thrashed in every direction all at the same time. My brain was nowhere to be found during this period.

As my vision cleared, I saw a white light. It was two angels motioning for me to come with them. I heard them speaking, but I didn't understand what they were saying. I hoped it was that I'd done well and it was time for my heavenly reward. But, as my mind began to clear, I saw it was just two L.A. motorcycle policemen staring down at me, asking if I was the driver of the van. I really don't remember anything they were saying—a witness told me. The police unbuckled my seat belt, helped me stand up, and told me to go wait somewhere. I don't remember hearing that either, but I do remember that every bone in my body popped trying to reshape itself into something that might be considered normal.

A witness said, "Man, we thought you were dead. You went through the windshield and skidded down the road. It's incredible that you're not a dead man. You should be dead."

Sorry to disappoint. I looked around and tried to shake the fog from my brain. Bystanders said they were talking to me, but I wasn't hearing them. I really wasn't.

It was then I noticed the freeway sign: "Mission Next Exit." I remember the sign, but not much else of that day. The Ouija board had predicted that we would be stopping at a church. Shivers went up my misaligned spine.

What happened in the immediate aftermath is a blur. One thing I clearly recall is the police asking me to help push the van back onto its wheels. When it was upright, a large bottle of beer, probably Glen's, fell out and broke on the freeway right in front of three police officers. They stared at it for a moment then looked at me, shook their heads, and kicked the pieces to the curb.

I don't remember Mike Bruce directing traffic. Dennis told me I attempted to cover Neal with a mattress. I definitely don't remember that. One of the strangest things, and I don't know why I would remember it, was that one of the band mothers had baked a very large and nice looking cake for us. She had packed in a sturdy box for the trip back to California. I carried it up front next to me on top of the engine compartment, wanting to keep it away from prying eyes and hands. I walked back to the wrecked van to retrieve it. The cake wasn't where I'd left it. It was everywhere I hadn't left it. It looked like it had exploded. The inside of the van was plastered with ruined cake and chocolate frosting. It was also on my clothing and in my hair. I noticed everyone else looked the same, as if during the accident we'd entertained ourselves with a massive food fight.

I can't recall how we got to the hospital. Dennis said that we each got an ambulance for the ride. I remember Dick had to have stitches in his scalp, and Neal hopping around, his gunshot wound aggravated. I must have seen and talked to a doctor, because I later found a prescription for painkillers in my pocket. I have no recollection who picked us up at the hospital. I don't know what happened to the musical equipment, or the washer, or how we got home to our place in Topanga Canyon.

My mother had given me a St. Christopher medal, the patron saint of travelers, to put in the Plymouth. I had transferred it to the van where I pinned it to the visor. St. Christopher must have been working overtime that day—it was amazing, possibly even a miracle, that nobody was seriously injured that April 12th 1968 morning. The Alice Cooper band could have tragically ended before they even got started. After the accident, I searched the wreckage for the medal but couldn't find it. I guess St. Christopher had enough. He was done riding with me. I couldn't blame him, but I really could have used his help a few more times after that. It was probably his way of saying, "You're on your own now." Thinking about it, he may have returned on those other occasions too, because we always survived accidents unscathed.

Photos Courtesy Toodie Mueller

Toodie Mueller atop crushed van

Michael Bruce (on top), Me, Les Braden (inside)

Michael Bruce

Me, Les, Mike Bruce

The accident proved to be a pivotal event in the history of the band. Our van was smashed. The musical equipment was smashed. The band members were smashed. The revenue stream was smashed beyond recognition and, to top it off, we would soon be forced from our Topanga Canyon home for failure to pay rent. Everyone felt disheartened. The band held a meeting to decide what to do next. The options on the table were: go home, break up, or pull ourselves together and ride out the situation in the hope we could turn it around. The band, along with myself, Charlie, Dick and Cindy, unanimously agreed to ride it out.

It was Alice who voiced what we were all thinking. "We don't know how to do anything else."

Much of the meeting centered on how to save money and get money. There was brief talk of selling instruments. This was counterproductive, of course, since they were a band and needed them. Another thought was to stop paying salaries, which was really a non-issue. Paychecks were few and far between. In fact, when we were paid, we would eye it and ask, "What's this for?"

We were in dire need of money just to survive and to continue as a band. There would be an insurance settlement, but a settlement would take time. In actuality it took months. I wasn't cited for the accident and, if they had caught the person responsible, my insurance company would have been on him like flies on stink. But that wasn't the case, and my insurer moved at a glacial pace to pay my claim.

In the end, hard decisions had to be made. The only way to get money right now, the band concluded, was for Dennis to sell his prized white 1964 Ford Falcon with the chrome rims and extra-large tires on the rear. He agreed because he recognized the need and the greater good. The band promised to pay back the money as soon as it was conveniently possible. After all these years he's still waiting.

Without Dennis's sacrifice, the newly named Alice Cooper would have ended before they even got started.

Glen, Alice Dennis, Neal. Using borrowed amps and drums
Courtesy Toodie Mueller

When she heard about the accident, Toodie drove her Mustang over from Phoenix and brought her camera. We needed photos at the wrecking yard for the insurance company. Mike Bruce and Les asked to come along, but they wanted to make a stop first, and it was in the same direction as where the van was stored.

Toodie said, "Sure," and off we went. As we were leaving Topanga she asked, "Where to?"

From the back seat Mike said, "We need to go back to where the accident happened."

Toodie chirped, "Cool!"

I asked the more important question, "Why do you want to go back there?"

Mike said that he had put a baggie of marijuana into the storm drain and he wanted to retrieve it.

"Cool!" Toodie said, again.

I, being the downer, said, "You know we will have to park on the freeway to get the baggie. You don't think that will raise some interest?"

Mike and Les promised it would only take a few seconds. I directed Toodie to the location of the accident, and she pulled up and stopped next to the storm drain. Les quickly jumped out of the back seat and laid on his stomach on the asphalt in front of the car. It literally looked like we had hit him. If you think we weren't drawing attention to ourselves, you would be so wrong. Les stuck his hand and arm deep into the drain and fished around for the baggie. After a quick search he shouted, "I can't find it."

Mike Bruce hopped out of the car and laid down next to Les. Now it looked like we had hit a second person.

Mike and Les lying on the freeway in front of her car was causing Toodie to get nervous. She said, "This is so not cool," while eyeing the traffic, afraid the police might show up.

All this time I'm waving at the approaching cars for them speed up, like there was nothing to see here. But traffic was still slowing and drivers and passengers stared at the two bodies wiggling around in front of the Mustang.

I had heard rumors about people who made their home in the sewers. Maybe they'd found the stash Mike had stashed. That would fall under the law of finders keepers.

After several nerve wracking minutes, Mike yelled, "I've got it," and he and Les dove into the car with their prize. Toodie, who was definitely not saying "cool" anymore, aggressively floored the Mustang and, with tires squealing, we sped away from the scene of the crime.

Making sure of our escape and certain we weren't being followed, we reached our destination, the wrecking yard. Toodie and I shot a roll of film for the insurance company and as souvenirs for ourselves.

Side Work

During those lean times, Alice and I had temporary employment making buttons with catchy slogans that were sold in the local head shops. Head shops sold beads, necklaces, posters, rolling paper, incense, and counterculture comic books such as *Yellow Dog, Mr. Natural, The Fabulous Furry Freak Brothers*, and others. A few of the buttons we made had phrases such as "Save Water, Shower with a Friend," "Peace and Love," "Make Love Not War." There was something for the "other side," meaning straight people, too. Notably, buttons with a peace sign that read, "Footprint of the Great American Chicken." This was during the unpopular Vietnam War.

Making and selling buttons must have been very profitable. The button manufacturer's house was located in the hills of Malibu and had a great view of the ocean. Alice and I worked in a large barn on the property. As we made the buttons, we'd gaze at the view and say, "Someday."

Food, or lack thereof, was a difficulty in our lives from time to time. Glen's sister Janice related a story about an incident that occurred before the accident during a family visit to Topanga. Tom and Jerry (I kid you not) Buxton and Janice had traveled to Topanga to check on Glen and the band. Janice was sitting by herself when Alice and Dennis came over to talk. The conversation worked itself around to asking for a favor. "Can you buy us a can of tuna?" Alice asked.

Janice, sixteen at the time, amiably agreed. They walked together down the road to the Topanga store-post office-gas station where she offered to purchase a can of tuna for each of them. They politely declined, saying one can was enough. She mentioned there were crackers in the car and asked if they wanted those too. Dennis said, "Definitely yes, let's do that." Back at the house, they retrieved the crackers from the family car and headed to the van, got in and closed the doors. The tuna and crackers were consumed hidden from sight. The reason for the cloak and dagger secrecy? They didn't want anybody to know they had food. They almost got away with it, too. The next day when I opened the van's doors, a faint fishy odor persisted, and the floor was littered with cracker crumbs.

Alice, Me, Janice (seated) Glen's mom Jerry
Photo by Tom Buxton

14

The Whisky

The band was booking more and more jobs at the Whisky a Go Go and at The Bank, where there was a little difficulty with family and friends crowding the band out of their dressing rooms. We had moved up from listening to music while standing outside the Whisky to playing inside. Some other group would now be outside listening to Alice Cooper's music, waiting for their chance. I have to admit that I retreated to the parking lot when Alice Cooper opened for Led Zeppelin. Led Zeppelin's music was deafening. You could probably hear them all the way to Pasadena.

Me, Dick, Charlie at the Whisky a Go Go January 2, 1969
Courtesy Monica Lauer

The Whisky was a famous club, like the Troubadour and Galaxy, but they all were surprisingly small. The Whisky had a tiny dance floor, with tables and chairs set up beyond it. The second floor balcony overlooking the stage was reserved for bands where they could listen to the other performers. It was also where bands waited between shows. Offices and storage areas were also located up there.

As long as the privilege wasn't abused, once you got to be known at the Whisky, you could come in for free and listen to whoever was playing. If you were famous, management wanted you to be seen there. I wasn't famous, but they let me in anyway.

Often, I would go during the day to make sure our musical equipment was still there—it was at the Whisky that Neal had his favorite drum stool stolen. The stool was unusual in the fact that it had a square seat instead of a round one, and it was pink. I was having a hard time trying to find a replacement.

One afternoon I went to check on the equipment, and there was a pretty dark-haired girl singing on stage. She was doing a sound check without her band. I didn't want to interrupt just to check our equipment, so I sat down at a table toward the back to wait. That young singer turned out to be Linda Ronstadt. Her voice was amazing. It was so pure and powerful a microphone wasn't needed. She didn't even need a band to back her up. She could have sung on stage all by herself.

She seemed nervous, and a person on the floor in front of the stage was looking up at her and speaking. I couldn't hear what they were saying, but the guy looked to be Michael Nesmith of the Monkees. It probably was him because he wrote the song "A Different Drum," which she recorded. I was thinking maybe I should leave. I could check on the equipment any time before the next show. Linda caught sight of me.

She called out, "How do I sound?"

I wanted to say, "I love you. I'm from Phoenix, and you're from Tucson. It's fate." But I didn't.

Instead, I said, "You will do great."

The stage at the Whisky was high off the floor and also small, matching the size of the club. Later that night Linda appeared on stage wearing a white dress, and she was barefoot, which was alarming because rock n roll stages were not the most sanitary places. Nor were the rooms where bands waited before going on.

When she performed the audience loved her. They rose to their feet, not to dance, but to crowd in front to hear her sing. Yes, I think she will do just fine. Her old band, The Stone Poneys, wasn't half-bad either. There might have been a young man by the name of Jerry Brown, soon to be Governor of California, at that show. It's been said that she gave him the nickname "Governor Moonbeam." They became quite the item.

Alice Cooper, Inc.

8814 SUNSET BLVD.
LOS ANGELES, CALIFORNIA 90069
PHONE (213) 657-8890

Dear Ellen,

This letter is arriving with Toodie by airplane. She will also have a small package with her. Remember about things in small packages? Well, don't you believe it. I hope you like it anyway.

I think I might be getting money also from the van accident from the insurance company, maybe, I hope. It will be the tidy sum of $80.90. Not bad uh?

By the way, I heard that you are crazy about me. So, I've been told. How about that, such an ego boost.

Alice and I have fencing swords, and we run around the house clanging away just like in an Errol Flynn movie. Alice wants to do something with them on stage. God help me.

Toodie and the boys seem to be having fun. They have been drinking, but not to excess. Oh, by the way, you told somebody what time Toodie was flying in, but not which airline. Shame on you. You made me and Dick look all over for her.

There's been talk of me, Charlie, and Dick coming back to Phoenix when the guys start recording, but it's only a rumor, so don't count on it.

So, have a real good time doing whatever you're doing. Within reason of course. Word gets to me about you, you know. Phoenix is not that far away. I've been really good while over here. Toodie can back me up on that. Just ask her. I told her what to say.

Well, I guess there is no more to say. I could say something about how much you mean to me, but I'm running out of room on the page to say anything. So, I can't.

Love,
Mike

Good Times and Hopefully Money, Money, Money

We had moved into the Landmark Hotel after leaving Topanga. Most of our broken equipment from the accident was finally repaired. The amps had been scraped up, Neal lost a couple of drums, and Dennis's bass guitar was damaged but fixable. It could have been a whole lot worse. I don't know who arranged this, Dick, Joey, or Shep, but Ampeg Musical Equipment gifted the group with amplifiers and a sound system. They were sort of our sponsor, like NASCAR, but the group didn't have to wear a product name label sewn onto their clothing. The sound system was good enough, but only for small clubs. We wouldn't look a gift horse in the mouth, though. Things were starting to look up again: bumps and bruises healed, new exciting jobs, new equipment.

It took four months to get the first and second checks for the accident from the insurance company and an additional two months for the third and final installment of the settlement. I received enough money for a good down payment on another van. I also received an $80 bonus check for expenses. The band members got money, too. It felt like Christmas! In fact, it nearly was, and I was filled with Christmas spirit, and a little cash. I purchased small gifts for Charlie, Dick, and the rest of the band, mostly records and novelty gifts. I bought a dress and a coat with a fleece lining for Ellen. My gifts, unfortunately, did not go over well with her parents. They thought it was inappropriate for me to give her clothing. Other than this, I think they liked me, or at least tolerated me. Until someone better could come along.

I bought a newer van: a yellow 1967 Chevy extended length with air conditioning and seat belts even. I had become a big believer in safety features since the accident. They were an upgrade option, but well worth it. The settlement didn't cover the whole cost of the new van, and Alice's dad, Ether Furnier, co-signed the loan with assurances from Joey and Shep they would make the payments. I hoped Alice's father wouldn't talk to Dennis about vehicle reimbursement.

The Chevy was longer than the Dodge with enough room for the equipment and even the band members, if they dared to ride with me again. Because we were extending our range for jobs further and further from L.A. and Phoenix, I constructed a single bed behind the front seats and installed a wood partition which I painted yellow to match the van. I cut in a window so I could see into the back and placed a gold eagle plaque above it for that designer touch. A royal blue curtain was hung in front of the window allowing me to nap on the road unseen. The wall and curtain also kept prying eyes from seeing the equipment inside.

It was around this time that Joey and Shep decided the Alice Cooper group needed something to boost its image, and they had a little money for it. The band was one hundred percent behind this idea, no matter what it was. Ideas occupied our thoughts every waking minute. Cindy dreamed of a larger budget, or any budget for that matter, for creating new band outfits. Most of the money came out of Cindy's pocket.

Perhaps better and more elaborate props for the stage—something with fire and massive amounts of smoke, Alice suggested. I guess he'd forgotten the "Cage of Death" and fire marshal experiences.

Maybe some money for Charlie for new lighting designs. Or even a better reel to reel to record practice sessions to help with song development.

All good ideas, but the image boost that Joey and Shep had in mind, which they determined we needed most was a......1956 Cadillac Fleetwood limousine. The Caddy won out on style, but practicality, that remained to be seen. The vehicle looked the part. It was long and black, though the paint was faded. It had lots of chrome and steel. It was almost as big as my old Plymouth Fury. The back seat was spacious and the carpet plush. It even had an extra bench seat that could be folded up or removed. Joey and Shep's selling point was that in order to be successful, you had to look successful. Nothing screamed success like driving up in a thirteen-year-old limousine.

The idea was to have the band arrive at the show in the limo, get out, and wave to the (hopefully) adoring fans. The spectacle of the limo, long hair, and sparkly clothes would cause a commotion helped along by our friends and a few of the GTOs. We hoped the people waiting in line would join in. Possibly a photographer would be there to catch all the action.

The only caveat was that the limo could be used for shows only in the Los Angeles area. The Caddy couldn't go on tour, perhaps because of safety concerns or other reasons. It's possible any of the band members getting behind the wheel, or me for that matter, was a factor. Too bad. I was psyched to wear a chauffeur's hat to add to the illusion. I did get to ride in it and also drove it a few times. It wasn't very good on corners.

Unfortunately, the limo only lasted a short time. While the band was on tour, we heard the Cadillac had been involved in some sort of an accident. I don't know who was driving, but Shep had an accident around the same time.

Another idea Shep had was advanced in a "secret" meeting between Shep, Dick, Charlie, and myself. We were hoping the meeting was to announce we would be paid on a regular basis. Instead, Shep explained, "We need to start treating the band like they are rock stars." He went on to say, "The band needs to concentrate on being a band and acting like stars, and by you doing everything else for them, this will help us achieve that goal."

We felt deflated. None of us had anything to say. We just looked at one another and nodded our heads in agreement, or disbelief. We had always thought of ourselves and the band as a family.

The three of us had the same vision upon hearing this announcement; the band's heads getting bigger and bigger until they exploded.

Shep concluded his talk. "Good meeting, and thanks."

Afterward, we sat down with the band. They asked two questions: "What was the meeting about?" and, "Is he going to start paying you?"

"No, nothing like that. We have to start treating you like rock stars and make all your wishes come true," Dick said. This news was enthusiastically met by those present.

"It's about damn time!" Neal said. And flicking his wrist in my direction, "Make me a sandwich and cut off the crust."

Mike Bruce added, "My dirty laundry is piling up. Have it done by morning."

Alice chimed in, "Wash my car, if I had a car, and draw me a bath."

This merriment went on for several minutes.

"We never said we were going to do it," Dick said, ending their fanciful teasing.

"Oh, man. It's not fair. I want to be treated like a rock star," Alice whined.

Reminds me of an old joke: A tourist in New York City walks up to a man on the sidewalk and asks, "How do I get to Carnegie Hall?" The man replies, "Practice, practice, practice."

Alice Cooper Goes Hollywood

Backyard and pool Quebec house
Courtesy Toodie Mueller

Eventually, we moved out of the Hollywood Landmark Hotel to the Hollywood Hills, a place with swimming pools and movie stars, where we rented a mini-mansion. It was 4000sf, located at 6225 Quebec Dr. I don't know who found this house, just that it wasn't me. I'm guessing Joey or Shep had as part of their "to be successful you have to look successful" boost the image scheme. The house itself had a very interesting history. It was built in 1927 by Hal B. Wallis, a movie producer and head of production for Warner Brothers Studio. Some of his movies were *Casablanca, Dark Victory, The Adventures of Robin Hood, The Maltese Falcon, Sergeant York, and Now, Voyager.*

In the early 1950s, Wallis hired a handy-man caretaker for the property. The handyman occupied a small apartment beneath the stairs leading up to the front door. He was a struggling actor named James Dean. It is rumored that he was discovered at the house during a party, which lead him to be cast to star in the movie *Rebel Without a Cause.*

The house was subsequently owned by John Phillip Law, the actor best known for playing the angel in the Jane Fonda movie *Barbarella*. The Alice Cooper group rented the house from Law. In 1973, the house was purchased by Doris Roberts, who played the mother on *Everybody Loves Raymond,* and she also made TV commercials for Glade Air Freshener. Around the neighborhood, the house was affectionately known as Casa de Glade.

The Quebec house was a large Spanish style building with a Saltillo tile roof and white stucco walls inside and out. It had wood floors, a living room with a large fireplace, beamed ceilings, and a large picture window to take in the view. There were several large bedrooms upstairs. The common word to describe the house was large, the largest we had ever lived in. No more sleeping in a closet for me! Mike, Dennis, Neal, Dick, and Charlie chose upstairs bedrooms. Glen claimed the closed-in balcony off the living room, which was surprising because a bank of windows let in a flood of light, and Glen was a night owl. His head rarely hit the pillow before 4:00 a.m.

Alice and I moved into the small basement room or, as we called it, "The Dungeon."

In the 1930s, the basement room had been a speakeasy. The ornate wooden bar still occupied one wall. The walls in the basement were made of boulders stacked one on top of the other. They were fake, but they looked real. The door leading into the room was secured with a push-button electronic lock, and there was another secret button in the living room.

For a while, the band practiced in the basement during the day and Alice and I slept there during the night or early morning. It was quiet and dark. I can truthfully say that no natural light ever penetrated the dungeon.

The main house was one story up, and you had to climb a flight of stairs to the front door. The bass player for Steppenwolf, and his girlfriend, a relation to Aldous Huxley who wrote *Brave New World,* lived in the small apartment under the stairs that James Dean had once occupied.

In addition to all the men in the new house, we also had a new woman. It was Neal's sister, Cindy, who had been with us on and off and on. She was our Wendy, and we were her Lost Boys. Basically, she took care of us. I don't think she had signed up for the job, but we gave it to her anyway. We really needed her. We were tired of talking to guys all the time. She was the proverbial breath of fresh air. It's a well-known fact that girls are smarter than boys—she explained that to me very soon, and often, after moving in. Cindy added a refreshingly different element of fun to the house. She made her bedroom off the kitchen in what would have been the dining room, if we'd had a dining table, or even chairs. She was the only one who actually had a real bed—a four-poster—to sleep in. The rest of us slept on mattresses on the floor. We didn't have much other furniture, but there were extra mattresses for guests.

Recently, Cindy reminded me of the time I picked her up, carried her to her bed, threw her on it and said, in my best Barry White voice, which probably sounded more like Gomer Pyle, "Let's do this thing." Hearing this story shocked me, because I would have never done that to Glen or Neal. She said I had just been kidding around with her. People described me in many terms, but I didn't think being a kidder would have been one of them. I considered myself more Spock-like back then. It must have been the fun element that she brought, or I was starting to behave like the band. Note to self: don't behave like the band.

Alice, as well as the rest of the group, loved old movies and theatrics. One of his favorite re-enactments was of a sword fight scene from *Robin Hood* where Errol Flynn and Basil Rathbone squared off. He was always trying to figure a way to incorporate a sword fight on stage without getting anybody hurt, emphasis on nobody getting hurt. During Alice's sword-play, I was a reluctant Rathbone to Alice's Flynn—reluctant because our previous sword fights had left me scarred. Since then, I had been hesitant to join in. Once bitten, twice shy comes to mind, as well as, it's better to run away and live to fight another day.

The minute he picked up the sword, Alice was the dashing and swashbuckling Errol Flynn. You may remember that his sword was the one with the jagged broken tip. If he connected with it, that would leave a mark, and it did. As his chosen adversary I would hastily grab a metal garbage can lid to use as a shield. When I picked up my sword, I was… Oh Crap! Alice would come at me like I was the last slice of pizza in the box, his blade slashing the air.

The house's old Spanish European design included an ornate wooden staircase, which helped Alice's Flynn persona come to life. Alice and I fought all the way up the stairs and charged into bedrooms climbing over mattresses occupied by people who, with urgent need, took cover. Pillows and salty language followed us on our exit. All through the house I yelled, "Help me" as Alice sparred, thrusting and parrying while I was ducking and covering.

Shep charged after us, shouting to get our attention. "Don't play rough," he scolded.

Looking at me, he warned, "And don't hurt Alice. There will be big trouble if you do."

Alice, hiding behind Shep, stuck his tongue out at me just like Gerald on the Wallace and Ladmo show, when he heard Shep's admonition. That order forced me into a completely disadvantaged position. Charlie would step in for me on occasion. He hadn't been permanently scarred—yet.

Alice was the essence of Mr. Positive. He never saw the danger in anything. On the other hand, I saw danger everywhere. Especially when a sword or a bullwhip and Alice were involved.

Alice liked to hand me a straw and say coyly: "Put this between your teeth."

I'd eye him suspiciously. "Why?"

He'd smile innocently and slide the bullwhip from behind his back and tell me he was going to knock the straw out my mouth.

Retreating, I'd say, "I thought we took that thing away from him!"

See, Mr. Positive. He was positive he could do it, and I was positive I would need to go to the hospital to have something sewn back on. If someone had said, "Those guys are coming over here to beat us up," Alice would reply, "Great. I'll make pancakes. Who wants bacon?" His attitude reminded me of those old Mickey Rooney and Judy Garland movies. When their situation was the darkest, Mickey would say, "Let's put on a show!" Problem solved.

Alice Cooper Makes an Album

In early 1969 after months of writing and rehearsing, the time finally arrived to record the album. During the recording process, Frank's schedule swung into high gear. As I recall, the album was recorded in just two or three nights of work. I knew nothing about recording an album, having never seen one made, but that seemed like a short period of time. There was a lot of, "Okay, we got that song. Let's do another one," from the engineer. The band countered, "I thought we were just rehearsing for a sound check?" The engineer replied, "It's fine. I will fix it later on." This was not the way Cayce, the engineer from Tucson, would have handled it.

During the session I fell asleep on the couch in the engineer's booth, and when I awoke they were just finishing their third song. One of the songs, "Levity Ball," was recorded live at the Cheetah Club instead of in the studio. I guess Frank was looking for an authentically real sound. What you hear on the record is what you heard in person. When the album was finished, it did sound like a live performance by the Alice Cooper Group.

Other than the quick recording time and the engineer acting like he wanted to be elsewhere, the only thing I remember about the session is that Mike Bruce wanted to play his guitar through a Hammond organ speaker cabinet. He had heard it could produce some unique sounds. I located one to rent and brought it to the studio. The question was how to run a guitar through it. The cabinet was crammed with electronics, wires, speakers, and whirling horns.

With a lot of luck, wire cutters, electrical tape, and a guitar cord, I managed to get it to work. The speaker only reproduced sound, but when you activated the whirling horns some unusual sounds came out. Everybody took a crack at playing through it. Even Neal tried to figure a way to incorporate it with his drums. After all the effort, I don't know if it was ever used on a recording. I spent most of what was left of the night sleeping or trying to find food at two in the morning. I only hoped the rental company didn't look inside the cabinet after I returned it to them.

Frank had a painting by Edward Beardsley that he wanted to use as the album cover. The painting is titled *Strawberry Cake.* The subject matter was a large man in a dark suit drinking a beer, a table with a dessert on it, presumably strawberry cake, and a girl hiking up her skirt to reveal her panties. Censors made the record company put a sticker over the girl's underwear. In the background, in silhouette, was what looked like a hearse, a bus and some cars lined up behind. The vehicles appear to be driving in a procession to or past a grave site. What it all meant, I have no idea. The band had hoped to use Dali's *Geopoliticus Child Watching the Birth of the New Man* for the album cover, but when you're a new band making its first album for Frank Zappa, and he says this should be your cover, and you'll be going on tour with Frank Zappa to promote that album, you choose wisely. And they did.

I have a sneaking suspicion, never proven, that Frank wanted to use the painting so he could write it off as a business expense. The picture, though, did work for the album, which was titled *Pretties for You.* Who doesn't like beer, and dessert, and girls lifting up their skirts? The artist referred to the painting as *Pretties for You* after the album came out. Sometime later, the painting was reported stolen.

> "Pretties For You." "Alice Cooper Pretties For You—Straight." STS 1051. Record World pick Album Reviews, *Record World,* May 31, 1969

> *Alice Cooper, a fellow, and four other fellows take a cue from John Cage and Frank Zappa and their own inclination for this package of strange, discombobulated sounds and songs. Just the thing for underground and above ground (in time) play.*

After months of delays due to record distribution and other issues, the album was released on the Straight label and not Bizarre June 25, 1969 to mixed reviews. Some critics liked it, some disliked it, and some liked parts of it. A little something for everybody. Over the years, the album gained acceptance and is now considered ahead of its time.

Frank gave a coming out party for all the groups signed under the Bizarre and Straight record labels. He rented the Shrine auditorium in L.A. The Mothers, Alice Cooper, The GTOs, and Wild Man Fischer performed. It was strange and wonderful all at the same time.

15

Easy Action

Alice was a fan of musicals, particularly *West Side Story* and, though it may be hard to believe, so was the rest of the band. Alice frequently broke into a spontaneous version of the Jet's song. The other band members joined in, but their voices trailed off because they didn't know all the words. Alice knew the words. His favorite song from *West Side Story* wasn't the romantic "Tonight," but the song "Cool." Alice sang the part of Riff. Everybody, even me, joined in snapping our fingers and bobbing our bodies up and down. Glen had a major part; he would bang his fists on a table and say, "*I wanna get even!*" Alice would reply, "*Easy, Action!*" and continue on with the rest of the song.

Easy Action just happened to be the title of the next Alice Cooper album on Frank Zappa's Straight Records. The album's songs were worked out and practiced in the speakeasy basement that Alice and I shared. *Easy Action* was released in March of 1970 less than one year after their debut album. Was the title *Easy Action* a coincidence? Nope. It was a tribute to West Side Story and the fun we had singing that song. If you listen to the song "Still No Air," you can hear the band singing parts of songs from West Side Story.

One song on the album "Lay Down and Die" is interesting. It was the B side on The Nazz's 45 record "I Wonder Who's Loving

Her Now." "Lay Down and Die" was recomposed as an eight-minute instrumental similar in style to Karlheinz Stockhausen's. Only at the end are there a few lines from the original rendition.

How the band wrote songs was a democratic affair. Majority ruled. This went all the way back to The Spiders and The Nazz days. An idea for a song, usually the lyrics, was presented and everybody would break off into pairs or by themselves to work on their part. They'd come back together and share what they'd done. That was when they had to be able to take criticism, because everyone was allowed to critique the work. Defending yours or approving theirs was part of the process. There was a lot of, "What if you do this" and "how about changing that." After hearing all opinions, a vote was taken, and the part receiving the most votes stayed in the song. But it was always subject to a revote once the piece was completed, or if the producer or engineer recommended, "Let's do this instead."

The *Easy Action* recording session was another whirlwind affair. *Pretties for You* was recorded in just three nights. With the *Easy Action* album, they attempted to break that record, but I believe it took four nights to finish. Frank liked to move things along. "Time is money" was one of his philosophies. The album debuted in March 1970. It wasn't all that well-received, at first. Again, this would come later. I'm not a music critic; I like what I like. What I heard on *Easy Action* seemed, to me, to be a building block, and they were headed in the right direction, getting closer to their musical destination.

The band was discovering the sound that would soon define them.

Cathode. T.V. Rock. *The Berkeley Barb.* University of California, Aug. 29 – Sept 4

In contrast to their female image, bizarre Barbarella costumes and lots of eye make-up, the music Alice Cooper plays is loud and powerful. The conflict between hard masculine sound and feminine clothes is accompanied by childlike clowning with various stage props. Alice describes the desired combination—"When the whole act is integrated—male, female, and child—it is always a growing thing."

It was during this time that Dick convinced us to try vegetarianism. I don't know why this happened, unless it was to keep grocery bills down. We reluctantly said sure. I think back then to say you were a vegetarian was a status symbol. It showed that you were deep, possibly even spiritual. Our vegetarian meals generally consisted of boiled vegetables over white rice with soy sauce. Not bad, but when you're used to and like eating meat, it wasn't that good either. Vegetables and rice alone took some getting used to. I may have lost fifteen pounds on this meat-free diet, but I cheated whenever possible. I'm sure everyone else did too.

Dick
Courtesy Toodie Mueller

Alice Cooper, Inc.

8814 SUNSET BLVD.
LOS ANGELES, CALIFORNIA 90069
PHONE (213) 657–8890

11-24-1968 10:00 p.m.

Well Ellen, at this point I don't know whether to say I'm sorry you can't make it, or I'm glad that you're coming. You didn't sound too definite.

If you do, it will be the same routine: long talks and walks. If I get the insurance from the van wreck this week things will be really different; I will take you out proper.

Nothing exciting is happening, everybody gets up and goes to practice and then comes home. The TV's broken. I can't even promise you entertainment if you come. I think Charlie is going back to Phoenix after the job at The Bank.

Everybody is busy now painting on Neal's drums. I'm even doing one. It's not very good, though, but the rest of the drums will really be nice with Vince and Dennis and Charlie working on them. They have talent. Me on the other hand not so much.

I'm glad to hear my last letter had some sort of effect on you.
Tell Toodie we found her coat and if you come over, which I hope, you can bring it back to her.
Dick just asked me if you can drop by Bonnie's and get his instamatic camera and bring it with you, if you come that is.
So, until I see you here, or I don't see you here.

Love,
Mike

Painting Neal's Drums

Because Neal's drums had been banged up in the accident—destroyed beyond recognition in fact—he bought a couple new ones using his insurance settlement. They didn't match what was left of his old set, and he decided we should paint them. Alice, Dennis, and Charlie were pretty good artists. Okay, they were real good artists, especially Dennis. Me, I could bend some wire, stick it in a mound of clay and call it Madonna with Child. Compared with the others, I really wasn't that good, but time was of the essence. I grabbed one of the standing toms and stripped it down to just the cylinder. I painted a space theme with stars and planets on it. I figured that if I painted a blue and black darkness for the background and then threw in a couple of planets and stars, I might pull it off.

Afterward, I looked at what I had painted. It didn't look bad at a distance, a very, very far distance, but it didn't look good either. I decided to throw a white Pegasus in the mix—that might make a difference. I actually added two, but what is the plural of Pegasus? Pegasuses? Later on, I learned Pegasus was the name of the flying horse, not the breed. Anyway, two flying horses added more interest, but not any more talent to my work. Neal could turn the drum toward the back.

Alice painted a mountain shape on the bass drum head, and what could be interpreted as a desert scene on the other standing tom. Dennis, showing his creativity, painted the other bass drum. His was a gray and black chorus line of people dancing in formation around the outside edge of the drum. The drum head, as I can best describe it, looked like a strip of movie film with Neal's face in the frame. Charlie and Neal did the fixed toms. One was painted with stripes and the other was a psychedelic mix of colors and shapes. To complete the makeover, Neal added a set of steer horns to the front of the set. His drum kit was definitely one of a kind.

When we were not working, and the band wasn't practicing, we watched TV. A lot of TV. At one time we had one sitting on top of another, just in case we wanted to watch two programs at the same time. We could have gone out, and sometimes we did, but being home and finding a comfortable mattress in the living room to lie on was so much easier. We were old before our time.

We watched *The Beverly Hill Billies, Star Trek,* one of our favorites—well, one of my favorites anyway—*The Invaders, Rat Patrol, and The Avengers.* We all were huge fans of Mrs. Peele in her body-hugging outfits. Other favored shows were *Lost in Space, Get Smart,* and *The Monkees.*

One evening we were watching an episode of *The Monkees* when they sang "Valeri." Referring to Mike Nesmith playing the flamenco-style guitar part, Glen complained, "He's not playing that right." He picked up an acoustic guitar and finished the song. Glen was good, really good. I never fully appreciated his talent until that night. Maybe I should have let him try to teach me again.

We also watched *I Spy* and *The Man from U.N.C.L.E.* We had a lively discussion, with Neal taking the lead, on the length of Illya Kuryakin's hair. We also enjoyed *The Smothers Brothers* and *Laugh In* for their comedy. Mike Bruce paid rapt attention when Goldie Hawn danced in a bikini with her body painted in psychedelic colors and patterns.

We watched *The Ed Sullivan Show* on Sunday nights when someone good was on. Alice had a genuine fondness for Topo Gigio, the Italian mouse puppet. Alice thought that he was the funniest mouse he'd ever seen. None of us could see the humor. We would glance at one another and think, *I don't get it,* while Alice rolled around on a mattress laughing.

Late at night, if the antenna was turned just right, bull fights from Mexico came in. Seeing animal blood and gore was disagreeable, but even more disturbing, after the bull fights were over, actual live surgical operations were broadcast. It was absolutely horrifying watching real people cut open. We saw amputations, and some patients had portions of their bowel and other organs removed. I found it particularly strange the Alice Cooper group were repulsed by the sight of blood. Most of the time I made some excuse to leave the room.

In the afternoon the TV was always tuned to the soaps, usually *Dark Shadows, Days of our Lives,* or a Dick Clark spinoff variety show called *Where the Action Is.* If we passed through the room, we stopped to watch without sitting down. Everyone denied tuning the TV to a soap opera, and we blamed Cindy for it, who insisted we were wrong. But, every one of us knew who Barnabas was, and the scandals in the city of Salem, and of the melodramatic misfortunes of the Horton family.

Mellow Yellow

During the late '60s there was a rumor going around perpetuated, perhaps, by the banana industry, that smoking the soft part of the peel produced a psychedelic effect that would make you high. And it wasn't illegal. This made it extremely hard to find a banana west of Yuma. This fad was called "mellow yellow," and it inspired a few bands to write songs about it. The interest in smoking banana skins for its purported high was widespread, which prompted the FBI and researchers at NYU to look into it.

The boys also thought this was an intriguing and cheap way to get high and wanted to see what it was all about. The process consisted of scooping the goop from the peel onto a cookie sheet to be baked. This was the longest time I ever saw the band together in a kitchen but, then again, I should talk. Once the peel, which I had a strong feeling was the same as the banana, was cooked, it was ready. Everyone, with the exception of myself and Ellen, was excited to find out if the effort was worth it. Meanwhile, I had a lot of freshly peeled bananas to eat. While I ate, they inhaled rolled banana joints. "Do you feel anything yet?" "Not sure, maybe." "Don't know." Then, someone said, "Yeah, I'm feeling it! Oh, wow!" And another would say, "Me too! This stuff is great."

Ah, yes, the old placebo effect on full display. Even though the high of smoking bananas was questionable and entirely subjective, the band planned to conduct a few more experiments to be sure. These guys were funny.

Alice Cooper, Inc.

8814 SUNSET BLVD.
LOS ANGELES, CALIFORNIA 90069
PHONE (213) 667-8890

Dec. 20, 1968 10:00 p.m.

Dear Ellen,

It's for sure now that I'm not going to be coming back to Phoenix for a while. It's not been our week. The band's amplifiers were stolen out of the van, right underneath Glen's window. Luckily, the drums weren't in the van.

Shep went to renew his car registration, and as luck would have it a car hit his from behind and completely wrecked his car. He's all right, but he has a big lump on his head. Dick just came in and said he got a speeding ticket. The guys just found out they have to do 3 sets instead of 2 at the Whisky. Glen spilled hot soup all over himself in the kitchen, scaring me causing me to spill a half a gallon of paint all over myself. So, as you can see, we're going to be lucky if we live through the week.

I really don't know what I can say except I wish I was coming back to Phoenix for Christmas. Mrs. Phillips will be returning Saturday or Sunday to Phoenix with some presents I gave her. Some are for you. I was wondering if you could pick them up and drop them off. If you can write or call me telling me that you will or you can't do it.

Well, I'm running out of room on the paper and I'm too lazy to get another piece.

Love,
Mike

After Christmas the band thought it would be fun, or maybe only Alice thought it would be fun, to gather up all the Christmas trees in the neighborhood and arrange them in the living room, where it would be like living in a forest. Alice, I don't think, grasped the concept of what fun really was. We collected close to twenty trees. They remained for months, littering the room with a blanket of dry needles. It looked like the floor of the forest in a stand of dead trees. Someone finally realized that Glen liked to relax in the living room smoking and having a drink at the same time. We let it sink in for a minute and came to the same conclusion at the same time. That day the trees were removed and the floor swept.

The backyard of the Quebec house resembled a tropical jungle overgrown with palm and shade trees, and flowering shrubs. It was that way because it had been neglected for quite some time, and was very unlikely to get any attention from us. In that jungle was an absolutely green with a thick layer of algae swimming pool. Mike Bruce would actually swim through the nasty-looking sludge. Climbing out, he looked like some sort of horrible slimy sci-fi swamp creature. We feared for his health and in the back of our minds wondered who we could get to replace him if the worst happened. I believe Cindy banned him from coming into the house until he'd hosed himself off with fresh water and Clorox bleach.

Mike had picked up a small stray dog he named Podgie. Unlike the mellow Dag, the good Topanga Canyon dog who showed up in the morning to sleep in the front of the couch and left at 2:00 p.m., Mike's canine brought no joy or love to our house. Podgie, the new dog, nuisance-barked nonstop in the house and nonstop outside the house. He also used the house as his personal toilet—at least I hoped it was him. One day we received a note from the neighbors. It was more like a three-page letter. They were not complaining about the loud music during practice, although that was certainly mentioned. Instead, their chief complaint was the dog's constant barking was driving them crazy and for us to do something about it and, by the way, what are you planning to do with all those dead Christmas trees on your property? It's a fire hazard.

Shortly after, the dog and trees disappeared. The city came by to pick up the trees, encouraged by our neighbors doing their civic duty. I don't think the dog was picked up by city. I just hoped he had gone to a good home.

Equipment Stolen

I was in a habit, when the band played two nights in a row but at different venues, of leaving the amplifiers and equipment in the van, although I always took the guitars and the drums out. The rear windows of the van were whited out, and a drape hung behind the seats, so all you could see through the front window was the yellow partition I'd built. It was impossible to see what was inside the cargo area. The Quebec house didn't have a garage. The driveway led to the front door, and Glen's bedroom on the enclosed balcony worked like a carport, covering most of the van. I felt pretty confident leaving it parked and locked in the drive, especially since Glen's room was directly overhead and he was a night owl. I felt certain that he would hear if somebody tried to break in. Plus, when they were in town, the bass player for Steppenwolf and his girlfriend lived in the ground floor apartment, which provided an extra layer of security, I thought.

I was wrong on all counts. During the night one or more individuals broke in through the rear doors of the van and removed all the new Ampeg amplifiers. Luckily, Neal's drums had been brought into the house to be painted. A truck or another van to haul the equipment would have been needed, and to do all that without anybody hearing anything was strange.

After 11:00 the next morning, I went down to throw something in the van. At first glance I didn't notice anything unusual, but I felt something wasn't quite right. Then it hit me: the van was completely empty. For a moment I thought the guys might have come down and gotten the amps. Only on a rare occasion had they ever done that, so I rejected the idea. Hurrying back to the house, I searched every room—no amps. I told everybody what had happened. They didn't seem that upset. They still had their old equipment, which they preferred anyway, they said.

We concluded that it was either dumb luck the van was full of equipment when the thieves struck, or someone knew my pattern of leaving equipment in the van. The police were summoned and arrived to make their report. Luckily, Dick still had the paperwork from Ampeg, including all the serial numbers. The officers said they would get in touch with us if anything happened. Dick notified Joey and Shep. They seemed more upset than the band.

The group acquired another amplifier sponsor. A new company, Acoustic Amps based in California, was just starting their business. They wanted Alice Cooper to represent the company to increase their visibility, which they hoped would generate sales. The band agreed. It was perfect timing as the band's previous equipment was gone. Probably forever. Never to be seen again I thought.

The new amps were all circuits and no tubes. The amp heads were as light as a feather—I liked that—and the six speaker cabinets were also manageable. They looked nice. They were actually pretty in a manly sort of way. The color scheme was sky blue and black. Unfortunately, the bass amplifier was another thing altogether. This enormous bad boy was very heavy and awkward to move. To make it somewhat manageable, this monster came with its own built-in furniture dolly. The bass amp had one large speaker housed in a special case mounted inside the amp's cabinet. That one speaker had a twenty-one-pound magnetic coil drive. The bass speaker was so powerful, instead of being mounted facing the front of the cabinet, it was installed facing the reinforced back of the cabinet. Purportedly, it was possible to blow the speaker cover off, knocking down small children. Okay, the last part was not true, but it could have been.

The amps also came with their own traveling cases. Packing the smaller amp cases was simple: grab hold of the handle on the speaker cabinet, put the speaker in the case, and put the top on. See, easy. Only you couldn't do that with the bass amp. It had to load wheels first. It needed either a block and tackle to lower it into its case or five or six beefy men to lift it six feet in the air before gently dropping it into the case.

I finally figured out a way to get the thing packed. I put the case on the ground wedging it against a wall, then moved the amp off the stage to the floor and, with the help of the built-in dolly, slid it on its back into the case. At that point I could shove the case upright. The final steps were to attach the top and load it onto another dolly to move it to the waiting van. No one would try to steal this thing! They'd be crushed under the weight of the amplifier.

Alice and I Get Out

Just to get out of the house, Alice and I would sometimes walk to Sunset Strip or Hollywood Boulevard. One day we wandered into a taping of *The Mike Douglas Show*. Someone must have recognized Alice, because he and I were invited backstage. We were separated when I left to search for something called the "Green Room." I heard food was in there. I found the room and went inside. First of all, it wasn't painted green. Second, there was an older man already in there keeping me from the food. I said hello to the person, who was waiting for his turn on the show. His name was Georgie Jessel. He was known as the Toastmaster General of the United States—I guess because he gave a lot of toasts at social or political events.

He asked what I did for a living. When I said I worked for Alice Cooper, a band that's starting to get known, he looked at me and put his hand on my shoulder, which made me just a tad nervous. He said he was going to give me some advice.

"You need publicity."

I agreed, but I was pretty sure we had already thought of that all on our own.

He repeated, "You need publicity."

Yes, I got the publicity part.

"Any publicity is good publicity unless it involves rape," he went on.

Politely, I said, "Thank you," not knowing if this was a joke or some serious advice he was handing out, and slowly backed out of the room leaving the food, and Mr. Jessel, behind.

I found Alice, who was wandering around backstage, and told him about my odd encounter with Mr. Jessel. We left without seeing the show.

Another time we went to a taping of *Playboy After Dark* hosted by Hugh Hefner. Joe Cocker was the guest entertainer and we wanted to see him even if he would just be lip synching.

The premise of the Playboy show was swingers swinging after dark. Since I wasn't much of a swinger, I focused on the lavishly set up mouth-watering all-you-could-eat buffet table. I felt it would be extremely discourteous to our host if I didn't partake of the bounty that was laid before me, and I was feeling a little protein starved because of Dick's "Let's all be vegetarians" phase.

The buffet included Swedish meatballs and shrimp wrapped in bacon, which meant it had to be really good, along with a salad and chips and dips. From my perspective, the only negative was how small the plates were. It was best that Dick, our vegetarian guru, not be any the wiser about my meat-eating relapse. I was feeling guilty and hoped there wouldn't be a urine test when we got home.

Holding a plate piled with food, I noticed Hef looking at me. He walked over. I was starting to feel nervous. I thought he was going to scold me, "Save some of the meatballs for somebody else!" Thankfully, that wasn't it.

He asked me to lounge around on the stage during filming and do nothing but look cool and interested when a performer or a guest was talking. I said I could do that. I intended to position myself on the staircase but thought better of it: too visible and too far from the buffet. I wondered if the caterer would be bringing out desserts.

I could do nothing. I was good at that. However, to do nothing *and* act cool *and* interested at the same time might be a bit of a stretch. We stuck around long enough to hear Joe Cocker. I saw Barbi Benton there—she was Hef's main squeeze at the time. Yeah, I can do cool. I guess the one minute with Hef rubbed off on me.

Tourists

Every once in a while, the group, or most of the group, would brave the daylight hours and go for a walk down Hollywood Blvd. Occasionally, there would be tourists out hippie-hunting. These individuals approached us with caution, as if they were on safari and didn't want to frighten the wild things. I could imagine a commentator's whispered voice: "*Look out there. You can see them in their natural habitat. Be careful now or they will bolt and run. Aren't they magnificent in the wild?*"

A lone tourist, usually a woman, would break from the pack. The others hung back looking down at the sidewalk, nervously fiddling with their cameras. The woman would timidly ask if she and her friends could take our pictures. They had no idea what, if any, band we were in. They were interested in photos of genuine hippies, or reasonable facsimiles. We obliged them and mugged for the camera. They would thank us and walk away commenting on how they couldn't wait to show the photos to Aunt Harriet in Dubuque, and did you see how disgusting those guys looked? Just awful.

Asian tourists were the best, very polite. They held their cameras up and pointed a finger at us. Once we nodded and said OK, they posed us, usually around a nearby expensive car like a Rolls Royce or Cadillac. We would tell them the cars were not ours, but they didn't care. One of us would be posed as if trying to enter (or break into) the car. A few of us would be positioned leaning casually against the hood, and another ready to enter through the passenger door. When everyone was set up, the cameras would click away. Satisfied, they would smile and wave at us. Some would politely bow. Then, they would walk off saying they couldn't wait to show their photos to Aunt Suki in Tokyo, and did you see how disgusting those guys looked? Just awful.

At Love-Ins, and especially in San Francisco in the Haight Ashbury area, tour buses lined up for blocks to film and photograph the strange subculture of society in their natural habitat, running wild and free. When the buses reached Golden Gate Park, the narrator might issue a warning: *Don't make eye contact with them. They might become agitated and attack.*

He would describe their tribal customs: the drum circles, the wild unnatural dancing, the colorful flowers and shrubbery in their hair, the paganistic painting of their bodies. *Look out there. They are in their nakedness. Oh, it's just a bunch of males. Nobody wants to see that. Wait. Some females are joining in. Cameras at the ready folks.*

The comments inside the buses would be universal. *"This is disgusting." "It's just awful." "Be sure to take a picture of those people behind the tree."*

Personality

Each member of the band brought his own unique set of skills and traits amplifying the dynamic of the group. And I envied each and every one of them.

Alice was the most genuinely optimistic, positive, and good-hearted person I'd ever met. He could speak on any subject for hours. And did. His glass was never half full. It was filled to the top and overflowing. The only other person who could match his outlook was Toodie Mueller. She was every bit his equal on the positivity scale.

The band had done shows, especially in Michigan, where bikers gathered in large numbers and did what bikers do best, which is not sitting quietly and politely clapping after each song. Nope. They liked to light fires and ride their bikes through the crowd and invade the stage. Generally, just raise hell. The band would look at one another and ask the question everyone, except Alice, was thinking: "Do we really want to go out there?" Alice would cheerfully reply, "Bikers love me." In unison we would think, "And you know this, how?" Most of the time he was correct, but there were some very close calls.

Alice was a natural born showman. He was Henny Youngman (you'll have to look him up), Groucho Marx, and Soupy Sales all rolled into one. He never let the facts get in the way of a good story. My girlfriend Ellen visited me and the band from time to time, and Alice had a new audience to entertain. His stories and antics had Ellen laughing so hard she was crying.

Dennis or Mr. Bass Man had the soul of an artist. This was because he was an artist. I took art classes with him in college and he was good. I mean really good. When I looked at the stuff I did, it looked like something a summer camper would make—if I'd ever been to camp.

Dennis was kind and thoughtful. He was a quiet thinker, reflective, introspective. He was contemplative on how art influenced everything, even Rock and Roll. Certain songs can trigger feelings in us, good, and bad, happy or sad. Remember how you enjoyed listening to the song "Timothy" by The Buoys and then found out it was about cannibalism.

Dennis felt that their, Alice Cooper's, music wrapped in the theater of the absurd was art and should be explored. Alice, naturally, was totally onboard with that idea. It showcased his talents.

Dennis enjoyed listening to old blues artists to discover how they conveyed their message. When Cindy Smith came into his life, I believe the blues took a back seat and his mind was opened to new contemplations. Cindy equals fun. Fun equals happiness, and happiness equals contentment.

Mike, he liked the ladies, and the ladies liked him. He, in a word, was smooth. If he'd had a Scottish accent, he would have been a Sean Connery 007 lady-killer. As it was, Mike could walk up to any girl and start talking, and she would hang onto his every word. In contrast, when I started a conversation with a girl, after I got through asking about her zodiac sign—I don't know why one's astrological sign was important to people in the sixties—and commenting that it was a nice day, I was done, completely out of ideas.

Looking to improve my prospects with females, I considered following Mike with a tape recorder to study his conversations. The only problem was, back then tape recorders were the size of a microwave, heavy, and required an extension cord. Carrying it in a wagon might appear to be a bit too much.

Mike cared very much about the music. He was the original multitasker constantly jotting down words for new songs. He worked on arrangements and kept them in his head or on pieces of paper stuffed in his guitar case to be trotted out at some future date. Truthfully, every member of the band did that, but not to the degree Mike did. He had ideas for albums far into the future, not just this week's work.

In the early days, everyone worked on their individual part of a new song, then they assembled it piece by piece. Maybe this was why

Pretties for You had more musical changes than a Las Vegas showgirl. Don't know, but could be. Whatever it was, it just worked.

I even attempted to write a song for the group, but I kept it to myself. Here it is for the first time, a song called "Crimson Skies."

"When red orbs light the sky at least we can say we tried.

If wishes were horses beggars would ride and we will take it all in stride."

What kind of post-apocalyptic nonsense was that? It scares me just to think I wrote it. No positivity there.

Neal was what I imagined a rock star god should look and act like: tall and lean, great posture—never slouching, and in total command in any situation. At least he gave that impression. In my mind I saw him as this Nordic god—actually, he was from Ohio—walking in slow motion, wind blowing his hair, dressed in satin and a flowing scarf, adorned with bracelets and rings, all the while exuding pure charisma and commanding attention. I may need to speak with a professional about these mental images. Yes, he gave the impression of complete confidence. Something I lacked in buckets-full. His presence on stage was palpable. It was not just his height, though the platform shoes might have helped. I'm 6ft 5in, and in a million years I couldn't pull it off. There was more to it than that.

He sat patiently behind his massive drum set, built more for an octopus than a man, twirling his drumsticks, waiting to start. When he played, the drums came through cleanly and smoothly. Sometimes, there was the appearance of reckless abandon in his movements. But that was all planned and part of the show. He was a great drummer and performer.

In the song "The Ballad of Dwight Fry," Monica Lauer, a friend of the band, voiced the child for the song on the album *Love It to Death*. Neal spoke the child's voice on stage. I know it's hard to believe, but that was his real natural speaking voice......just kidding.

Glen had perfected the role of rebel, disdaining authority and anyone he didn't know who tried telling him what to do. The smirk or scowl on his face in photographs exemplified his reaction to people asking him to "smile." His natural inclination was to do the opposite.

Aside from being a rebel, he was also something else. He was a great guy. Like Alice, Glen was a larger-than-life personality, but he kept it hidden most the time. He would give you the shirt off his back, but it would probably be the shirt he had borrowed from you and hadn't returned. I've seen a lot of photographs of Glen, and I would swear he's wearing clothes that look like the clothes I used to own.

Glen loved old movies, especially in black and white. Since many programs and all our TVs were black and white, there wasn't any choice. The older the movie, to him, the better, and he also loved 1960s sitcoms. *Leave it to Beaver* was a favorite. I think he identified with, if not idolized, the Eddie Haskell character. He perfected impressions of W.C. Fields and Wolf Man Jack, and tried a few I couldn't readily identify.

I found out the hard way who one of his favorite actors was. I was driving down Hollywood Blvd with Glen. He was in the passenger seat commenting on the lousy music on the radio. Where we were coming from or going to, I don't remember.

All of a sudden Glen shouted, "Stop the car! Stop the car!"

Panicked by this sudden outburst, I slammed on the brakes, partially sending us onto the sidewalk. I didn't know what was happening. I thought Glen was ill, and his shouting had scared me.

"It's him! It's him!" he yelled.

Despite being thankful that he wasn't sick, only crazy, I was still unnerved.

I'm shouting back, "Who's him?"

Glen yelled, "That's him, Slip!"

I shouted, "What's Slip?" This was starting to sound like an Abbott and Costello routine.

Glen gestured excitedly across the street at a not-too-tall guy. The man was dressed to the nines in a black suit and matching hat. There were two tall, beautiful, I assume showgirls, wearing matching white sequined dresses on each arm. He was wearing the biggest, happiest smile. He turned to see why a van was on the sidewalk and to hear what the crazy man inside was yelling.

Glen, still excited, but more under control now, said, "That's Leo Gorcey. He plays Slip in the old *Bowery Boys* movies."

I didn't really know. I wasn't a connoisseur of *The Bowery Boys* work. Gorcey was a master of mangled English and Glen began to imitate him. It was either that or he was having a stroke.

"I depreciate your comment. I resemble that remark," Glen quipped.

I asked, "Do you want me to turn around so you can meet him?"

"No, just seeing him was good enough."

He mimicked Leo, again. "Your eyes are bad. You need to see an optimist." Then he smiled and chuckled to himself.

I won't dwell on Glen's problems. They are well documented. I would rather remember his friendship, his kindness, and his humor. He had a great sense of humor, even when he was mad about something. The madder he got, the funnier he became. He reminded me of an R rated Gabby Hayes. He was also a real charmer. He could really pour it on when needed.

Oh yes, one other thing. He was one great guitar player. He tried to make every lead on a song better than the one he played on the last. And he made it look easy.

Glen had tried teaching me to play guitar. I think he gave me two or three lessons, but I didn't put in the work. Glen Buxton, one of the greatest guitar players ever, offered to teach me, and I just shrugged it off. I was really, really stupid.

Glen was a multi-talented guy. One of the more obscure talents he put on display was his ability to blow smoke, literally, out his...

tear ducts. He inhaled cigarette smoke, pinched his nose, and blew the smoke out through his tear ducts, or lacrimal ducts if you prefer. This feat brought about two possible reactions; the first was, "Wow man! That is so cool." The second was to find a receptacle to vomit into. The latter was the one most often chosen by me.

The Dating Game

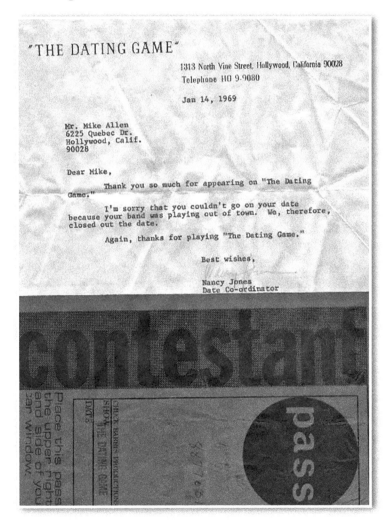

At the Quebec house one day, Cindy took a phone call. She said they were asking for me, Alice, and Neal. It was *The Dating Game* calling. They wanted us to come down and test for the show. Incredulous, my initial response was: "Are you sure they want me and not Mike Bruce?"

That would sure make more sense. Nope, they wanted me.

"Let's do it. It might be fun," Alice said enthusiastically. What else would he have said?

I did not share his enthusiasm, but said OKAY. Neal said yes. I believe his exact words were, "Hell yes!"

I have often wondered who suggested us for the game show. I assumed *The Dating Game* just didn't make random phone calls to random strangers and ask them to appear on the show. I accused Cindy of setting us up, but she protested that she had not. Why me? Why not Dennis, I wondered. It struck me then; there was something going on between Dennis and Cindy and they didn't want anybody to know. It made sense Cindy wouldn't want Dennis to appear on a show called *The Dating Game*. Ellen had asked me if there was any-thing going on between the two of them. Women must have a sixth sense about such things. I said something like, "What! No, they are just friends. We're all friends. Friends like each other. I don't know." I played it real cool. Hef would have been proud. Ellen said okay, but in some small way I think she doubted my sanity.

Selection for *The Dating Game* required we go for an interview and a mock show with staff members. What were we to be graded on? I had no idea. Personal hygiene, maybe? The three of us auditioned as people checked boxes on the form on their clipboards. They thanked us, told us to go home, and wait for a letter or a call. I was hoping that letter or call would never come, at least not for me. Neal was flashier, Alice was funnier. I was neither, really. My only qualification was I changed my turtleneck every once in a while and lived by the motto, "It's better to sit in silence and be thought a fool than to open one's mouth and remove all doubt."

The letter came revealing they had chosen me and only me. Everyone, except me, thought it was very funny. Joey and Shep thought there could be some nationwide publicity for the group, and I was to mention Alice Cooper as many times as possible. All I could think was, I'm going to make a fool of myself on national television. My instructions were to be at the studio at a certain time, dress neatly, and don't talk about race, religion, or politics on the show. Be spontaneous and have a good time. This cannot be happening to me.

Cindy took charge of what I would be wearing. She refurbished my old Spiders jacket, and commented that I had the same-sized shoulders as Mike Bruce. It would have been better, I thought, if she said Mike Bruce had the same size shoulders as me. She found a green paisley shirt in the closet. Contestants were directed to wear a solid color shirt, white or light blue. Maybe I'll be thrown out for violating the dress code. Cindy made a pair of blue velvet bell bottom sailor pants with a button bib front. I'm in hell. I must be in hell.

"You look great!" she exclaimed.

And I probably did. I would accept her fashion sense over mine any day, but I was just so far out of my comfort zone. The whole world would be watching. My family. My friends. And Ellen. What would Ellen think of me trying to convince a girl to choose me as her date? Would she think I wanted to win *The Dating Game*? But if I lost, what would I be? Either way she might have to rethink our relationship. I was screwed.

The big night came—two strangers and I were herded into a room. Each of us was thinking the same thing: *Why am I here?* The show assistant frowned at my shirt. He told us once more what the rules were, and he admonished us, "Don't mention anything about Christmas."

The date the show was to air was scheduled for some time after December 26. Great. We had already been told not to talk about race, religion, or politics. Now we can't talk about Christmas. What's left—the weather? Oh, that's right. I live in California. We don't have weather. We were led out of the room and told to stand behind the curtain and wait. When the signal came, we were to sit in the chair that had been assigned to us. I was in chair number two. Once again, we were told to have a good time. Once again, I was thinking about bolting out of the nearest door.

The snappy music cued up, the curtain opened, and the announcer announced. He talked about the first guy. I don't remember what he said. All I could think was, *Don't run. Don't run.* Then he talked about number two. That would be me.

"He works for a rock and roll band. He likes John Wayne and girls. He's a Scorpio," he said in his peppy announcer voice.

Please somebody shoot me. The total summary of my life: I work, I like John Wayne, and I'm a Scorpio. And according to James Garner, John Wayne wouldn't like me. So, if you take that out of the equation, I only work and I'm a Scorpio. Could things get any worse? Oh, yes, I have to somehow mention Alice Cooper with every answer.

Then came the third guy. He was a doctor, volunteers to help people, coaches a little league team, won the Nobel Prize, and is one of the world's greatest human beings! Well, that wasn't exactly what he said. I wasn't really listening. I was still going over the sum total of my life, or lack of one.

Then, they brought out the girl. Her name was Smokey. I assumed that was a nickname or alias. You mean we didn't have to use our real names on the show? Why wasn't I advised of this? That was all I remember about her, and she had blonde hair. I was thinking my dad named every dog he ever owned Smokey. Who names every dog the same name?

We all said hello to Smokey. I hoped I didn't sound like I was calling one of my dad's dogs. Then came the questions.

Number two, "What would you do if I told you I was seeing someone who paid attention to me, bought me presents, and was a total gentleman?" she asked.

"He sounds like a great guy!" I quipped.

The audience roared with laughter. Jim Lange, the host, was laughing, giving me a thumbs up.

The next question came. "Sing a song with my name in it, and it can't be "On Top of Old Smokey."

I responded, "Where there's smoke there's fire. My heart is filled with desire. Then, I start to perspire." Pure gold. I hoped somebody was writing this down. It had number one hit written all over it. The audience laughed again. They were easily entertained.

She asked the next question, "Where did you get your muscles?"

"They came with the suit," I said, coolly. I was staring to relax.

More laughter and two thumbs up this time from Jim Lange. *I'm killing it,* I thought. There were more questions, but I honestly can't remember any of them. Then came the part of the show when the girl chooses her date. Please don't let it be me. Please don't let it be me. Please don't let it be me.

It was me, number two. Damn my charming and witty personality. Who knew? The drapes separating us from the girl were drawn back, the lights came up, and she got her first look at us. I think she was reconsidering her decision, but it was too late. She was stuck with me. Next time choose more wisely. I hopped off my chair and gave her the requisite peck on the check. The date was described: "You're going to Tucson, Arizona, where you'll ride with the Grand Marshal in the Tucson Rodeo Parade!"

I'll get killed. I really did say that, but I don't think anybody heard me. My date and I blew our kisses to the camera and audience and were led to a room offstage where we could get acquainted.

"I don't think I'll be able to go with you to Tucson," I said. "We'll be on tour." It was lucky that I had a built-in excuse. Smokey seemed genuinely nice, but the thought of riding in an open car in a rodeo parade in Tucson, Arizona, home to cowboys and rednecks, had murder written all over it.

"That's okay. My boyfriend wanted me to do the show. I didn't want to," she replied.

"Me neither. Maybe you and your boyfriend can go on the trip to Tucson," I suggested.

I don't know if they went or not. I received a gift for partici-pating. It was a Samsonite briefcase and some assorted turtlenecks. It worked out all right after all. The briefcase went to my dad. The turtlenecks went with me and my newly improved fashion sense.

16

A Day at the Beach, Well Maybe a Couple Hours

One night after a show in San Diego, some local girls invited us to go with them the next day to the beach and go surfing. Just what San Diego needed to see, eight ghostly-white bodies soaking up the sun. We could quite possibly burst into flames. Correction: there would only be seven white bodies on the beach. Mike Bruce was always tanned.

Most of us spent the day trying to stay out of the sun, while Neal's efforts to surf kept us entertained. He's up, he's down, he's up, and he's down. We thought he would eventually be brought in by the waves and deposited on the shore, face-planted on the sand. He took a pretty good beating. We, including the girls, amused ourselves placing bets on whether Neal could stay on the surfboard for more than three seconds and ride it all the way to shore. I let one of the girls apply silver spray paint to my hair from some sort of hair product can. She said I looked distinguished. Great, just what every twenty-one-year-old needs to hear, "You look distinguished."

The day was going pretty well—so far. The girls had thoughtfully brought sandwiches, chips, and drinks. The day was warm, the ocean was blue, and we had food. It had all the makings of a great afternoon. Then the police showed up. There had been numerous complaints, they said, that we were being disruptive. The nearest persons were at least twenty yards away and on the other side of a large boulder, and we couldn't see how that could be true. I was sure the police had observed us for some time, and knew it wasn't—unless Neal falling off a surfboard gave surfing a bad name.

It must have been quite an effort to summon the police. Cell phones hadn't been invented. Someone had to leave the beach, get in a car, drive to a phone booth or business, call the police, and complain that the very sight of us was ruining their little day at the beach. It was probably some poor man who couldn't have cared less set upon by his nagging wife pleading with him, for the sake of the children, to do something about "those degenerates." The police, in so many words, said we were spoiling everybody's day and politely told us to get off the beach.

The girls squawked in protest. We explained we'd been down this road before. Quite a few times to be exact. "This isn't right," they complained. We agreed but still left.

Anyway, Neal may have had a concussion from all that surfing. Well, actually from all that falling off the board.

I'm Going to Disneyland. For Real.

Toodie and Ellen drove to the Quebec house from Phoenix on a Friday night and stayed until Sunday. Our habit of staying up all night and sleeping all day was pretty boring—we weren't the most exciting people to be around. On Saturday morning they surprised me by saying they were taking me to Disneyland. I said I couldn't go, even though I would've liked to. I really did want to go to Disneyland. I couldn't get enough of the place, and that's true to this day.

I explained the reason: it was Disney's policy to exclude males with long hair from entering the park. It would spoil the fun for the normal people. I had heard rumors that long-haired hippie type males had jumped off the Jungle Cruise boat and were living off the land in the Adventure Land jungle and on Tom Sawyer's Island. There were other rumors of long-hairs attacking Mickey Mouse and throwing him into the lagoon. I believe these stories all to be false. Despite these reasons, they insisted that I was going, and they would get me in. I just had one question for them: I didn't have to dress as a girl, did I? Disney probably had a policy about that, too.

Toodie drove Ellen and me to Anaheim in her blue Mustang, and we arrived at the Disneyland parking lot close to opening time. The girls wet my hair down with a spray bottle of water, swept it up over the top of my head, and covered it with my baseball cap. I looked like someone with a lot of hair stuffed under a hat. A little more water and combing, and presto! Now I looked like a guy with a *lot* of wet hair stuffed under a hat. People might think I was running a high fever with all the water dripping down my face.

"We will get the tickets. You just stand behind us," Toodie said.

"Stand behind you? I tower over you by a foot and a half."

"Put your collar up to hide the back of your head. Once we get inside, they can't throw you out," she said. I wasn't reassured.

"When did you ladies have time to become lawyers?" I asked.

"Trust us," Ellen said.

I suppose there were worse things in life than going to Mickey Mouse jail.

Toodie and Ellen went to the window and ordered three packs of tickets. I stood back, looking down, hunching over, water dripping from under my cap, knowing everyone was watching me. In a few seconds it would be all over.

Then, I heard the ticket seller say, "Have a magical day!"

I worried that she needed her vision checked. We walked through the gate and stopped just past the train station.

"Now, take off your hat," Toodie said. I did.

"And do something about your hair. It looks awful," she said, laughing.

Looking around nervously, I brushed my hair down to my shoulders and put my baseball cap back on bracing for the worst, but nothing happened. Miraculously, no one recoiled in fear. Mothers didn't shield their children's eyes. It truly *is* a magical place! Nobody cared. We spent the day going on as many rides as we could. We even used the lowest A and B tier tickets. We did not ride the Tea Cups, though. I don't ride the Tea Cups. I had an unfortunate mishap as a child, which likely traumatized a lot of other children. I vomited into the river at Storybook Land in front of everyone.

During the course of the day, I saw no evidence of anyone living on the Jungle Cruise islands or on Tom Sawyer's Island for that matter. Mickey Mouse wasn't being protected by the Mouse Militia, though his eyes followed me suspiciously as I walked by.

I actually did come across a fellow long-hair. He had a big smile on his face, flashed me a peace sign, gave a thumbs-up, and went happily on his way. He must have hidden his hair under his baseball cap, too. We stayed for the fireworks, rode the train around the park, and headed home. A perfect day. A magical day.

On the Road Again

On longer trips, Charlie rode with me in the van. I did most of the driving. The band and Dick flew and rented a car at their destination. Depending on the distance, Charlie and I would leave two to four days ahead of the band. When traveling cross country from Los Angeles, we drove the southern route, always stopping at the A&W in Dodge City, Kansas. It appeared our arrival made their day, because they would always play "Hair" by The Cowsills, sometimes more than once, after we pulled into a spot. It was a visit they looked forward to as much as we did, we thought.

When we crossed into Texas, I would let Charlie drive. On one trip, in the middle of nowhere, he drove straight through a two-way stop sign, narrowly missing a car that had the right of way. In a small town a short distance away, he grazed the bumper of a parked car. It was literally a scratch. We stopped. The police came. I told Charlie I should tell them I had been driving because I had insurance. I followed the police to the courthouse, where I immediately went before the judge. I told him I had insurance and wanted to call my agent.

"That will be one hundred dollars to pay for the damage," the judge said, ignoring my request.

"I'll call my insurance agent," I repeated.

The judge looked sternly at me and answered that I needed to give him the cash. Right now. I looked at him skeptically but paid the hundred dollars.

"You're free to go," he said.

I thanked him and we left. I wasn't given any type of paperwork—not even a receipt for the money I shelled out. I had no idea if it would ever reach the car's owner.

As we drove out of town, Charlie admitted, "I don't really drive much."

That was the last time I let Charlie get behind the wheel.

Traveling through Texas another time, I came to a bridge that was built over train tracks. The speed limit was forty-five miles per hour. The second you drove past the high arch of the bridge, there was another speed sign. This one read fifteen miles an hour. I slammed on the brakes, but it was too late. Two policemen were pulling drivers over for speeding. This was what was known as a speed trap.

An officer approached the van and told me I had been speeding. *Along with many others*, I thought sourly. The fine was forty dollars.

I stood beside the van with my hands in my pockets waiting for the ticket. He stood in front of me waiting for the money.

Looking annoyed, he said, "I need you to pay the fine."

"I give *you* the money?" I asked. I was a little confused. This wasn't the normal paying-a-fine procedure.

He said, "That's right," and stuck out his hand.

I gave him the forty dollars in cash.

He looked flatly at me and said, "You can go. You paid the fine."

I drove off, still confused. I had paid the fine, but I never received a ticket.

Seattle Pop Festival button given to band members to go between the stage, back stage, and the hospitality tent. I was given one, but the term artist was a bit of a stretch, in my case.

The Seattle Pop Festival lasted three days. Big-name groups such as The Doors, Led Zeppelin, The Byrds, Guess Who, The Who, Chicago Transit Authority, Bo Didley, Vanilla Fudge, and many more were on the playlist. Buying a three-day fifteen dollar ticket gave access to see just about every famous rock group there was, including Alice Cooper.

There are a few things that I remember from that Pop Festival. One was an airplane circling low overhead. When it was directly above the crowd, the plane's door suddenly opened, and a parachute wrapped around what looked like a person was jettisoned from the plane. It hit the ground hard. The first guy who reached the scene screamed to call a doctor. In the end, it was just a sick joke, which was what I thought it had been in the first place. Later, another plane flew over and dropped flowers on the crowd. I guess this was an attempt to compensate for permanently scaring the crowd by pretending to dump a body on them. All that great music, and all I recall is the plane and a parachute, the dummy and the flowers.

To be honest, I don't remember a lot of the music at concerts, unless something happened while Alice Cooper was playing. That would stick in my mind. One of the reasons I don't recall much is the band played with the same groups over and over again. And the sets were usually the same, unless there was new material or a new album coming out. When we saw each other again it was like old home week. There was a lot of, "Where'd you guys play last?" "What was that like?" "How are you liking America?" "When is the next album coming out?" "Next time you're in L.A. stop by."

It was like working and doing the exact same thing every day, except in a different city and your coworkers were rock stars. It was hard to keep it all straight.

Over one weekend, Alice Cooper played with Chicago Transit Authority at the Boston Tea Party concert venue in Boston, Massachusetts. It had originally been a church, then a movie theater, and now a club. Chicago Transit Authority, the band, was coming off the success of their first album, eponymously named Chicago Transit Authority. Unfortunately, they were being threatened with a lawsuit by the original Chicago Transit Authority and the City of Chicago over the album's title and the band's name, which were both called Chicago Transit Authority. Chicago Transit Authority, the band, in the face of the impending lawsuit from the Chicago Transit Author-ity and the City of Chicago, decided to change its name to just plain Chicago, which made all three "Chicagos" very happy. That week-end, though, we hung out with the original, but soon to be the for-mer, Chicago Transit Authority. Peter Cetera, the band's singer and bassist, had to sing through his wired-shut jaw. He had been attacked while attending a baseball game in Los Angeles. It definitely was not the era of peace and love any more.

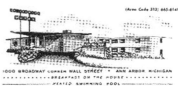

Dear Ellen

I think I'm coming back to Phoenix on the 14th a Sunday to take my draft physical on Monday. I don't even know if that's legal. Currently, I'm registered in three states for the draft: Arizona, California, and Michigan. Shep doesn't think that's right, so he's taking me to see someone who will hopefully straighten it all out. The states will be fighting over me pretty soon. If all goes well, I'll be flying to Buffalo on Tuesday. Can you ask Bonnie if I can stay at her place Monday? I'll call if I'm coming. I just have to find out which state wants me the most. I know by now not to take anything for granted. Haven't really got too much to say except that I'm a little nervous about the 15th, but you know how hyper I can be sometimes.

After Buffalo we're going to do a couple of weeks up in Canada again. I think we will be going on tour with Jimi Hendrix up there for 7 days.

I would talk about the weather, but that would be too much. I'm running out of things to say. We haven't got a house yet and we probably won't at this time. I did enjoy talking to you. I'll have to consider doing that more often. So, I'll try and see you in Phoenix if I can figure out which draft board I'm supposed to show up at.

Love,
Mike

17

The Draft

The Draft. The two words that struck fear into the hearts of most, if not all, eighteen-year-old boys. To the government, we were men but not quite men. In most states during the 1960s, at the age of eighteen you couldn't vote or drink or get married without your parent's permission, or buy cigarettes or gamble, either. In some states you couldn't get a driver's license. But you could be inducted into the Armed Forces.

There was fighting in Vietnam, Cambodia, and Laos. But it was called the Vietnam War. It was immortalized in a little anti-war ditty by Country Joe and the Fish, "I-Feel-Like-I'm-Fixin-to-Die-Rag."

The conflict went on from the late 1950s until 1975. Other countries had gotten in on the action early. In 1964 it was the United States's turn.

I was the son of a retired U.S. Marine officer, and I was prepared to go if called, but I wasn't hoping for the call. It's like that old adage: everyone wants to go to heaven, but they're not in a hurry to get there.

I got the call. Well, I actually received a letter. We were in Detroit when the government requested that I come to Phoenix for the pre-induction physical and aptitude test. At the time, I was registered with three different draft boards: Arizona, California, and Michigan because eligible males were required to register where they were living. Arizona got to me first. The other two draft boards would be disappointed.

The band wished me well, and said, "We'll see you in two days," but they were thinking about who they could recruit on short notice to replace me. The night before my appointment, I flew back to Phoenix on a red-eye and arrived at the pre-induction center on time, with a bag packed and ready for what could come next.

I was scared to death, but I meant to be truthful during the test and physical. The tests were of the IQ and psychology variety. There were general questions on history, math, and a few questions with a bunch of straight lines. You were supposed to determine what those lines made. There were several questions like, a grape is to blank as a gun is to a revolver. The answer is raisin. There were other questions about how you felt about your parents and authority figures.

The physical part, after first removing all your clothes and carrying them in a bag around your neck, entailed listening to your lungs, turn your head and cough as somebody shoves a finger up your scrotum (the hernia test), a hearing test, and an eye test. I was surprised at the hearing test. I thought it took a long time before I could hear any sounds. Rock and roll music really does destroy your hearing. It may destroy your brain, also. After the physical test part, we were told to dress and sit in another room to wait.

The processing part commenced with the shouting of names. When a name was called, the person was pointed to either door A or door B. It was totally nerve wracking. By now, my bowels were in an uproar, and I was spending a good part of the time visiting the bathroom. When I returned to the waiting area, the room, and my bowels, were empty. All the names on the list had been called, except for one, mine. I was worried that I had missed it while I was in the restroom. I walked to the desk and told the man that I didn't hear my name.

He said, "We know who you are. Go back and sit in a chair until we call you." This was not a friendly request. I guessed I would have to get used to it.

I waited nervously for what seemed like forever, but was probably only fifteen minutes.

At last, I heard one word, "You." I looked up to see a man pointing his finger at me. I thought they knew my name?

"Leave your bag here. Go through that door," he said, but where he pointed was neither door A nor door B. "Go down the stairs and outside. You will see a van with the back doors open. Sit in the middle seat."

I asked, "Do you know where I'm going?"

This was met with a stony stare and silence. I followed the instructions: down the stairs, second row in the van, sit in the middle seat. Out of nowhere I was joined by a driver, and two MPs (military police) slid in on either side of me.

I nervously asked, "Where am I going?" I was only told to relax.

Even though they told me to, I was not relaxing. Quite the opposite. The MPs did not carry side-arms; they carried batons. Another name would be billy clubs. I had a fleeting thought maybe I'd done so well on the test and physical they were taking me to O.C.S. (Officer Candidate School), but concluded that was doubtful.

The van drove up to a nondescript red-brick building where I was led inside to a room with three chairs and not much else. I was directed to sit in the middle chair. My two traveling companions sat on either side. After a few minutes a man in his late forties came through the door. He was dressed in black pants, a white shirt, and a dark tie. He wore heavy black-framed glasses and was balding. They took me to see a Jehovah's Witness?

The man greeted me and asked me to follow him into his office. The guards stayed behind. The office had white walls and was sparsely furnished: a metal desk and chair, a bookcase, and another chair. Venetian blinds covered the windows. There was no nameplate on his desk, no pictures on the wall. The bookcase had a few books. Medical books to be exact.

I realized the military was sending me for a psychological or psychiatric evaluation. Were they afraid of me because of the way I looked? Those guys were morons. I couldn't have been the first person with long hair to go through pre-induction. The man motioned for me to be seated and read a file, I guess the military had a file on me, then he looked steadily at me. He got the big question out of the way first.

"What type of drugs do you take to get high?"

I replied, "I don't do drugs."

With what sounded like total disbelief, he asked, "What do you mean you don't do drugs?" Then, he proceeded to name every drug in the hospital formulary, some of which I had never heard of, pausing after each one for my answer. I wondered if he was just making names up.

"I don't do drugs," I repeated, "and I don't drink or smoke either. Because I drive a lot, I will take a 'No Doz' to keep me awake."

"So, you take uppers," he persisted.

"No, I take a No Doz on occasion so I don't fall asleep when I drive. The commercial says they are equal to drinking a cup of coffee, which I also don't drink."

He asked another question. "Are you a homosexual?"

"No. I am not a homosexual."

"Why do you wear your hair long, if you're not a homosexual?"

"I wasn't aware that only homosexuals wear their hair long. To me it is just a choice of how I want to wear my hair. I choose to wear it long."

"Are you depressed?"

"Well, everybody gets depressed every once in a while," I answered.

"Have you ever thought of suicide?"

"No, but I have thought of what it might be like to be dead, by lying still with your eyes closed and clearing your mind."

"So, yes on suicide," he said, and wrote something on the form in front of him.

"So, no on suicide. Pretending to be dead is not the same as wanting to be dead," I said.

"Are your parents ashamed of you?" he asked.

"I don't believe my parents are ashamed of me. They may be disappointed in my current choices, but they know I'm a good kid and a hard worker. I always have been."

"Are you a conscientious objector?"

"No."

"Are you a pacifist?"

"Well, I would like all conflicts to be resolved peacefully, wouldn't everybody?"

I told him what my dad had said about the Vietnam War. My dad said it was an unwinnable war and if you can avoid it, don't get involved. We will kill a lot of people, but we won't win because there was no plan or strategy to win. We will just bomb them until they get tired. If that doesn't happen, we will say we won the war and come home and nothing will have changed, except that a lot of good soldiers will have died.

"So, your dad's a pacifist?" he asked.

"He's a realist. He's a retired Marine Corps Major who served in the South Pacific in World War II and in the Korean War. If he heard you call him a pacifist, he would want to kick the crap out of you."

I was getting irritated, but was trying my best to keep it under control.

"Do you own any guns?"

"Yes, I have several, pistols, rifles, and shotguns. Which are you most interested in?" I said.

He seemed confused. "What's a pacifist doing with guns?" he asked.

Frustrated, I answered, "I'm not a pacifist, but even if I were, a pacifist has got to eat. I use guns for hunting."

At this point I was starting to lose it. I wasn't yelling, but I could hear the tension in my voice. I was desperately trying to get myself under control and calm down. I was not a person prone to anger, and I was surprised that his questions could provoke me. I calmed myself by thinking that it couldn't last much longer. But the questions continued for some time. Questions about my relationship with my parents, rebelliousness, being a troubled youth, going to Catholic school, and church on Sundays. He revisited the drug questions a few more times, and last, but not least:

"Do you have a hatred toward women?"

This confirmed my opinion that this guy was a moron.

Finally, it was over. I was actually happy to see the two guards again. I even asked them if they missed me. No answer. We drove back to the pre-induction building. I went upstairs to the waiting room, got my bag, and sat in a chair. The room was empty. There was no one to tell me what to do or where to go. I realized I was hungry. I found it hard to believe, but I hadn't eaten anything since the night before. I'd been going through this draft hell for more than eight hours. Finally, a soldier came out, looked at me long and hard, then told me that I could go.

I asked, "I can go where?"

"Anywhere you want," was the curt reply.

I still wasn't sure. "Am I finished here? Can I leave the state? I don't have to return tomorrow?"

"If we need you, we will contact you."

I thanked him and hurried out the door. I felt relieved and free. I took a taxi to the airport and caught the first plane to Buffalo.

I don't know why the military didn't take me. Maybe the psychiatrist thought I was crazy. I know I thought he was crazy. Possibly the way I looked and the way I spoke didn't match his or the military's preconceived idea of how someone like me should act. In their judgment, maybe I had concocted some sort of elaborate plan to get into the military by pretending to be normal.

But I really didn't care. I couldn't wait to see everybody and tell them about my day. And tell them to take the ad out of the help wanted section. I was back.

Alice Cooper, Inc.

8814 SUNSET BLVD.
LOS ANGELES, CALIFORNIA 90069
PHONE (213) 657-8890

Dear Ellen,

Since my last letter we've been in Philadelphia and New York—exciting. I guess we'll be heading back to L.A. in about two months. Everybody is going crazy here. New York at this time is not among the Cooper's favorite spots. New York must be home of the Blues.

Ellen, if you're glad to see me, why do you wait 3000 miles to tell me? Wouldn't it be easier to say when I'm about a foot away from you? It wouldn't boost my ego that much. I might be unbearable to live with for a couple of days, but it would pass. Don't be afraid to let your feelings show a little. Look who is giving relationship advice.

Going to Toronto next weekend. Looking forward to that. Charlie dropped an amp on his foot and broke his big toe and he has to use crutches for six weeks. I bet he's probably using his plight to get himself out of doing work. Though his toe does look quite bruised and swollen and it's minus the toenail. So, he might not be faking. Oh, by the way I had an accident, but nothing happened to me. I fell off some wooden boxes, which were about six feet off the ground. Two of them fell on me, but nothing happened. I have all the luck. I guess my next letter will be sent to Camp Counselor Ellen. I hope your father has a happy Father's Day. We're not staying at the Albert. We have a new place one step below the Albert. It's called The Earle. Oh well, make the best out of what you have.

This is it. It's 3 a.m. in the morning and I'm tired. I'm going to go to sleep. No offense.

Love
Mike

Dear Ellen

Having a wonderful time in Buffalo. Wish you were here. That's good so far, how do you like it? Actually, I'm lying about having a good time in Buffalo. It's cold, it's damp, and it's dark. I think I saw the sun once, but I could have been dreaming. I think everybody has a secret desire to leave. They had a chance to go to New York City for a couple of days. They didn't, because they don't like it there either. They decided to stay in their present misery rather than to go to a fresh misery.

It's so different back here. Everything is so drab, and the weather doesn't help. Everybody here dresses so colorlessly, if that's a word. I wore a flowered shirt to the college. I was the only color in the school. The school has one form of dress. It's ripped jeans, beards, and army jackets, and that goes for the women too. Just kidding.

I think everybody finally realized that if it wasn't for the boys getting drunk and high every day, I think they would be climbing the walls by now. We'll be here until Thursday then we will go to Philadelphia. We were supposed to be getting a house in Buffalo. I think after the band's experience up there, I believe that idea to be shelved for further deliberation. I hope.

You can keep your eyes open and find a place for the band in Phoenix, a place where they can live and practice, maybe a ranch outside of town.

It was nice talking to you the other night, but then it always is. So, I hope to see you soon so I can stop writing letters. Seeing you is better than writing to you any day.

Love,
Mike

"A LANDMARK OF N.Y.C."

HOTEL CHELSEA
New York

AT SEVENTH AVENUE
WEST TWENTY THIRD STREET
NEW YORK, N. Y. 10011

CABLE ADDRESS • HOCHELSEA • NEW YORK
TELEPHONE CHELSEA 3-3700

Dear Ellen

Still nothing much to report, we've just finished playing the Electric Circus in Toronto, and we're leaving tomorrow for Cincinnati. Then it's back to Detroit. And sometime in April out to the west coast, maybe. I've started saving money again after my spree in Canada, got $100 saved so far.

The album is out soon. The only thing I've heard is that there are 8000 advanced copies sold in Detroit. That's a start.

I'm running out of things to say— there hasn't been a whole lot to do, but I'm sure things will pick up when we go to Cincinnati. That's a real friendly town. There's not even anything on television, doomed! I paint a dark picture, don't I?

Shep just walked in and said, "We're spending too much money on phone calls." Referring to me I believe, though by far I'm not the worst.

So, I guess this puts an end to another exciting "day in the life."

Love,
Mike

Detroit

Morphy, Ken. "An Experience in total sound."
The Spectrum, State University of New York at
Buffalo, Friday, June 27, 1969

*Alice, Glen, Dennis, Michael, Neal and Char-
lie (the light organist) looked like another Blue—
cheerish group.*

*The occult charms, the black knight, the warrior
king, the poet, the artist and the witch all added
up to a big put-on. Alice Cooper is honesty and that
is all.*

*The purpose of Alice Cooper was not to show how
mystical they were, how groovy they moved or how
nifty their clothes were.*

That fall we traveled and played a never-ending circuit: Detroit to
Ann Arbor, Cleveland, Cincinnati, New York City, Buffalo, and into
Canada, then back to Detroit. I referred to it as the rainy, overcast
tour. We wouldn't see the sun for months. We're from Arizona—
we had minimal experience with dreary, wet or snowy weather. In
Detroit we lived at a cheap motel near the Playboy club—never went
there—but it was close by. The motel did have one feature: a 24-hour
coffee shop. We ate there a lot. The accommodations consisted of
two shabby rooms with two queen beds and either a roll-away bed or
a broken down couch. The eight of us used the motel as our home
base, returning there after road trips. Dick was suggesting that we
might get a house in Buffalo as our new base. We hoped it was a
cruel joke.

We opened a show for the British band, The Who. They were doing their *Tommy* tour. During the Alice Cooper set, Keith Moon came out to listen. He set his drums up behind the curtain and, during the last song, played along with Neal. It made for a very unique duet. After Alice Cooper finished, I thought I would get a jump on loading up the van before The Who got started. I was nearly finished; just a few minutes before The Who were to play. As I opened the stage door to take the last pieces out to the van, a blast of freezing winter air rushed in. Pete Townshend was standing nearby and felt the full effect. He glared at me. That look spoke volumes: do that again and I will kill you. So, I didn't. Instead, I found a chair and sat backstage and listened, and I was glad I did.

The Who were great. Pete Townsend was wind-milling up a storm. I'm surprised he didn't dislocate his shoulder. Roger Daltrey sang and swung a four-pound microphone over his head like a lasso, which was appropriate because he was wearing a leather-looking western shirt with long fringe. He could have killed somebody, or himself, with it. John Entwistle, just stood in one spot, only his fingers moving. He played some great bass. He also plays a mean French horn, but didn't that night. Keith Moon played like a maniac in need of sedation, I thought. Sticks, drums, cymbals, blood, sweat all went flying.

The Who shot way up on my greatest-of-all-times band list, even if Pete Townsend had given me the death stare. After their show, Pete walked past me and said, "Thank you." I don't know if that was meant for me or the audience.

Did Everything Change Because of a Movie?

While living in Detroit, we ventured out a few times to go to the movies. The movie theater was built in the 1930s and was impressively decorated. The screen alcove was very elaborate with three layers of curtains, one of which used up most of the red velvet in the city, I thought. The wall of curtains was part of the experience. Just before the movie started, they opened one at a time to reveal the screen. The interior of the theater had a main floor and two balconies. The floor was carpeted and seats were covered in a dark plush material. On each side of the theater a medieval city, complete with knights in armor, had been built into the walls. The town had light effects that changed from night with twinkling stars to sunrise.

The movie we came to watch that night was a cartoon. One that had a profound effect on the band, I believe. Are you wondering how a cartoon can affect the direction of a band? If I told you the movie was Walt Disney's 1940 *Fantasia,* would that help?

We took our seats on the second-tier balcony along the rail with an unobstructed view of the screen. After settling in we began to notice a few things. One, the theater was quickly filling up: the movie looked to be sold out. Two, most of the attendees were in their late teens to early twenties. And three, a very distinct aroma of marijuana permeated the theater.

The movie opens: musicians in silhouette against a blue background. A cacophony of discordant sounds came from the pit as the orchestra tuned their instruments. I found out many years later that those were Walt Disney Company employees who acted in that scene. The conductor, Leopold Stokowski, climbs the stairs to the podium, raises his hands and the orchestra begins to play Bach's "Toccata and Fugue in D minor." The music, in a word, was phenomenal. The theater had great acoustics and a first-rate sound system.

A little something for you music history buffs. *Fantasia* was the first movie ever composed in stereo, although it wasn't called stereo. It was developed by Disney Studios and called "Fantasound."

The visuals kicked in. They were stunning. I won't try to describe what I was seeing. I couldn't begin to do it justice. With the opening visuals and music, the audience, including the people I'm sitting with, were transfixed. There was no such thing as "turn the music down" here. It was turn it up, way up! When the first segment finished, the audience cheered.

With the exception of the narrator, who sets the scene for what's coming up in the next segment, not one word of dialogue is spoken. I won't elaborate on every segment because I can't recall all of them. A few that made a lasting impression on me, and the audience, were the appearance of the Oriental mushrooms dancing to music from Tchaikovsky's "The Nutcracker Suite." The audience must have thought there was some drug culture symbolism and howled with laughter, and again, cheered. "The Sorcerer's Apprentice" by Dukas brought the house down. I always thought it was a little on the dark side, especially watching it as a child. During "Night on Bald Mountain" by Mussorgsky, the audience was absolutely quiet. When I watched this piece years before it scared me to death. People in the audience wept as "Ava Maria" by Schubert played.

As I said, I won't go into every segment, but the dancing tutu-attired hippos and their crocodile partners were a crowd favorite. When some movies end, certain members of the audience might clap to show their appreciation, but this was not the case with *Fantasia*.

The audience rose en masse to give the movie a lengthy standing ovation, cheering and clapping. Their admiration may have been brought about by marijuana, and what other drugs may or may not have been consumed. No matter, to this day I believe *Fantasia* had the greatest impact on an audience I have ever seen, drugs or not.

I glanced over at Charlie, who was sitting next to me, to gauge his reaction. He appeared to have thoroughly enjoyed himself—he had a huge smile. Charlie had a great smile. It reminded everyone of the Cheshire cat from *Alice in Wonderland*, also made into a Disney movie.

On the other side of me were Alice, Dennis, the rest of the band, and Dick. Alice and Dennis were leaning far over the rail intensely observing the scene below. The others were also watching. I could almost see the wheels in their heads turning. What did we just see happen here? A large audience of teens and twenty-year olds that we want to buy tickets to our concerts had just sat through a two-plus hour, dialogue free cartoon, and listened to classical music. And they liked it…a whole lot. Most young people, if put in a room to listen to classical music, would have jumped out a window. Some time ago in Phoenix there was a loitering problem in a shopping mall parking garage. Kids gathered there to party, ride their skateboards, spray paint graffiti, vandalize property, and break into cars. The mall solved the problem not with force or extra security, but by piping classical music into the garages. It drove the kids, like lemmings to the sea, out. At the same time, the soothing music somehow made adults feel safer.

What was reinforced with the band that night was the correlation between music, which is an art form, and the related visual art forms of light and design and theater. They wanted to create the same conditions on a stage. But it wouldn't be with classical music. It could be any music—even their music. What was needed a corresponding stimulus.

The problem that presented itself was how to replicate conditions in the theater on a concert stage. Drugs weren't going to be the problem: fifty percent of the people at concerts were stoned anyway. Well, better make it seventy-five percent. The music part was easy. It would be Alice Cooper's music. The visual stimulus element would take some time to develop. They had already started wearing flashy clothes and had incorporated light effects, doors, crutches, and swords into the act. Soon, feather pillows and chickens and fire extinguishers would be added. In a few years everything would come together with giant stage productions. Did a movie bring about their transformation? I don't know, but just maybe.

Holiday Inn OF ST. LOUIS-NORTH
4545 NORTH LINDBERGH BOULEVARD
P.O. BOX 768
BRIDGETON MISSOURI 63042

Dear Ellen,

We're now in St Louis. Nothing like starting out with something interesting. Newest fact. We will be in San Francisco the last week in April. That will be the closest to Phoenix I'll get. And then it's back to Detroit. I just found out the band will be playing at the Whisky again in L.A. in May. Something to think about. Everybody wants to go back to Phoenix, even me. I was the last holdout, you know. Just kidding. Anyway, there isn't any time to come back because we'll be working constantly until June, so maybe then.

I went down to my last remaining draft board in Detroit to turn in some paperwork. I was told that I would probably have to come back in May sometime for a pre-induction physical. This is starting to get real. I think I'll start praying. I'm going to need all the help I can. I have to go to the club now, sorry I had to stop writing. I know I can do better.

Love,
Mike

YOUR HOST FROM COAST TO COAST

Chicken Feathers

The city where Alice first attempted to rip open pillows and toss feathers, much to the consternation of the janitorial crew, was Detroit, Michigan. First there were feathers. Live chickens came out later. Their inaugural feathers and chickens stunt thrilled the crowd, the exception might have been a few asthmatics who didn't appreciate the plumage storm.

I had positioned myself by the exit door to observe the crowd as they left covered in feathers. Two people left with chickens, probably leghorns, under their arms. Everyone was laughing at themselves and at the other feather-plastered people. What could possibly have made it a more successful night? Feathers, check. Chickens, check. Entertained concert goers, check. We hoped the hotel didn't inventory their pillows anytime soon.

The problem we had found with chicken feathers, other than the loathing directed at us by the cleanup crew, was that they didn't distribute very far into the audience after being tossed around by Alice. Most of the feathers came to rest on the stage and the first couple of rows. Some might have managed to make it to the third or fourth row. We wondered what could be used to send the feathers further into the audience. Mike Bruce came up with the solution: high pressure CO_2 gas. In other words, CO_2 fire-extinguishers. Brilliant! Blasting the chicken feathers with an explosion of gas would propel them far into the audience. As a bonus, the feathers would stick to everything and everyone. The feather finale was a spectacular success, a showstopper. Except for, once again, the loathing of the cleanup crew.

Alice Cooper, Inc.

8814 SUNSET BLVD.
LOS ANGELES, CALIFORNIA 90069
PHONE (213) 657-8890

July 10, 1969

Dear Ellen,

Just finished the Saginaw Festival. It was outside of the city on a farm quite an event. According to the TV, two people were injured by shooting—a crazy farmer shooting at the crowd. Motorcycle gangs accosted girls and caused fights, the fence surrounding the festival was burnt along with the adjoining woods, the security team was run off by the gang, the state police and other agencies surrounded the hills, and in the middle was—me. Was I scared, hell yes, but I didn't bite my nails. The guys left right after they'd played because the bikers didn't control all the roads then. They were overturning equipment trucks and beating up a lot of people. So, Charlie and I were left to take care of ourselves and the equipment, but our good vibrations and reckless driving saved us. Others weren't so lucky. It was quite a day.

Will be in Phoenix for one glorious day—Saturday. Friday in San Diego, Saturday in Phoenix, Sunday in L.A.

A weird thing happened to me in Chicago. I walked into a club—it's like the Whisky—and this girl came up and started talking to me, and I guess she thought I was someone else, or something. She started grabbing at my turtleneck. Some other girl, a friend of hers I guess, started pulling her off me, because the guy she was with was getting mad at me. I guess he thought I was trying to take his girl. I was trying to climb over the railing so I could jump to the dance floor because I knew I was going to get killed by the other guy. The other girl got her off me. I lost a side of a good turtleneck. Needless to say, I then departed. Life in the big city. Who needs it? I really can't wait to get back to the west coast. I never really appreciated it until now. People out here are crazy.

Looking forward to your letter, and the usual stuff I put at the end of a letter to sound funny, but not today. Strictly business, very formal.

Love,
Mike

18

Saginaw Michigan

We left our home base of Detroit. This made the concert's janitors very happy, and the hotel could restock their dwindling supply of feather pillows. We had jobs lined up in Canada, Ann Arbor, Saginaw, Saugatuck, Grand Rapids, and Dubuque, Iowa.

The Dubuque, Iowa show was at a high school with Alice Cooper and Vanilla Fudge headlining. The most interesting thing there was the name of the place we stayed; The Hotel Cornfield. Our rooms had a great view of a billboard with a very large three-dimensional cow's head. I believe it was a Holstein cow. At night it was lighted, which brought tens of thousands of swarming moths to the lights. The moths descended onto the cow head, covering every inch of it. This was such a sight to see that people would come from all over just to admire it. A room and a show. I was so impressed I took one of the hotel's towels as a souvenir.

At our next show in Saginaw, Michigan, feathers were not used. This concert was in the middle of nowhere on someone's farm. The main attraction, besides Alice Cooper, was Arthur Brown, who had a hit called "Fire." The show was billed as *The Crazy World of Arthur Brown Tour.* It would be just a one-day concert for us.

In order to get there, we traveled off the highway and down some back roads. Along the way we stopped at a roadside farm stand to buy a bag of cherries. Charlie noticed, beside the stand and across the road, the ditches were filled with marijuana plants. Instead of corn, maybe this was their new cash crop. Charlie was eager to help with the harvesting, but the concert awaited us.

We continued a long way down a dirt road with fields on either side. I don't remember why, but I was driving a U-Haul truck. Up ahead I saw some sort of obstruction. As I approached, I saw two motorcycles partially blocking the road and members of a motorcycle gang holding up a long line of traffic. When it was my turn, I stopped next to them.

A biker asked me, "What's in the van?" These guys sounded just like the police.

"Musical equipment for the Alice Cooper group," I said.

The reply was, "I've heard of them."

He handed me whiskey, or some sort of alcohol, in a bottle. I didn't drink, so I passed it over to Charlie. He took a swig and passed it back to me. I was ready to hand it to the motorcycle guy when he asked, "What about you?"

"Oh, sorry. I forgot." I took a swig.

There's a reason I didn't drink. It's the taste. You could use whatever this stuff was to start a lawn mower or strip paint off the side of a building. It burned going down, it burned coming back up, and it burned going back down again.

"Smooth," I lied, handing back the bottle of vile, brown fluid. *Don't ever give it to me again,* I thought, but said, "Thank you. I needed that."

"More?" he asked.

I declined, saying, "I think you'll need it more than me. Looks like rain."

We drove on, confused why the biker guys were stopping cars. Where was security? Or were they the security? Soon, we came up to a large open field bordered by low forested hills. A very picturesque place, with the exception of twenty or thirty bikers tearing up the ground with their bikes. I had a feeling this was not going to be a good day.

The bikers had built several fires in the field and were warming themselves by riding through them. I guess they actually weren't providing security. The security we saw looked to be about sixteen years old, and most of them had already had their security hats taken away by the bikers. I estimated around three hundred people had come for the show. The concertgoers seemed nervous because of the gang's antics. If they were not, they should have been.

The concert got started, and we'd be going on soon.

Concerned, I asked the group, "What do you think?" nodding over my shoulder at the bikers raising hell by riding their motorcycles roughshod through the crowd and the bonfires.

The security team by this time had retreated and were hiding behind the stage or in other places unknown.

Alice said it would be fine. I believe his exact words were, "Bikers love me!"

The rest of the band and I thought, *since when*? That Alice, always the optimist. You gotta love him.

"I'll back the truck behind the stage. I can leave it parked there after I unload the equipment in case I have to throw it, literally, back in the truck if things go south," I said. Like say if we need to leave for some reason such as imminent death.

Alice Cooper began playing. So far, so good, up until the last song when someone threw a stuffed animal onto the stage in front of Alice. Alice and Glen immediately took turns kicking and stomping it. This threw the bikers into a frenzy. Up until then they had been satisfied riding through the crowd and the bonfires on their bikes. A couple of them got off their bikes and jumped onto the stage.

Alice looked wide-eyed at me. I looked back at him, my eyes clearly conveyed my message: you're on your own, brother. Besides, bikers love you, remember? I like to think, if the bikers had gone after Alice or the band, I would have intervened. Well, maybe, possibly, probably. But, luckily for everybody, and this would include me, the two bikers were only interested in flattening the battered stuffed animal. Alice picked it up and drop-kicked it off the stage and the bikers jumped after it like dogs chasing a stick. On the ground, a few more joined in. They feverishly stomped on the stuffed animal, or whatever it used to be. You never would be able to identify the body.

The group finished—no encore, just a rapid stage exit. Charlie and I hastily threw the equipment in the truck. I locked it up and drove to a more unobstructed area so we could make a quick getaway if needed. Everyone was happy, we were alive, so far, and now we could enjoy The Crazy World of Arthur Brown. I told Charlie that if things turned bad to get to the truck and we would get out of there, one way or another.

I don't know if it was the real Crazy World of Arthur Brown that showed up, but the Arthur Brown on stage appeared to be slightly inebriated or it could have been part of the act. The back-up group looked like teenagers with brand new Fender amplifiers and matching black jackets—just like The Spiders had worn in Phoenix a few years earlier. They didn't add much to the crazy-world image. The singer stumbled around the stage as he performed. I was only familiar with one of Arthur Brown's songs, "Fire," so I don't know if that was how he was supposed to sound. He had a good voice, though, and could put some volume in it, not really needing the microphone.

His stage persona was that of Joe Cocker wearing face paint suffering from vertigo. When he shouted, *"I Am the God of Hellfire"* you could easily believe him. After this declaration, he put a crown on his head, lit it on fire, and proceeded to sing the song. During the part *"I want you to burn!"* he whipped the crown from his head and threw it over the group's equipment at the back of the stage. Black smoke began rising, then flames appeared. This piqued the biker's interest more, perhaps, than the stuffed bunny had.

Charlie's eyes met mine. I signaled him and said, "We're out of here!"

Everyone in the crowd thought the same thing. The last I saw of Arthur Brown's band was their amps being tossed off the burning stage. I never knew if the fire was put out. I hadn't seen anything else burst into flames, but that was a moot point now. My focus was on getting out of there.

Because the road ahead was still blocked by the two bikers, with more coming to join them, the dirt road was jammed-up by exiting concert goers. I inched the U-Haul along for a time. There were still twelve or more cars in front of me when I finally had enough—must have been the liquor talking.

The road was built up a little higher than the fields on either side. I pulled the wheel sharply to the right and drove down the grassy slope of the shoulder crushing the gas pedal under my foot. The U-Haul surged forward, riding the shoulder at a steep angle. I'm sure the company wouldn't approve. I had done an incline maneuver once before, only it was up instead of down. What could possibly go wrong? Oh yeah right, something about an accident on a freeway. I glanced over to see that Charlie had rolled his window up. He probably would have fallen right through it otherwise. I wondered if he would want to ride with me any more after this.

The back tires slipped on the wet grass as I headed straight for the bikers and open road. I just needed a few more seconds. By now, the speeding van had caught the bikers' attention, but I doubted they could do anything except run for their lives. The U-Haul began to slide sideways, its wheels spinning, just before I hit the dirt road and straightened out. There was no stopping until I reached Detroit.

I never knew why the bikers were holding up traffic. Maybe they were taking a survey on how everyone enjoyed the concert? Was there anything they could do to make it a better experience? That would have been nice, but I didn't care.

As I drove back to Detroit and our motel that was close to the Play-boy club, with the 24-hour coffee shop, I thought about the day and how badly it might have ended. And I hoped the room had been resupplied with fresh pillows.

When I went to my room, I discovered someone had broken in and stolen all my clothes. Nobody else's, just mine. Either I had great taste or the thieves were my size. Well, they didn't take all my clothes. They left one white shirt with French cuffs, but they took the cufflinks. I don't know why they didn't take the shirt. It looked great with jeans and a leather jacket. I mean, if you are going to steal someone's clothes, you might as well steal everything! Their loss.

We were in Grand Rapids, Michigan, famous for furniture making and Gerald Ford. He became president when Nixon resigned. Some of Charles Manson's followers attempted to assassinate him. But enough history.

Charlie and I had arrived a day early, ahead of rest of the group and checked into the Pantlind Hotel, which was built in the 1920s, or perhaps earlier. It looked old and tired now, but you could tell it had been THE place to be in its time. We decided to have dinner at the hotel's restaurant. We walked downstairs, found a booth and sat down. There was just one other occupied table. We waited, and waited for service. No one came. The lone waitress took care of the other patrons but ignored us. I stood to get her attention. No luck. I told Charlie I would find someone and would be back. I approached the clerk behind the front desk and explained the situation, his back stiffening as he listened.

"Come with me," he said angrily.

I followed him back to our table where Charlie waited unat-tended. He told me to sit down and someone would come take our orders. He headed straight into the kitchen and shouted at the staff. We could hear him clearly from the dining room. He did all the talking and they did all the listening.

He ended his tirade saying, "You never treat people like that. Do you think you're better than them?" A minute later he walked back to our table.

"Someone will be with you momentarily. We don't allow prejudice in this hotel," he said. His voice was still hard.

Did I fail to mention that this man was black?

"Maybe it was just a misunderstanding on their part," I said helpfully.

"There was no misunderstanding. This is prejudice. I know more about that than anybody else in this room. They didn't like you because of the way you look, and nothing else. Stupid kids."

We thanked him for his help. I never did get his name. As he walked away, he was shaking his head muttering to himself. He turned around once more to give the wait staff THE LOOK.

A young waitress hurried over to take our orders. She looked to be seventeen or eighteen, not too much younger than me. When she returned with our food, I made a point of talking to her. I asked if she knew where such and such place was. I already knew where it was—we had passed it coming into town. She gave us directions.

"The group we work for will be playing there tomorrow," I said.

"Really? Who's that?"

"Alice Cooper."

"I've heard of them." She left to finish up with the other guests.

She came back later to see how we were doing and brought along a co-worker who was about the same age. They asked us about music. Asked if we'd ever played with this group or that group. We answered yes to each of their inquiries and elaborated on some of the groups. I asked them to pull up chairs, and we talked for about half an hour.

The girl said, "It was the cook who didn't want us to serve you. He thought you were weird and probably perverts."

"What? Do you think we're weird?" I asked. I skipped the pervert part, but for the record, no, we are not.

"No," she answered. We all agreed the cook was a jerk and they should not listen to him anymore.

I told them a story about Alice when he was first starting out, about how he would be mistaken for Tiny Tim and people, usually children, would ask for his autograph. He signed it "Tiny Tim," because he didn't want them to be disappointed. For those who don't know about Tiny Tim, he was a guy with long black stringy hair. He wore a checkered suit, played the ukulele, and sang "Tiptoe Through the Tulips" in falsetto. He spoke in a high effeminate voice, too. He married Miss Vicki, who was seventeen and he was thirty seven, on the Johnny Carson show. He didn't remind me too much of Alice, although Alice could do a pretty good impersonation of him.

After dinner we stopped at the front desk to again thank the man who'd helped us.

"We talked to the staff and they ratted out the cook as the troublemaker," I said.

"Yeah." He paused. "That guy's an idiot."

We agreed.

Saugatuck, Michigan. The Town Will Remember This.

The concert was to be held near the shores of Lake Michigan outside the small town of Saugatuck, where 700 to 800 souls resided. The town folk had no idea what was in store for them.

It was a very humid, warm weekend. Rain fell off and on. Inclement weather of any kind was not a musician's or outdoor concertgoer's friend. Alice Cooper was scheduled to play one or possibly both days, but their name never appeared on the poster or handbills. The groups booked to perform were wide and varied. Representing the blues were: John Lee Hooker, Muddy Waters, and Big Mama Thornton, though she never appeared. From Michigan: Bob Seger, the

Amboy Dukes, MC5, Brownsville Station, The Stooges, and many others. Representing bands from other countries were Procol Harem and Arthur Brown. The Arizona contingent were: The Red White and Blues Band, originally from Phoenix, now from San Francisco, who would later merge with The Beans to form The Tubes and, of course, Alice Cooper, even though their name was left off the roster. As I drove the truck onto the grounds, I noticed two things. One was a giant crane that seemed out of place, the other was bikers, lots and lots of bikers. Bikers and Arthur Brown. Deja vu all over again.

From time to time during the concert, the bikers climbed onto the stage and screamed obscenities at the crowd, warning them to keep clear of their bikes and that touching them would not be tolerated. When they weren't blasting obscenities at people, they were mostly content to hang with their group and party heavily. Occasionally, they ventured away from their gathering and walked through the crowd to intimidate people. They were experts at intimidation. Unsurprisingly, the undersupply of facilities at the concert didn't seem to concern them.

Procol Harem finished out the first night and were able to mellow the crowd with their music.

Alice Cooper earned some appreciation from Saugatuck. The crowd really loved the group. They really, really liked them. They received a standing ovation in fact. Truthfully, there was no place to sit, but the crowd's enthusiasm for a not so good weather-wise, biker-wise, too-many-people-in-a-small-area-wise, and nobody-going-home-soon-wise performance was amazing. The crowd's reaction, simply put, was tremendous.

This remarkable reception was a major turning point in the band's evolution. Most notably, because of the success in Michigan, the band made the decision to make Detroit their base.

Closing out the weekend festivities was Arthur Brown and his crazy world. He made his entrance by descending from the heavens suspended from a cable attached to the crane I had noticed earlier. His head looked like it was on fire, thanks to his famous flaming crown. He was screaming "Fire!" at the top of his lungs, which I'm sure caused the Saugatuck Fire Department some unease. After a few adjustments by the crane operator, Arthur landed on the stage. A group of people, some with fire extinguishers, unharnessed him. As long as he wore the flaming crown, people with extinguishers would be at the ready. There would not be a repeat of the Saginaw disaster on their watch.

After Arthur Brown finished, the crowd remained where they stood, because there was no where they could go. By the end of the weekend, it was estimated that more than 30,000 people had attended the event.

Vehicles were unable to exit the parking lots because the roads that led to them had turned into another parking lot. The massive number of people and vehicles overwhelmed the police and effectively shut down the streets all the way to the freeway. Then, the police closed down the town, preventing any vehicles from going in or getting out. Other than that, it was a pretty nice weekend.

One day Mike Bruce, in which city I don't recall, was reading a musician's magazine and became quite excited. He told me a speaker company was replacing their speakers for free if something was wrong with them.

"We should take advantage of this. The factory is just a short way from here," he said. "We can go down there and have our speakers checked out."

I felt he was using the wrong pronoun, rightly proven the next day when the "we" had morphed into me. I really didn't mind. It got me out of the motel room shared by four of us. So, I left a city I don't remember, traveled to a city I also don't recall, and headed for a speaker factory the name of which has long since vanished from my mind. And the "not too far away" was close to 100 miles.

Arriving at an old red-brick building, I parked the van in the nearly deserted lot and headed inside and to a young lady sitting behind a desk.

As I approached, she smiled and said pleasantly, "How can I help you, sweetie?"

I hadn't been called sweetie in a long time. My grandmother called me that, and she did not look like my grandmother. I explained about the ad for free replacement speakers. She called me sweetie again, but this time there was a hint of sadness in her voice.

"The ad says take the speaker with the bill of sale to where you bought it," she explained. "The store will check it out and, if anything is wrong, they will replace the speaker. We reimburse the store or, if they don't have the speaker, we will send them one."

As she was telling me what the ad really said, I recalled what Mike Bruce *told* me it said, and thought *BRUCE!!!!!* She may have noticed the sudden change in my disposition and offered to go back into the factory and see what she could do. Ten minutes later she returned.

"It's not usually done this way, but they will do it for you," she said, which really meant they would do it for her, "but it could take a while."

I thanked her, went back to the van, drove around back to the receiving entrance, and unloaded the amps. A guy told me that he wouldn't be able to check them out for another couple of hours.

"No problem. Take your time and thank you for doing this," I said.

I went back to the lobby-girl and said I was going to walk around the town.

She asked, "Do you want to go have lunch?"

"Sure, but won't you get into trouble for leaving?"

"I have the easiest job in the world," she said. "We don't do any sales here. We just make speakers. Just ship and receive goods and that's all done in the back. I sit behind the desk and talk with anybody who comes through the front door, by accident usually."

We walked down the street to a restaurant she chose, were seated in a booth, ordered, and started talking. I asked if she got bored doing nothing all day. Sometimes I don't believe what comes out of my mouth.

"No, because I have plenty of time to study for the college courses I'm taking."

She said her dream was to be a veterinarian. I told her that I had thought about doing the same thing, until I found out it was easier to get into medical school than it was to be a vet. She said she had heard the same, but she was going to do it. I believed she would, if drive and determination meant anything.

She asked the name of the band I worked for. I told her it was Alice Cooper. She said she had read about them and asked if he was the guy who dressed like a girl. I explained how the band got its name and what the show was about. She looked relieved. I paid for lunch as thanks for helping me and for not throwing me out when I arrived. When we got back to the lobby, a note on her desk said that they were finished with the amplifiers and one speaker had been replaced. It had the possibility of going bad sometime in the future, maybe, they said. Now, that was what I call a warranty. It was more like a gift. I got the original speaker back, and the new one they installed, plus they threw in another new speaker, just in case. Every band I meet I'm going to recommend they show up at the factory for free speakers. On second thought, I'll keep this to myself.

I walked back into the factory and thanked everyone I saw for helping me. I thanked lobby-girl again, and wished her the best of luck on her career choice. I finally thought to ask her name. It was Susan. I drove back to the city I can't remember the name of. I wasn't even upset with Mike Bruce for sending me on this fool's errand. It turned out to be a very good day indeed. Except now I have to find a place to carry two extra speakers.

Alice Cooper, Inc.

8814 SUNSET BLVD.
LOS ANGELES, CALIFORNIA 90069
PHONE (213) 657-8890

Dear Ellen,

I am now in Phoenix, and this is my last night. I was here for two days, not quite the week I hoped for.

I talked to Mary. She seemed alright and is happy. I guess she and Cindy are going back to Ohio, though I can't understand why. When I came back it was Cindy's birthday, and I had bought two necklaces from an Indian trading post up north. I bought them for you and Mary, but it was Cindy's birthday, and I didn't have anything for her, so I gave her yours. I hope you don't mind. I don't know why I just told you this.

I don't know if you're getting my mail or not, because I asked you to write me at Bonnie's and no word. Which leads me to believe one of three things:

1. You're not getting my mail
2. You're too busy to write   } *confusion*
3. You don't want to write

I did want to talk to you, because I've been doing some thinking. This was brought about by my last visit here, and when I saw Mary she looked at me as though she was looking at my grave. Remember I told you about eyes, and how I can tell certain things? Well, it's true. Even though she was happy and smiling, there was something wrong. Also, I picked up a strange feeling.

Also, the night I took you to see Funny Girl there was something weird in your eyes. This is beginning to sound like a 1930 Dracula movie with all this looking into people's eyes. Anyway, when I come back to Phoenix, I feel we ought to talk. Then you can tell me if I'm right or wrong, and don't hold anything back. I don't want you to. If we can't be honest with each other…I'm going to feel really stupid if this is all my imagination. You're probably thinking I've flipped out. Well, I haven't. At least I don't think so.

I don't know why I'm sending these pictures. I don't even look good in them. I guess I want to show you that my hair is getting good in the back. Anyway, you can trade them with your friends. They make lovely gifts suitable for framing.

Will be in California for another month, so you can write me at Joey and Shep's new address. It's on Beachwood. I don't know the full address. I think I might have given it to you in my last letter.

Steve told me you were in town Tuesday. I was still driving to Phoenix. I'll call you when you get back to Phoenix. I'm still leery of calling you at Prescott.

Oh, don't worry about the middle of my letter. Anyway, I'll look forward to seeing you again.

Love,

Mike

Ellen,

First thing, I want to apologize for my last letter. I was just upset about not receiving a letter from you. I also had not had any sleep, and I drove all the way back from St. Paul.

But I do want to talk to you. It's about us. It's nothing tragic. I think it will help us. I know this is going to hang over your head till I see you, but I can't write it down. It would take too long, and I couldn't explain it right. You know how I am when it comes to explaining things.

Tonight, Neal hit me in the eye with a drum stick during the last song where he throws his sticks at his drums. My eye is all swollen above my eyebrow, and my eye keeps watering. It's hard for me to focus it. I guess I'll go to the doctor Monday. That information is for Nurse Ellen.

We'll be in L.A. for a week and a half starting Sunday. You can write me at

2449 Beachwood
Hollywood, Calif
c/o Shep Gordon

By the way, I got your letter Saturday. Thank you. I do like to hear what you're doing. They do a lot to make me happy.

We won't be in Phoenix for a least a month, but I will call you when you come home from camp.

Love,
Mike

Dear Ellen,

We're now in San Francisco for four days rest then we go to Portland and Vancouver.

The plane we came over on had a fire in the kitchen and I was sitting right next to it when it happened. I was waiting for the food, as usual, but I was very heroic.

I may be coming back on the 28th, but I'm not sure. Which means if I am there, I'm there. If I'm not…

Not really doing much now, just have a sack full of dirty laundry, but that's nothing new.

What are you going to do when you finish up at Camp Friendly Pines? Go back to nursing school? I think you mentioned that you weren't going to make enough money to pay for next semester. Well, I'm rolling in the chips now and if you need anything you have only to ask.

So, is Bonnie back yet? If I come back, I hope she'll let me stay there. The last time I was in Phoenix I slept on the floor there. It's not too comfortable.

You're now asking if anything exciting has happened to me, aren't you. Well, no.

So, I guess that's it—another big letter. I hope to see you in Phoenix sometime. If not this year, maybe next. How do you like going with a guy you never see? Don't answer that.

Love,
Mike

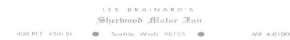

PHONE 965-1820
(Area Code 313)

1316 E. JEFFERSON AT RIVARD
(5 Blocks E. of the Civic Center)
Detroit, Michigan 48207

The Shorecrest Motel

Dear Ellen,

Not much to report, just going along. We're in Detroit now, next week Canada. I won't be coming back to Phoenix the 22nd. We'll be in Chicago.

We may not be with Bizarre Records much longer, so we are going to have to find another record label.

I've had some sort of rash on my face, and I didn't shave for about three weeks. I shaved today, and I now have a moustache and sideburns. I look real dashing, like Errol Flynn. I looked like a mountain man before.

We'll be back east until Oct 31, then they are playing at a Black Cats Festival on Halloween. It should be interesting.

You should be pulling out of Prescott soon? Relieved, aren't you? I know I would be. I believe you finish on the thirtieth. Use E.S.P. to send answer.

So, as you can see, I'm running out of things to say, as usual.

So, this brings to a close another fun-packed letter.

Love,
Mike

Dear Ellen,

Nothing is happening. We'll be back in L.A. on the 18th, I think.

In Portland, they have rain and then they have more rain. I was told the sun comes out, but I saw no evidence of that. We went out to Dennis's grandparent's farm while we were there. I really enjoyed it.

I called Mary while I was In Portland. We talked for about fifteen minutes. I told her about my accident, big deal, and she talked about going to Ohio with Cindy. She still wants to go there. Bonnie's still not home yet.

We just got back from going to London. Canada, that is. It was great. I really like Canada every time I see it.

We're in Detroit right now, going to do another Michigan Pop Festival.

Here's a bit of news: we got a raise as of this week. I now make a big $50 a week sometimes. That means I can take you to twice as many movies.

So, I guess that's about it. Not very interesting, but it's something. Oh, tell Mary that I saw Steve Kahn from the Steve Miller band and they'll be playing there in Phoenix in August sometime and that he will call her, and that he's "sorry he hasn't written because he's been busy." End of quote.

Love,
Mike

Dennis Dunaway, Michael Bruce, Charlie Carnal, Alice Cooper,
Shep Gordon, Neal Smith, unknown, Me,
Glen Buxton at Dennis's grandparent's farm
Courtesy Dennis Dunaway

19

Back to the West Coast

Alice Cooper had bookings for multiple dates at The Whisky in L.A. and other shows in San Francisco, Washington State, and Oregon. While The Alice Cooper group and Dick were jetting off to the cities, I was doing the driving. Charlie as usual was my wing man.

One such trip was to Oregon to play at the Eugene Pop Festival with The Doors, Them, The Youngbloods, Alice Cooper, and a host of other big-name bands. After the concert, somebody decided it would be fun to visit Ken Kesey on his farm outside Eugene. Ken Kesey is the author best known for his book *One Flew Over the Cuckoo's Nest*. He and his friends, who were called the Merry Pranksters, lived together on the farm. They traveled in a bus painted with psychedelic designs that they named *The Further* and did whatever Merry Pranksters like to do which, I guessed, would likely involve getting stopped frequently by the police. We drove to the farm where I took myself on a walking tour to check things out. Everyone else went in search of Mr. Kesey.

The farm was a nice setup: a white wood-sided house and a barn on a large piece of land, perhaps forty acres, that had been cleared, but I didn't know if it was all his. Except for a few acres being tended by people in white linen shirts, slacks and sandals—not the typical Midwestern farming outfit I was used to—none of the other fields had been planted. There was a pretty good-sized vegetable garden with different varieties of squash and melons, along with corn, green beans, carrots, onions, and radishes. A variety of fruit trees were growing in long, straight rows.

I noticed, or more precisely, I heard voices coming from the garden, but nobody there was speaking. Very strange. Were the gardeners communicating with the vegetables and they were talking back? The source turned out to be speakers hidden in the trees and the bushes. Someone was having a discussion with, I assumed, someone that I couldn't hear. I walked back to the farmhouse listening to the odd one-way conversation.

When I got to the house, Ken Kesey was sitting in a chair on the back porch. It was his voice I'd heard broadcasting to every area of the farm. There were three people on the porch with him. I wondered if he was conducting a class of some sort. The Alice Cooper group and Charlie stood on the ground in front. I joined them.

"What's going on?" I whispered, and received numerous shoulder shrugs in reply. When Ken Kesey finished talking about the weather and breakfast and whatever else was on his mind, he turned the microphone off. I never heard him speaking to the assembled visitors, but maybe what I'd heard earlier in the field was that conversation. We thanked him for taking time to see us. He didn't reply, but sat quietly on the porch a few minutes longer. Then, he abruptly rose and went through the old screen door into the house, never to return.

As we walked to our vehicles, I turned to Charlie and said, "What the Hell was that?"

At the time that was pretty strong language for me—I wasn't much of a user of swear words back then, but I have since outgrown that part of my personality.

Charlie said he didn't have any idea. Maybe it was something he did to prank strangers to keep them from coming back. After all, he was one of the Merry Pranksters.

McLeod, Brian. "Unmatched talent of Mother-hood" Popscene, *The Province,* Vancouver, B.C., Saturday, April 19, 1969

Alice Cooper, (a group) however, proved to be little more interesting than sitting in on a jam session in an insane asylum. Light show excepted, these freaks pranced and skipped around the stage like the house band at a spastic reunion.

Our next concert was at a festival in Squamish, Canada. We flew to Seattle rented a truck and loaded up the equipment. One of the festival's crew drove the truck into Canada for us. The promoters then boarded us onto a seaplane headed to Vancouver. Seaplanes were a novel experience for the band. I had flown in them a couple of times. The last time was from Hawaii to California on a military seaplane called the Hawaiian Mars. At the festival all the equipment trucks had been parked in a special guarded area. Event drivers gave us rides from our hotel back and forth to the site.

The day before the concert, I needed to check on the equipment. The huge canopied stage was ready and the equipment for the first three groups had already been set up on it, one band's equipment behind the other.

One of the most challenging things to do at these concerts, once a group had finished playing, was to get their equipment off the stage and get the next band's equipment up and ready to go. It would sometimes take up to an hour just to switch from one group to the other. These guys had a plan which consisted of an army of people to quickly move equipment off and on as many times and as needed. It was a nice, and very welcome, change.

As I walked around the area, I saw a pretty girl laying out electrical cords with inline plugs spaced three to four feet apart. I thought it would be excellent for the band to have some of these. The hardest things to find at a non-concert venue were enough electrical outlets to plug the instruments and Charlie's lights into. I usually had to string miles of extension cords and cables running everywhere to different outlets. These multi-outlet cords would be neater, and I wouldn't need as many. I asked the girl where she had gotten them. She smiled and said her brother had them made. He was doing the lights for the concert.

"He's on the stage right now setting up the rest of the lights, if you want to talk to him," she offered.

"I don't want to bother him if he's busy."

"He's not busy. He's just setting up some lights for a couple more bands who want their own light show as well as the regular light show."

"You have your regular light show and then groups pay you for an individual light show?" I asked. She nodded her head. I never really thought about that until just then, but that's exactly what Charlie did when the band played at a concert: he used the light show the concert venue provided and added another layer with his lights.

She asked if I would like her to show me around.

"That would be great, if you're not busy?"

"No, it's fine. I'm getting hungry, and there is a tent with free food."

My two most favorite words: free and food. Lead on. We got something to eat, sat down at a nearby table, and started talking. I introduced myself and said I worked for Alice Cooper. She said she knew of them, and that her brother probably had done some of their lights. She worked part-time to help him and got to listen to a lot of great music for free. I asked what she did when not stringing lights. I thought she would say student, but she said modeling.

"You're kidding me?" I blurted out. The only model I could think of was Twiggy, and she did not look like a Twiggy.

She laughed, and I said, "I'm sorry. So, you're a fashion model?"

She giggled again. She had a nice laugh.

"You could be a model. You look like you could be," I stammered. By this time, I could tell she was enjoying seeing me make a fool of myself.

I said, "I'm going to shut up now so you can talk."

"I'm a print model for magazines, but mostly for commercials," she explained. "I hold things or stare at stuff and smile. I'm not the glamorous type. I just dress in jeans and a t-shirt. I did a photo shoot a month ago, and the ad is out now in magazines."

She talked about the photo shoot and I remembered the ad, because it caused me to do a little thinking when I saw it. The photo was of the interior of a nice house on a lake. It was taken in a living room and had been shot from a second story, or a tall ladder, looking down. The room was quite large with big windows and a view of the lake. A fire burned in a stone fireplace. The sun was starting to set, and the light was dimming. The girl stood in front of the window. In the distance there was a small boat moving toward the house. In one corner of the room, near the window, was an easel with a blank canvas on it. Was she going to start painting? When she walked toward the window did she see the boat? Who was in the boat? Her husband, friend, anyone one she knew?

Impressed, I asked, "You did that ad? You were the girl looking out at the boat? Who was in the boat?"

"I don't know," she replied. "The photographer just told me to look out the window. I don't usually know what the photos will be used for. Sometimes they just take pictures and find a client for it later."

About this time Mike Bruce and Les Braden showed up. I introduced them to the girl and said that she was helping her brother with the light show and was showing me around.

Les, always angling for the girls and in competition with Mike, said something like, "Why don't you show us around?" She replied with something like, "I'm fine here."

There was a little more talk, then Les and Mike got up and left. She said she needed to get to work, and we walked back to where she'd left her cords.

She asked, "Are you leaving after the show tonight?"

"No, I'll lock the truck up and come back tomorrow morning to drive wherever we go from here."

"Well, stop by to say goodbye. I'll have my brother write down where to get those electrical cords."

"Thanks," I said. "I forgot all about them. See you tomorrow, and it was nice talking to you."

She waved. "See you tomorrow."

The concert went off without a hitch except for an intermittent light rain. I didn't see the girl—she was probably busy helping her brother with his lights. The next day I stopped by the truck. She was outside. I walked over to say goodbye.

"Are you leaving now?" she asked.

"In a few minutes."

"I have something for you," she said.

I thought it would be the address for the electrical cords. I was half-right.

She said, "It's a gift for you," and handed me a pair of orange tinted sunglasses.

"What's this for?"

"These are for you."

"I can't accept them." I searched for something I could give her. All I had was a pocket full of change, and a couple of guitar picks.

"You don't have to give me anything. I want you to have something to remember me by, and say thank you."

Thank me for what? All I did was talk to her for a couple of hours. I didn't even buy her lunch. It was free.

"Thank you for the sunglasses." I put them on. "How do I look?"

She smiled. "Great."

"They make everything seem brighter. We'll probably run into each other again," I said.

She replied, "We probably will." But we never did.

THE RED CAFE MOTEL

10-10-1969

Dear Ellen,

It was nice hearing your voice all the way from Phoenix. Yes, the telephone is a wonderful invention. I'll have to use it again sometime. We're still in Detroit. We're all going crazy. Right now, it's 3:30 in the morning and we're watching the movie The Naked City. I have to drive down to the airport to pick up some records at 6:00 so I'll be going to sleep when you're just getting up.

List of items you can put under your "can believe it or not" column.

1. *Premier Booking of Europe is lining up a tour for us in March and April in Europe*
2. *We're playing in Puerto Rico in December*

Well, that's it in the Alice Cooper rumor department.

Will be playing in San Francisco up until Halloween for four days. Then I don't know where we'll probably be, but I believe it will be Detroit again. Well, how are you anyway? You always ask me to write to you and tell you how I am and how I'm feeling, now you have to do the same. You know I've got a pretty big shoulder to lean on.

Vince and I went to a place where they sell old Ice Capades outfits. I bought a flashy sequin European style military jacket with epaulettes and gold braid. Pretty fancy for Mike Allen, isn't it?

Well, I'll write again.

Love,
Mike

San Francisco

Alice Cooper was scheduled to play in San Francisco at Bill Graham's legendary Fillmore West. The billing included Alice Cooper, It's a Beautiful Day, and Ike and Tina Turner, who everybody was excited to see. Ike and Tina did not disappoint. Tina and the Ikettes must have sweated off 10 lbs. doing their show. They did not stop singing, accompanied by very energetic dancing, from the minute they walked onto the stage till the minute they left. When they did "Proud Mary" the audience experienced a once in a lifetime moment of pure nonstop energy. I was exhausted just watching their act. I had a similar reaction seeing Janis Joplin with her dynamic raspy singing style. My throat hurt just listening to her.

In my mind I had built the Fillmore up as this mythical place imagining marble floors, granite columns, and stained-glass windows. I envisioned it as sort of a Gothic Cathedral, only dedicated to rock music. However, my mental image quickly dissolved when I climbed the stairs and saw what it was: a basketball court with bleachers along one wall. The stage was no more than three inches off the ground. The worst part was trudging up three flights carrying equipment just to get there. What was promoted as a great concert hall was underwhelming, I must admit, until I really took a look at the space. The bleachers along the wall provided a perfect view of the stage, and the audience could sit on the floor until the music moved them to get up and dance.

For a large place, it had a very intimate feel. Concert-goers in the first few rows on the floor were practically sitting on stage as the greatest present and future rock legends performed: The Grateful Dead, Jefferson Airplane, The Doors, The Who, and Led Zeppelin, and Alice Cooper. You saw them up close and personal. You could hear them talking among themselves or speaking to the audience. It was as intimate a venue as it could get. It didn't need to have granite columns. It didn't need to have a grand façade. The Fillmore didn't need any of it. The people who went there had understood what it was all about, and now, I also understood.

I feel sorry for fans who pay big money for a bad seat at a concert with 50,000 of their closest friends and can only see the musicians on stage where they appear to be four inches tall, or to watch them on giant Jumbotrons. I wish that they could go back in time and attend a concert at the Fillmore West, or any other great concert venue. And pay five dollars to see The Who or Alice Cooper. Unfortunately, the Fillmore West closed after only three years.

It was alleged that Bill Graham disliked Alice Cooper. You can probably take out the alleged part and the disliked part and replace it with hated. Why? I don't know. Maybe he only liked the San Francisco sound: The Grateful Dead, Jefferson Airplane, and Moby Grape. Come to think of it, It's a Beautiful Day was from the Bay area. Maybe he didn't like the Phoenix sound. Bill Graham's disdain for the group was communicated through the event posters. The print size on the poster for the show featuring It's a Beautiful Day and Ike and Tina Turner was very large, while Alice Cooper's print size is quite small. On the second show's bill with Iggy and the Stooges the print size is the same, but Alice Cooper's name was last, below the people putting on the light show.

A little information about Iggy and the Stooges. They were from Detroit. Iggy often assaulted the audience verbally, physically, and always musically. His look was that of a skeleton that hadn't yet lost all its skin. When he wasn't insulting the audience from the stage or in the audience getting into fights, he was entertaining and scary all at the same time. There was a *"what is he going to do next"* coupled with *"do I want to be anywhere near him when that happens?"* quality about him. I always imagined him giving a half time speech to a losing football team: "*go out there and fight!*" He would have been great at it, but he also might have scared the team too much.

Truthfully there wasn't much of a sound coming out of Phoenix at the time, but that would change very soon. The late 1960s Phoenix main sound was Alice Cooper and The Beans, who later joined with members of The Red, White and Blues Band to form The Tubes.

By far the most popular band in Arizona, especially with the younger teens, was Hub Kapp and the Wheels who signed with Capital Records and had national success with the song "Work, Work." Mike Condello's Salt River Navy Band was also popular. Both of these bands were created by and for the Wallace and Ladmo Show.

Backstage after the show at the Fillmore, the band heard that The Beatles were in town and were at a party. The band, including Charlie and Dick, wanted to go. How this information was come by I don't know, but I was in total agreement. The thought of meeting the most famous band in the world made us as giddy as a group of teenaged girls—except we could be much cooler. The Beatles? Sure, we'll meet them.

Everyone piled into the van, which was already crowded with equipment causing a déjà vu moment. We ignored the feeling because we were going to "Meet The Beatles!"

I asked, "Where to?"

A voice behind me said, "Don't know. Just drive around San Francisco until we find the party."

Normally, being the sensible one, I would have had more than a few reservations about that, but the possibility of seeing The Beatles defeated common sense. It just might work.

"Let's go!"

To make a long story short, we cruised around the city for an hour and a half. Then a sane voice from the back of the van said, "Let's go back to the hotel. I'm tired." Turns out The Beatles hadn't been in town after all.

Driving from San Francisco

The next day Charlie and I started the drive back home to L.A. We had decided to take the scenic route down Highway 1, which followed the coast almost all the way to Los Angeles. We were in no hurry, nothing pressing to do and no place to be so let's see the sights. There were great views and overlooks, and we stopped often to take in the incredible panorama of ocean and cliffs.

About a third of the way home, something ahead had happened. The traffic in both directions had come to a complete stop. Neither of us could see far enough ahead to know what the situation was. We simply assumed it was an accident. Infrequently, the traffic would move. Sometimes one car, sometimes five or six cars sped by, and we moved forward. As we came closer, we saw that it wasn't an accident at all. There was a landslide—in progress.

The highway crew was working to clear the road with a bulldozer and shovels. When rocks and mud fell onto the roadway, the bulldozer pushed the rocks and the mud over the edge of the road, briefly clearing the way for a car or group of cars to pass the slide area. Drivers watched the highway crewman, who stood looking upward studying the hill intently. He held up his hand for stop, or he motioned real fast with his hand, and that meant go and don't stop.

To say I was tense was an understatement—I was petrified. I had already witnessed several huge boulders tumble down the mountainside. It was a long way to the bottom, but it would take a vehicle a very short time to get there if something went wrong. At last, it was our turn—we were the lead car. The guy with the all-important hand approached the van.

"Don't look up," he said. "When I tell you to go, you go, and don't drive over the center line because cars will be coming from the opposite direction." He was standing right next to me as he spoke. I did not look at him. I stared at the road ahead. It was less than a hundred feet to the other side of the slide, but to me it seemed like a hundred miles.

He shouted, "Go, go, go!" and banged his hand on the side of the van, which scared the-you-know-what out of me.

I pushed the gas pedal hard and the van sped, as fast as a fully loaded van could, to safety. I was afraid for the people following behind me. About five miles past the landslide, we stopped at an overlook and got out to gaze at the ocean.

"Well, that was fun. Do you want to do it again?" I asked Charlie.

"No. No. I do NOT want to do that again."

"Me neither," I said, "But think of the story we have to tell!"

I'm pretty sure nothing like this would happen today. Traffic would be held up for hours at a complete stop and backed up for miles in both directions while numerous agencies discussed the best way to handle the situation, and then they would report back to the higher-ups for further discussion. Life was much simpler back in the 60's. All the road crew needed was a bulldozer, a couple of guys with shovels, and someone to signal drivers when the time was right.

Alice Cooper, Inc.

8814 SUNSET BLVD.
LOS ANGELES, CALIFORNIA 90069
PHONE (213) 657-8890

June 6, 1969 12:00 a.m.

Dear Ellen,

We are in New York City now. Charlie and I drove straight through from L.A. We're staying at the worst dump ever. It was built in the early 1900s and is filthy. The sink has a habit of falling off the wall and doesn't work most of the time. The toilet also doesn't work. The shower has low water pressure, and the walls are covered with dirt. There are rats in the elevator. They are the size of cats. Looks like a flop house. The beds are great if you don't like sleeping and you're a masochist. Everyone, needless to say, is upset.

I almost didn't make it here. I was passing a semi going about 70 when one of the front tires blew out. I handled it like a pro, but in stopping the van I ruined the tire, broke a shock absorber, and smashed up a rim and damaged a tie rod that helps control the van. So, it took a good five hours to fix and a good hundred dollars to pay for it.

The show tonight is with Jimi Hendrix at the Felt Forum.

Notice I didn't tell you that I loved you this time around. I figured if you've heard it once you've heard it a thousand times. This would be reinforcement theory. Alice thinks you're neat and you're too good for me. A lot he knows.

Mike

Off To The Big Apple

We had made multiple trips back east to New York City and the surrounding areas. Playing the east coast was kind of a big deal for us. We were already fairly well known on the west coast, and the Midwest, and now at last on the east coast. This road trip to New York was mostly uneventful, thankfully. Charlie and I stopped in Dodge City, Kansas to eat at our favorite A&W. As always, we were serenaded with The Cowsills song, "Hair." We never got tired of that friendly greeting.

We made it to New York City in two and a half days, with a brief stop—five hours—somewhere in the Midwest for a tow, tire, shocks, and a piece of the suspension. Never pass a semi doing 70mph and have a tire blow out. It can ruin your day. I had acquired a few new driving skills by now, and I was able to slow and stop the van without swerving too much—but a lot of sparks flew.

Arriving in New York City, I found a parking space right in front of the hotel that had been booked for the band. Joey and Shep had arranged for our rooms. We checked-in and advised the front desk clerk of the group's arrival the next day. This hotel, like many we stayed in, was kind of a dump. We were pleased, however, to find that our room was quite large, with five or six single beds, a couple of dressers, and nightstands with porno magazines in the drawers. We had reading material, at least. The sounds of the city were clearly and loudly heard day and night. I guess that's why New York is called the city that never sleeps. I can attest to that.

When Joey and Shep arrived, I was roundly scolded for parking the van on the street where it was unsafe to leave it, they said.

"Where should I park it?" I asked.

"In an underground parking garage," Shep informed me. They were New Yorkers and knew how things worked in the city.

I drove around, eventually finding one, but it wasn't close to the hotel. The garage attendant collected nine dollars. *Nine dollars a day!*

That was just a little less than our room at the hotel, I thought. At least I hoped we were not paying much more for the crummy room.

The Alice Cooper Band was booked to play at several clubs in New York City. The only one I remember was the Felt Forum, or Madison Square Garden as the locals knew it. To be more precise, we were playing *beneath* Madison Square Garden. I parked the van in the loading zone, found a dolly for the equipment and started unloading. I was startled by a loud irritated voice behind me.

"What are you doing?"

I looked around to find four burly guys glaring at me.

"I'm unloading musical equipment for the Alice Cooper show tonight," I explained, confused about what the problem was.

"No, you're not. We're with the Union, and nobody moves this equipment into the building except union members. Are you a union member?"

"No, I'm not," I said. "You're telling me I can't unload this van, and you have to take the equipment to the stage?" I asked incredulously.

"You point, and we lift," was the reply.

"Where have you guys been all my life?" I exclaimed. "I'm sorry, I didn't know how things worked here. We're going on first. We, I mean you, can set the equipment up now."

Thirty minutes later, the van was empty and the equipment was set up on stage.

"Will you guys be taking it off the stage then, and putting it back in the van?" I asked, hoping they would.

"We will. You don't lift anything," they told me.

I love New York City. We're never going to leave!

After the show, Charlie and I made it back to the hotel at almost the same time as the band, thanks to the union guys. And that wasn't counting parking in the underground garage and walking the two blocks back to the hotel.

The guys asked, "How'd you get back here so fast?"

"Unions." I paused and said it again, smiling broadly, "Unions."

Alice Cooper, Inc.

8814 SUNSET BLVD.
LOS ANGELES, CALIFORNIA 90069
PHONE (213) 657-8890

3:00 a.m.

Dear Ellen,

I'm trying hard to find something to like about New York City, but it's not easy. Besides our wonderful hotel accommodations, Glen's guitar was stolen out of our room as we slept. We all feel so safe in this town. Paranoid. Playing at The Scene Wednesday and Thursday, and Friday in Philadelphia, and somewhere Saturday, then Sunday for a love-in at the park.

Central Park, by the way, is one of the dirtiest places. I see garbage everywhere. The lake stinks so bad you can't get near it. Times Square with its strip clubs and bars and adult sex stores is neat only at night. Which raises the question, do you want to be down here at night? In the daytime it looks just like Central Park with a lot of garbage thrown around, but at night it's one big light spectacle with one billboard trying to outdo the other for being the most elaborate.

I made two deposits already in my new bank account. Keep up the good work, Mike. As for myself, I'm doing alright. I really must have changed this past week. It would have really gotten to me a month ago. I'm just groovin' as the song goes. I rode the subway. It's a trip filled with fear and delight. Fear because you're afraid somebody will kill you while you're riding it. Delight when you get off and go upstairs and breathe some of that wonderful New York air.

By the way, write — if I ever get an address that you can write to and tell me when you're graduating, okay?

Well, sugar babe (sickening isn't it), I guess that's it.

Love,
Mike

Guitars Stolen

After the show it was still relatively early in the evening, and everyone decided to get something to eat and explore a little of New York City. The band changed out of their show costumes, and we walked to Washington Square and the Village, coming back to the hotel well after midnight.

The next morning, we were awakened by a furious Glen. "My guitar was stolen!" he shouted. Not in those exact words but with more colorful language. You get the picture. He was in a rage.

Apparently, someone had come in while we were out, or less likely while we were sleeping, and stolen his much-loved Gretsch guitar that he had stored under his bed. And this was no exaggeration: he truly loved that guitar. The burglar hadn't come in off the fire escape; the windows were locked. He had to have come through the door. I pulled on some clothes and rushed downstairs and asked the day clerk to ask the night clerk if anyone had left with a guitar case during the night. He said he would. The answer was no.

Glen was upset and had every right to be. It's said lightning doesn't strike twice, but it was about to. After Glen's Gretsch guitar was stolen we changed hotels. When the band arrived by taxi at the new place they deposited their luggage on the curb, and went inside to check the hotel. There was not much to see. It was shabby and run down, like most we stayed in. You felt rat eyes following you wherever you were. If a rat was occupying the elevator, you let him have it. It was proper etiquette at this hotel.

After stridently complaining "what a dump" followed with colorful earthy expletives, the band went back to the curb to retrieve their luggage. Almost all of it was there, with the notable exception of Glen's guitar case. His Les Paul guitar had vanished, just as his Gretsch had a week earlier.

This guitar was quite unusual, a pink Gibson Les Paul, and to be honest, I don't even know where he'd gotten it. He'd owned it for less than two months.

"You need to get another guitar right now, Glen!" Shep said emphatically. "It may not be the one you want, but you'll have to use it until what you want comes along,"

I told Glen I'd go with him to look at guitars, and that we might possibly find one or both of the stolen ones. "I'll find out where the pawn shops are in this area, and we'll search until you find your old guitar, or a buy a new one."

And so, out we went. I had no idea how abundant pawn shops were in New York City. We spent the better part of the day roaming the streets around the hotel, which was now referred to as Hotel Hell, searching pawn shop after pawn shop.

I've often wondered why Glen didn't pick up another Les Paul or a Gretsch when he saw one, and we saw many. Perhaps he was in a state of shock, having both of his guitars stolen in the span of a little over a week. He considered quite a few, but none struck his fancy, and we returned hours later empty handed. Later, Shep picked Glen up at the hotel and drove to a music store. Shep told Glen to "just pick one." He settled on a Rickenbacker. I guess a Les Paul guitar was just a Les Paul guitar, unless it was *your* pink Les Paul. I could understand that.

A few days before Glen's Les Paul guitar was stolen, the Alice Cooper group appeared in a movie. The scene lasted only a few minutes, but it was a movie, and it was a BIG deal for them. The movie was *Diary of a Mad Housewife* starring Richard Benjamin, Frank Langella, and Carrie Snodgrass. Carrie received an Oscar nomination for her part. Frank Perry directed.

The premise of the band's scene was that Richard and Carrie had gone to a club where the Alice Cooper Group was playing. The club was packed. Carrie doesn't want to be there. Richard ignores her and tells her to stop clinging to him. She lets him go and stands by the exit door where Frank Langella approaches and basically insults her. The music grows louder. The band gets crazy and the dancers go crazy. Feathers fly, and Alice unexpectedly throws olive oil on the dancers then the CO_2 fire extinguishers come out. Total chaos. Cut and print, as they say. I didn't know if Frank Perry was expecting a Gallagher type performance of exploding watermelons or what. I also didn't know if he knew what to expect from Alice Cooper, but he got quite a performance.

I almost had a talking part. Frank Perry asked me to say a line to Frank Langella, who wasn't actually present that day. The line was something like, "She's over there," and then point in some direction. It had Oscar written all over it. Unfortunately, an assistant interjected, "He's in the band." Before I could tell him I was not in the band, just with the band to set up the equipment, Frank said, "Oh," and chose somebody else. I don't know why he asked me in the first place, unless he knew talent when he saw it. More than likely it was because I was already wearing makeup. Earlier, Mike Bruce told me that if they had to wear makeup so did I. I noticed Charlie was being made up, which was fortunate because he had the only close-up: a shot of him sitting cross-legged on the floor, flipping his lighting micro-switches.

I did have my moment in the movie, though it was fleeting. I'm standing on the far-left side of the stage. Sadly, only a few would recognize that it's me. During the scene, I found a pillow and tossed it into the crowd. You can see the pillow, but not who threw it. I picked up a second pillow intending to throw it across the stage, but thought better of it, afraid I would hit one of the band members. So, I waved it around in the air a few times and threw it on the floor.

Before the scene got underway, Mr. Perry said, "Have fun and show me lots of energy," He told everyone how he wanted it to go:

lots of enthusiastic dancing, the people in costume go up front, people wearing their own clothes stay in the back. The partiers were costumed in a way people in the 1960s were thought to have dressed, according to movie people. Loud multi-colored nylon shirts, head scarves, neck scarves, beads, chain necklaces, bell bottom pants, and jackets with very wide lapels. I was definitely not in style.

Dear Ellen

This is the last letter you're going to get from me until our new address in San Francisco. Least I have the advantage over you. From now on I'm the only one who's going to be doing the talking. You'll just have to listen to what I say, because you won't be able to reach me. True male supremacy.

How come you're quitting work? You know you're just going to be bored with nothing to do.

If you want my opinion and you're going to get it, I don't think you and your sister taking off this summer and traveling around the country is a good idea. I can barely survive driving around the country. I don't feel you could take care of yourself. I think you would end up getting in some sort of trouble you couldn't get yourself out of. I mean take a good look at your sister, and think about her. Then, have your sister do the same to you. I rest my case. Pretty convincing...

The police found the Ampeg amplifiers that were stolen some time ago at the Quebec house. I had to go downtown to the police station to pick up some papers. I was a big hit. I had to walk right past the Narcotics Division before I got to where I was going. I had to drive down to the pawn shop where they were found and get them back myself. The area around the pawn shop was very depressing. The people at the pawn shop seemed ready to kill me. They finally let me have the amps when I told them the police were coming down to find out if I had gotten them. I think that was the only thing that saved me from having a very rough time.

Anyway, I'd like to reserve one or two nights when I get back to Phoenix. I thought you might want to see a new group called Alice Cooper. They're very good I hear. So, I will end this letter now, so that we can both get some sleep. After all, it's 3:30 in the morning.

Love,
Mike

20

Equipment Recovered

The band was back in L.A. for a brief stay working at the Whisky, the Cheetah Club and a few more places. Cindy took a call from the police and passed the phone to Dick, Thanks to Dick giving the police the serial numbers, they had recovered the stolen Ampeg amplifiers. The equipment had been located at a downtown pawn shop. Dick took down the address.

The owner would be expecting us, meaning me, to come pick up the equipment. The caller asked if the police needed to meet me there. Dick said that wasn't necessary, that I could handle it. I had been out most of the afternoon running around or dropping equipment off at a club. When I returned home, he told me about the call. I said, "No time like the present."

The van was already empty, and I headed downtown stopping first at the police station to pick up paperwork for the pawn shop. I had a very good relationship with the police. I religiously stayed out of trouble, and the police could stop me anytime they wanted.

This was the first time, though, that I'd ever been inside a police station. The experience was not an enjoyable one, but this was largely due to my nerves. There was nothing to worry about, I told myself. I spoke with the desk officer and explained why I was there. He told me to walk down the hall until I came to a bench by a door and sit down and wait. Everyone who walked by stared curiously at me. I spent a lot of time looking at my shoes. Finally, after what seemed like days, I was called into the office. The officer handed over a folder with three sheets of paper inside. His instructions were to give the top two pages to the pawnshop people and keep one for myself.

Leaving the station, I felt relief just being outside and headed to the pawnshop. Along the way, I perceived that it wasn't the safest looking part of town. In fact, in the daytime, let alone after dark, you would not want to be there. The streets were lined with very run-down bars and seedy looking places that advertised beds for rent. People, mostly men, were sitting or lying on the filthy sidewalks. A strong urine odor permeated the air. I'd never seen anything like this in my twenty years on the planet. I had seen down and out before—people hoping a break would come their way giving them the means to crawl out of their present situation. But these people on the street were different. They had given up on life, and life had given up on them.

I parked on the street, got out of the van, and walked into the pawn shop. All three employees ignored me.

"I'm here to pick up the stolen musical equipment," I said. I was sure they were thinking I had to be more specific. "The police said you were notified, and they would meet me down here," I lied. Secretly I wished Dick had said yes to the police, and had them send S.W.A.T. also.

Silence. They didn't look happy to see me. I slid the folder with all three sheets of paper across the counter. This place was starting to creep me out. They examined the forms and mumbled something to each other that I couldn't hear, but I'm sure it was derogatory and about me. I had a hunch they felt I was stealing the Ampeg amplifiers from them. The very same amps that had been stolen from us!

Finally, one of them said, "It's in the back," and waved his hand in the general direction of the rear of the store.

Great, it was in the back. Why couldn't it be up front where I might at least be seen through the dirty windows? I walked past dusty cases of pawned tools, jewelry, and other items and went through a swinging door. Our amps were stacked in a back corner, and they had police tags on them. One by one I carried them out to the van. The pawn shop guys watched sullenly, not volunteering to help, which was fine with me. As I worked, the people across the street became aware of me and began to stir, but they never approached. After the last amp was loaded, I called out a thank you to the men inside the shop. No response. I hadn't expected any.

Safely back at the Quebec house, I was thankful my body had not been discovered dumped in an alley. And thankful I hadn't given up on life. Hopefully, I never would.

Alice Cooper, Inc.

6614 SUNSET BLVD.
LOS ANGELES, CALIFORNIA 90069
PHONE (213) 657-9890

Dear Ellen,

I'm going to the doctor tomorrow, but not for my eyes. Seems like I happened to get into another automobile accident. Odd for me to do that. I'm alright except for back trouble, whiplash, and my nerves are shot.

Now I'll go into epic detail about the accident. I was in the fast lane of the freeway going south. There was a dirt median going across two freeways so people could turn around. There was a car stopped on the median. The car pulled into the fast lane going about five miles an hour. I slammed on my brakes and headed for the ditch. My speed was about 65. I had to miss some concrete pillars that were along the side of the road. I missed them and headed straight for a telephone pole. I missed that, then the truck started going into a spin, the back tires blew out, and the truck was going to tip over. I pulled the front wheels straight and slammed the truck into a huge freeway sign. I knocked it completely down, and it fell on top of the roof, crushing in the top. I then promptly passed out. Charlie caught me before my face hit the broken glass from the windshield. Charlie's alright. He was just grooving when it happened. The driver was cited for not yielding to traffic, driving too slow, and hazardous driving. I have to go to the doctor for back treatment. Shep says I can make some money from the accident, but I don't care really. Well, I guess that's it. I just bought a leather coat and a pair of fake leather pants. I'm looking like quite the star. Oh well!

Love,
Mike

flying the friendly skies of United

Dear Ellen,

I've been to the doctor, and I'll have to see him every day except Sunday for two and a half months for treatment for my neck and back. For my back I get heat and whirlpool. For my neck I get it stretched out of shape. They put some straps around my neck and then they pull me out of my chair. I also get heat. I actually feel pretty good. I think they're just trying to milk the insurance money. Plus, I've never been anywhere in one place for two and half months.

Right now, 25,000 ft. up, flying to Seattle for a festival. Big time, you know. Been flying almost everywhere, now. If you get another letter from me, that will mean I've made it.

You ever wonder why I don't say "How are you?" or "How's your job?" If I ever did, by the time I heard from you I would have forgotten the questions.

We'll be on the road for the next month until the middle of August, then back to L.A. I don't feel too bad injury wise now, but my neck keeps hurting. The lawyer says I ought to get about five thousand dollars for the accident, but he's nothing but a crook. I'll be satisfied with $50.00.

Going to Canada again. Maybe there will be an official Canadian gift in it for you.

Love,
Mike

Coast-to-Coast…and to Hawaii

Not Again

The band played another successful concert tour in San Francisco, Portland and Oregon. Once again, Charlie and I headed home to L.A. on the 5 Freeway. We had briefly discussed using Highway 1 again but, remembering the previous trip, that was quickly vetoed. So, the 5 freeway it was. We were somewhere south of Frisco and everything was going fine. We were traveling along in a grouping of cars with a Highway Patrol vehicle on my right side. Everybody was going the speed limit—a nice and legal 65 miles per hour. However, I was starting to get paranoid about the police next to me because I had been pulled over so many times. The police routine was: stop, license and registration check, ask questions, back to the police car's radio, come back, and "You can go." Most times I was not given any reason for being pulled over in the first place.

Anyway, I'm cruising along minding my own business, with the officer on my right, anticipating the lights and siren. A little way ahead I noticed a car with its brake lights on sitting in the dirt median. I really didn't think too much about it as I was almost on top of him. Without warning, the driver pulled out into my lane directly in front of me. According to the highway patrol, the car entered the freeway going 5 miles an hour. I slammed on the brakes, pulled the wheel hard to the left, and steered the van onto the dirt median.

Instead of stopping his car, the other driver continued right into the path of the highway patrol car one lane over. It's the old physics thing again: no two objects can occupy the same space at the same time. To avoid a collision, the police officer braked and swerved into the lane that only seconds before had been occupied by my van. The police car did a complete 180 on the freeway and stopped facing in the wrong direction, into oncoming traffic. Cars rocketed off the freeway. It looked like a demolition derby: cars sliding, spinning, and going sideways.

I was still moving forward and quickly running out of options. Vehicles all around me were careening out of control. They were in front of me, coming up behind, and beside me. Rocks flew and clouds of dust rose from the median obscuring much of what was happening. In my view, continuing across the median onto the northbound freeway into oncoming traffic was not the option I wanted to take.

By this point I couldn't tell if I was driving with a purpose or the van drove itself. Either way, the van was headed in the general direction of a large highway sign and then went straight at it. For a moment I thought we would miss the sign altogether, but a rear tire blew and control of the van ceased to be a factor. There was nothing I could do now to stop. Luck or divine providence would have to intervene. I hoped the van would pass through the sign posts avoiding a collision with one or both of them. Unfortunately, the van was a few inches wider than the opening between the supports and slammed into the wooden columns which shattered on impact. The highway sign plummeted down on top of the van and snapped in two, one large piece landing alongside the van making it impossible for Charlie to get out. A length of the fractured support exploded through the front windshield neatly lodging itself four or five inches away from impaling either me or Charlie.

The van, with half the sign still sitting on top, stopped just feet away from oncoming traffic. Stunned, Charlie and I sat there, unable to process what had just occurred. I had developed a habit of shutting my mind down after car accidents. I sort of remember people banging on the door telling me to unlock it and asking if we were hurt. I clearly remember someone standing on the front bumper pulling the sign support out through the windshield, and others moving the large section of the sign that was blocking Charlie's door.

We climbed out of the van, but I remained in shutdown mode for a while. I saw six or more cars strewn haphazardly around the median. Another half dozen had stopped on the shoulder to help.

Drivers and passengers gathered in small groups to recount their near-death experience. The highway patrol officer said that if I hadn't pulled off the freeway when I did, he would have crashed into me.

The driver who caused the accident had also stopped, and the police were speaking with him. Someone in the crowd who was angry suggested we "*hang that guy.*" Since I had obliterated the only structure capable of that, I felt it was an empty threat.

After a while, a California Highway Patrol officer approached and handed the driver's name and insurance information to me. He said that in my dazed condition I probably couldn't have gotten it myself. He was right. I don't remember taking pictures of the van for insurance purposes, but I must have—I always carried a camera and an 8mm movie camera with me. I used them to document our trips and concerts.

As my confusion resolved I began to understand what had just happened, and what could have happened. Once again, everyone escaped without a scratch. Mine was the only vehicle that sustained damage and, once again, it could have been so much worse. At least sixteen men, women, and children were involved, plus the individual who caused the accident. Divine intervention, St. Christopher, Guardian Angel, Karma, or fate. It was hard not to believe there was something, or someone, watching over us.

The California Highway Patrol officer took statements from everyone. One of the other drivers had thoughtfully put my spare tire on the van. We stayed at the scene for a while longer, letting the adrenaline dissipate. People conversed about where they had been going, what they planned to do once they got there, and what they would have to do now. And how lucky we all were. Eventually, everyone continued on their way.

Charlie and I drove on toward Los Angeles. After a few miles, we stopped for something to eat and to recover from the event. After that stop, things looked a lot better—that was until sixty miles farther when the California Highway Patrol pulled me over and gave me a ticket for having a busted windshield! The end to a not-so-perfect-day. So much for Karma. Or maybe St. Christopher has a weird sense of humor.

I drove the van to the Landmark Hotel in Hollywood. Joey and Shep came out to assess the damage. I walked with them to the partially-underground parking lot and explained that the damage wasn't too bad. I was trying to sound as optimistic as I could: busted windshield, front-end and bumper dented, the doors didn't close right, roof damage, side view mirror broken, and headlights. It would need a wheel alignment, shocks, a new front end paint job, another tire, and there was interior damage caused by the post slamming through the windshield scraping the dash and the inside engine cover. Plus on the drive home the van's steering was not as good as it should have been. To top it off there was possible frame or suspension damage. It really wasn't in the best of shape. The good news was the van was somewhat drivable, I said as cheerfully as I could, but I knew it was lost cause.

They stood back for a moment surveying the damage. To my astonishment they began kicking the van with their boots, working out their frustration over losing another vehicle. I felt it was better for them to kick the van a few times than to take their anger out on me. They knew it wasn't my fault.

"The van is totaled. How you even got it back here is a miracle. We'll make an insurance claim. It might keep the band afloat for a couple more months," Joey said matter-of-factly.

"From now on you can rent trucks, or you can fly if we're playing farther away or if there isn't enough time to drive," Shep added.

I never understood their reasons for not buying another van. Perhaps they thought renting would save money, but I really didn't think it would. Maybe they had lost faith in my driving ability. I believed the latter to be most true.

That was the last Alice Cooper owned van I ever drove for the band. From then on, Joey and Shep had me renting trucks from U-Haul, or some other company. The insurance company totaled the van and sent me to a doctor for back and neck injuries, because I was sore and in pain moving around, or even standing for that matter. A lawyer was retained to file an insurance claim for damages.

Renting trucks was a mixed blessing. The positive: all the equipment could easily fit inside, and I could sometimes fly with the band. The negative: I would fly with the band. I recognized there were some real and inconvenient problems now, most notably the van was our sole source of transportation. We'd be stuck at home, unable to go anywhere unless it was within walking distance. Relying on

Toodie to drive over from Phoenix to chauffeur us around was not a long-term option.

The maiden voyage using a rented moving truck was not the positive experience that I hoped it would be. We, meaning Charlie and myself, left L.A. around 10:00 at night. Our destination was Detroit. The truck's hard seats and stiff suspension were not as comfortable as my old van. My van also had a partition behind the front seats where I had a mattress for naps, plus it had an 8-track tape player, and automatic transmission. The rented truck had none of these features. That behemoth had a one-position barely cushioned bench seat in front and a giant box behind for the equipment. Because of its size and height, it swayed and swerved with every cross-breeze. The van shook, rattled and rolled. The suspension, or rather the lack of one, made for a bone jarring ride. After a ten-plus hour trip we felt and moved like we were in our eighties.

The transmission was a 4-speed manual. It had a first gear, but I never got around to using it. The absolute worst was that it lacked air-conditioning. This one critical feature was, to us, essential. On a summer night crossing the desert, the temperature still hovered at 100 degrees at midnight and felt double that in the daytime. We always traveled with a large ice-filled cooler placed between us on the bench seat. To get a little relief from the oppressive heat in the cab we periodically splashed water on our clothes or submerged whatever body part we could in the ice. The cooler also held our water or soda and food. Because there was no cab insulation, the decibel level was deafening. Separated by three feet, Charlie and I were forced to yell at one another to converse. Eventually, the effort was too much and we remained silent unless absolutely necessary. All these things made for a long, tedious, and uncomfortable trip.

Somewhere between Blythe, California and Quartzsite, Arizona around 1:00 in the morning, the moving truck succumbed to a slow, painful death coughing and sputtering along the highway. A final colossal backfire lit the night sky before the truck coasted silently to a stop. Attempts to start the engine failed. It emitted a low, pitiful moan in response to turning the key and pumping the gas pedal. Eventually, we surrendered and got out to diagnose the problem. Everything still seemed to be there—no major pieces of engine were missing. After a brief discussion, Charlie decided he would stay with the truck, and I would hitchhike to find help.

First, I had to make myself presentable to someone who might consider helping instead of running me over. I retrieved my trusty baseball cap from the truck and, using some of our precious cooler water, soaked my hair, combed it straight back and folded it beneath my cap. I thought if I put on a jacket, certainly unneeded because of the heat, and put the collar up, any loose hair mistakes would be hidden. I stood on the shoulder of the road and waited. Forty-five minutes later a semi-truck approached, slowed down, and stopped.

The driver leaned out his window and asked, "What's the problem?"

I said, "Don't know. Just stopped running and won't start."

I was careful to stay in the shadows so he couldn't get a good look at me. Charlie was hunched down in his seat out of sight.

"Got gas?" he asked.

"Says half a tank."

"Hop in. There's a truck stop twenty-five miles away. They should be able to help you."

I climbed inside, leaving Charlie behind and hoping I would see him again. The truck driver looked at me and gave me the once over. I don't think he liked what he saw. What I knew about truckers was gleaned from watching movies: they all were from the south, they all traveled with shotguns, knives, and baseball bats, and they didn't cotton to long-haired hippies. As I gripped the door handle in case a quick exit at 60 miles an hour was necessitated, I started talking to him—almost nonstop to keep him from focusing on my appearance.

"Where are you from?"

"Texas."

Great. All the movies I'd seen about truckers were true.

"What part of Texas?"

"San Antonio."

"Great city. Home of the Alamo. My parents took me there." I had never been there in my life. "How long have you been hauling freight?"

"Ten years."

"Is that Patsy Cline on the radio? I really like her."

After my nervous chattering and his one or two-word answers, something happened: we both calmed down. The tension that could be cut with a knife that I was sure he had, and I didn't want to see, had disappeared. He relaxed and began talking. He said he drove all over the country, traveling from job to job. He was married with two kids: a boy and a girl. He was on the road so much he didn't get to see them very often, but he tried to call every night. He spoke of his father, who was also a trucker. He wasn't surly any longer. He was lonely.

I told him that I was also constantly on the road driving from job to job, but it was easier on me because I hung out with the band for company. He said he had never heard of Alice Cooper, which was totally fine with me. I wasn't about to tell him anything about the band. I allowed him to assume the band was comprised of a female folk singer who sang with a gospel group. He said he was driving so much because he wanted to pay off his rig. It was a Peterbilt. He wanted to slow down and spend more time with his wife and kids. A half hour later, he dropped me off at the truck stop.

"It was good talking to you," he said. "Do something with your hair. They won't understand in there," he advised, nodding toward the station.

I thanked him for the ride and wished him luck with his plans.

Inside the service center, I greeted the attendant and explained my situation. He thought I was probably out of gas. I told him that the gauge read half full. He said it was probably faulty and asked if I had checked inside the gas tank. I hadn't. He filled a gas can and drove me back to the truck. The lights were off. I figured Charlie was asleep. I was wrong. Charlie was very much awake. While I had been gone, a car passed the truck, turned around, and parked behind it. Several men exited and walked around the truck. They messed with the lock on the rolling door trying to open it. To warn them off, Charlie flashed the lights on and off and laid on the horn. Luckily, that worked. The only causality, besides Charlie's nerves—the battery was now drained.

The truck stop attendant said, "No problem. I can jump the battery." He put five gallons of gas in the tank, then attached the battery cables. The moving truck shuddered once and came to life.

He said knowingly, "The companies that rent these things don't really take care of their equipment. Get them in and get them out as fast as they can."

I thanked him. Paid for the gas, the $10.00 service charge and a $5.00 tip and we were on our way once more. By now it was after four in the morning, and we still had a lot of driving ahead. But first, we'd stop at the service station for a fill up.

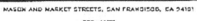

HOTEL OXFORD

MASON AND MARKET STREETS, SAN FRANCISCO, CA 94101

778-4400

Dear Ellen,

Just got your letter. Quite an ego boost. Oh, you're slipping. If you wait for me to come back so you can wear the dress, I'm afraid you'll be too old to appreciate it. I'm glad you liked it, and you're right: I do have good taste. But the sales people helped me a lot so I can't take all the credit.

I'm studying for my driver's test. I have to take it on Monday. I can't go on driving without a license much longer.

I would like to come back to Phoenix for that festival you mentioned, but things like that are out of my hands. Still dealing with the lawyers over the van crash outside of San Francisco. At this point I don't care what happens. These guys are really crooks, and I don't think I like getting money this way. Imagine me with morals over money.

Will be here for another two or three weeks, so keep those cards and letters coming in. Take care of yourself, and don't go getting any better grades in school trying to make me feel inferior, never! I won't allow it. Try to ruin my image. You better start flunking and be ignorant like me.

Love,
Mike

Fear of Flying. Not by Myself, But with the Band

One of my clearest memories of sending our equipment by plane was the pained expression on Joey's and Shep's faces when I presented them with the freight receipt. I wish I had taken a picture, but my cameras were neatly packed away with the equipment. They told me that I would have to find a way to get the cost reduced, and I did. More on that later.

On one flight, as Mike Bruce boarded the plane, he spoke a single word to the fight crew. That one word set off a chain reaction that could have gotten us in a boatload of trouble with the Feds—along with some serious jail time. That one word was, "Hijack."

In the preceding years, there had been a bunch of flights commandeered by people with guns shouting "Hijack!" Hijackers had taken over flights in the U.S. and demanded to be flown to the Middle East, Cuba, and Russia. One U.S. hijacker extorted money from the airline and, with a bag stuffed with the ransom, parachuted out of the plane somewhere between Seattle, Washington and Portland, Oregon. Neither he, nor the money, were ever found. The Federal Air Marshal Service was established because of those hijackings.

The word "hijack," as expected, caused quite a response from the stewardesses who were welcoming passengers on board. I had just stepped inside the plane two people behind Mike Bruce and was trying hard not to look like I belonged with the people in front of me.

Alarmed, a stewardess asked, "What did you say? Did you say hijack?"

Did he really say "hijack?" He really did say "hijack." Maybe we can all have adjoining jail cells. If this was meant as a joke, as I'm sure it was, nobody laughed. One of the pilots appeared, and he wasn't smiling either. I had a feeling this could get real ugly real soon. I seriously considered backing out of the plane, going through the terminal, and out the front door after I heard a menacing threat:

"Were going to make an example of you," and, "You won't think it's so funny later."

Dick was in line behind Mike. He quickly stepped forward and did all the talking—very fast nonstop talking. The word "hijack" was now being nervously repeated throughout the airplane. I expected to see Mike escorted away by a federal agent, never to be heard from again, or for twenty years at least. Dick was doing his best to explain Mike's unfortunate utterance in hopes of getting his imminent multi-year sentence reduced. Dick said Mike thought it would be a funny thing to say. That he just wasn't thinking. Along with not thinking, he was really, really sorry. Luckily, the crew bought it. At least the not thinking part. Not because it wasn't the truth, it was, but because they had wasted too much time already on this discussion. There was a schedule to keep and more passengers to board, and they were starting to get anxious about that. If there had been an air marshal, Mike would have been expelled from the plane or seated very, very close to him, probably in handcuffs. I so wished I could drive the van again. It seemed safer if this was to be the new norm.

On another late-night flight, we had a scheduled layover. The crew announced it would be a thirty-minute stop, and if you wanted to leave the plane, you could. I have to tell you that flying in the sixties was not like it is today: no metal detectors or TSA screenings. Heck, you could even fly on someone else's ticket. They didn't care. Airports weren't open 24 hours a day or even secure. In those days, you could roam all over the airport without any restrictions.

When a plane taxied to the gate, it was no closer than a hundred feet from the terminal. A truck with a set of stairs attached waited on the tarmac and drove out to the plane so passengers could either board or deplane.

When the stair-truck arrived to service our plane for the layover, the band bolted for the door, eager to explore an empty airport. I stayed in my seat.

Dick was not with the band during this time, and his replacement was unsatisfactory. Actually, I think the band didn't bother to wake him and we left him sleeping in his motel room. It was now my responsibility to get them back on the plane. Twenty minutes came and went. The stewardess announced, "We'll be leaving in ten minutes."

Okay, just great. I've got to put shock collars on those guys—they'll be easier to find if they're twitching on the floor. I hurried off the plane and ran through gate's door into the terminal. I spotted an employee at the check-in desk and asked if she could page throughout the airport. She said she could. I had her announce: "Will the Alice Cooper Band please return to the gate for immediate departure."

I paced nervously until I could wait no longer. I raced through the airport looking for them. As I searched, I realized I might also miss the plane. I was determined to be on that flight, with or without them. Joey and Shep would not be happy if I arrived and the group didn't, but I figured the group could get on a later flight and still make the show on time. I was getting on this plane, no matter what.

Sprinting back to the gate, I told the attendant that she could tell the band to catch the next flight to our destination. She said, "The plane is taking off now." *What!*

Panicked, I saw the only thing keeping me from the tarmac and the plane was a white rope with a Do Not Enter sign hanging from it. I jumped over the rope and raced toward the truck with the stairs, which had pulled away from the plane and was moving back toward the terminal. The plane was taxiing now, heading for the runway. I leaped onto the moving truck's stairs, charged to the top, and pointed urgently while shouting to the driver, "Take me to that plane!"

I wondered if this was not an uncommon occurrence, because the truck driver never hesitated swiftly reversing course nearly catapulting me from the top. It didn't seem to be a big deal to chase down a plane with a passenger clinging to the stairs poised and ready to vault onto a plane moving down the runway. Miraculously, the plane stopped. I don't think the pilots or crew were amused. As I boarded, the passengers, who had been attentively observing my antics from their window seats, welcomed me with thunderous applause. Everyone, including the band, clapped. They had gotten aboard as I searched the airport for them.

A stewardess took pity on me. "We gave away your seat," she said apologetically, then led me down the aisle to an empty row. She showed me how to make a bed out of the seats. I thanked her, and she said, "It looks like you've had a tiring day."

"I have." I replied wearily and quickly fell asleep.

When I woke up, we were still in the air. I noticed that there was a blanket covering me. The stewardess must have done that. She walked by and said cheerily, "You're up!"

"I am." I said. "Thank you for the blanket."

She smiled and asked, "Are you hungry? I saved you a meal."

I didn't hesitate. "Yes," I answered, and she quickly brought it. My meal was steak with potatoes and green beans. I thought this must be what the people "behind the curtain" were served.

"Thank you. This looks great," I said, appreciatively.

She said to enjoy it, and I did. I passed on dessert, though. I was full and didn't know if she would be in trouble for feeding me. I took some photos of her with the band and promised I would send her copies, which I did. It was a pretty good flight after all.

On another flight with the band, we were forty-five minutes in the air when the galley suddenly caught fire. I was seated across from it. To my knowledge the band had nothing to do with the emergency, but I wasn't watching them all the time. The only thing I witnessed was Glen pilfering liquor from the beverage cart. He possessed the dexterity of a magician. As the cart passed, Mike Bruce and Neal distracted the stewardess with polite conversation, and Glen went to work.

Meanwhile, the other stewardesses were occupied using CO_2 extinguishers on the fire while asking passengers to remain calm. The billowing white smoke from the extinguisher reminded me of the Alice Cooper show. All that was missing was the chicken.

After my other experiences on planes, I thought that if this was all they had to throw at me, I was really fine with it. I have a lot of stories where I'd have to tell them to "remain calm."

Joey and Shep had given me instructions to find a way to get the equipment onto a plane at a lower cost. If I could manage that, I'd achieve hero status. They would smother me with praise and possibly a raise, as well. I can dream, can't I? As it turned out, it really wasn't hard after all, but it did involve losing sleep.

Airports at night, especially after midnight, were all but deserted. A few airport staff were on duty, and that always included a Skycap or two. Skycaps were there just in case anyone showed up.

After a concert, if we were flying out the next day, I'd pack up the equipment and drive straight to the airport. Locating a Skycap, I'd tell him that the equipment needed to be checked-in for the flight we were taking later that day. The Skycap obliged by hopping into my truck, and we'd drive to the buildings where the luggage carts were stored. As I unloaded the equipment, he tagged the pieces and wrote the flight information on a card attached to the luggage cart. I'd drive him back to the front of the airport and tip him forty dollars. In 1969 forty dollars in cash was a lot of money, but it was much cheaper than paying the freight charge for the equipment. When I was finished, I might return the truck to the rental lot and take a taxi back to the airport where I'd find some uncomfortable chair to sleep on, or I might take the truck to the hotel and turn it in the next day on the way to the airport.

One night I decided to return the rental truck after dropping the equipment off. Everything went as planned: drop off the equipment and save the company some money. From the airport, I could actually see the business where I would be returning the truck.

A one-way road lead into the airport, and a one-way road lead out. Driving on the road heading out, I came to a long tunnel. Unsure of the tunnel's clearance, and because there was no other traffic on the road, I stopped to read the sign mounted above the tunnel's entrance. The sign read: "No vehicle over ten feet." The sign inside the cab of the truck read: "Don't drive under structures lower than ten feet." Naturally, I figured exactly ten feet must be okay.

I started through the tunnel. All was going well until I heard what sounded like popping sounds. It was hard to tell given the noise the truck made. Confused but not overly concerned, I kept driving, but I rolled the window down and turned the radio off in order to better hear. The road ahead looked okay, and I couldn't see anything on the road behind, so I kept driving. I was three-quarters of the way through before I realized the reason for the popping: the tunnel ahead was lit by rows of fluorescent lights, but behind the truck it was completely dark. I had destroyed every single fluorescent light in the tunnel with the roof of the truck! Because it was one-way, and I didn't want to back out, I sped up and smashed the remaining fixtures on the way.

Arriving at the rental drop location, I parked the truck and walked nonchalantly back to the airport, hoping there were no witnesses who could put two and two together. As I settled into a booth in the airport's coffee shop, I prayed I would make it onto the plane before security discovered who was responsible for the destroyed airport property. In the end, I figured the tunnel itself had been built to a height of ten feet, but, when the lights were installed, they effectively lowered the ceiling height to around 9ft 8in. I couldn't be the only one who had ever made that mistake unless the tunnel had just opened, or perhaps I failed to see a sign that no trucks were allowed on that road.

On a night flight from Phoenix to join the band in Cincinnati, Ohio the plane arrived at the gate around 9:00 p.m. I collected my bag and walked outside to find a cab where I was greeted by two police officers who were very curious to hear all about my trip.

"Where are you coming from?" one inquired.

I said, "Phoenix."

"Where are you going?" the other asked.

"To a hotel by cab."

"What city is the hotel in?" he pressed.

"Cincinnati," I answered.

"Well, this is Kentucky. The Cincinnati airport is in Covington, Kentucky," the first one said.

I really had no idea the Cincinnati airport was not in Ohio.

"Let's see some ID."

I handed over my driver's license. He took it inside the airport. The other officer entertained me by staring at me without blinking. After a long wait, my ID was returned. They told me to leave the airport and go to Cincinnati. Which, strangely enough, was what I intended to do forty-five minutes ago, but I kept that to myself.

I hailed a cab and, as I was getting in, one of the officers said, "Don't let the sun hit you on your back in Kentucky." I had no idea what he was talking about, since it was now close to 10:00 in the evening. I thanked him anyway and got into a cab. I told the driver where I needed to go.

He said matter-of-factly, "You got hassled by the cops." I didn't know if that was a question or a statement. I said I was used to it.

We were almost to the hotel when the driver muttered, "Well, would you look at that."

I did. It was a man standing in the middle of the street with a shotgun in his hands. I decided at that moment to look for spare change on the cab's floor. As he drove past, the driver waved at the man, then asked if I was still in the back—he didn't want to be stiffed on the fare. I said I was, and I liked it fine down here on the floor. "Let me know when we arrive at the hotel." I added.

I needed to have a conversation with somebody about booking better hotels in better areas.

Crossing Borders

The U.S./Canada border in Detroit is a Port of Entry. It was possible to be stopped for inspections on both the U.S. and Canadian sides. There never was any problem driving my old van to and from Canada through Detroit, but with the rental truck it was always a problem—it was a whole different ball game, in fact.

Driving the van, I would stop on the U.S. side for the inspection. They always asked the same questions: Where are you going? Where are you staying? What is the purpose of your trip? How long will you be there? Show some ID. The U.S. Border agent would then peer inside the van and wave me on. On the Canadian side, I would be welcomed with, "Have a good day. Drive safely." And, "You are on your way."

After we began using rental trucks, the U.S. Border agents would still pull us to the side for inspection, ask the same questions, and I'd give the same answers I'd always given. The difference now was the agents had me empty out the truck. They watched me work and had a good time with each other laughing about it. When I finished, they walked to the truck, peered inside to make sure everything was out, and said, "Okay, load it up," without ever even checking anything.

I would reload the truck and drive to the Canadian side. The Canadian official would say, "Have a nice day. Drive safely," and wave at me as I drove past. Canadians are really nice people.

On one such border-crossing trip, Charlie and I were crossing from the Detroit side. As usual, we stopped and emptied out the truck. This time the U.S. Border agents searched the truck and the cab and found nothing concerning. We put everything back in the truck. Two hours passing through the U.S. side. Five minutes for the Canadian side.

As I was driving away Charlie commented, "That was close."

"What was close?"

"When we stopped on the U.S. side, they searched the cab."

"So?"

"Your camera," he said.

I always traveled with a camera. It was kept in a case with a strap to which I'd clipped little metal canisters of undeveloped film. The photos on the film were mostly of the group playing, and at play, and other groups that we played with. I'd also taken photographs of places we had been and scenery.

"I took the film out of the canisters and put my weed in them," Charlie confessed.

I sat quietly contemplating what would have happened if we had been caught at the border. A cold sweat dampened my shirt, but I was calm when I spoke.

"Charlie, please don't do that again. If we'd been caught, we would have done some serious jail time, and the truck and the equipment would have been confiscated."

I think I may have needed a change of underwear after that.

Dennis tells a story about when he and the band were stopped at the very same border crossing. They were ordered out of their vehicle and followed an agent to a large bare room. There were four concrete walls, a concrete floor, and a camera. The room was freezing cold. They were instructed to remove their clothes and the agent collected them. It would have made for a very funny scene: the five of them standing around in their underwear, except I imagine no one was laughing.

As this was going on, the agents were tearing the vehicle apart, even dismantling a tape recorder and leaving it for them to put back together. After what must have been an agonizing period of time, their clothes were returned, and they were free to go. "Have a nice day," they said. I made that part up.

After this experience, we traveled in the middle of the night whenever we could. Fifty miles away from Detroit, there was another border crossing into Canada. Those men would wave us across the border after telling us we were far from where we wanted to go and the Detroit crossing would be a lot closer. We would smile and say, "We don't mind."

Toronto

Alice Cooper had played the Varsity Stadium in Toronto the previous June at the Toronto Pop Festival, but their name didn't make it onto the poster. They were in the additional-groups-to-be-added-later classification. They were also disadvantaged by an early afternoon time slot, which meant no light show. The Revival would hand them the opportunity to be noticed.

The Toronto Rock'n'Roll Revival in September 1969 was going to be big, really big. This was Canada's first major festival, and was just one month after Woodstock.

The Revival was held at the Toronto Varsity Stadium, which had a capacity 21,700. Shep worked a deal that the band would play for free if they could perform right before John Lennon, and they would also back up Gene Vincent.

The groups performing were many, and eclectic: The Doors, Bo Diddley, Chuck Berry, Little Richard, Blood Sweat and Tears, Jerry Lee Lewis, Chicago, Gene Vincent, and Alice Cooper. John Lennon and the Plastic Ono Band with Eric Clapton would have their one and only performance together. This was going to be a really great concert.

After the carnage of the Alice Cooper Group's performance, Gene Vincent came on stage. I believe he was thinking, "What did I get myself into?" As Gene Vincent performed "Be Bop a Lula" the local biker group, the Vagabonds, who had provided John Lennon and The Doors with a multi-biker escort to the arena, stormed the stage and danced to the music, which was quite a sight. Thankfully, the bikers exited the stage right after the song.

The Alice Cooper group clearly understood that if they did well at the Toronto Rock'n'Roll Revival more bookings in large venues would follow. The group had worked many times in Canada, but at much smaller places and events. They were understandably nervous. This could be a very consequential show for the band.

We prepared for the show by packing several feather pillows and CO_2 fire extinguishers. A chicken would be arriving later. Alice, however, wanted something more, something special, but he didn't know what. Since we had arrived a few days early, I suggested we go out to see if we could find whatever it was that would be Alice's "something more."

The next day was drizzling and overcast, but the gloomy weather didn't stop us. Alice and I made our way downtown and wandered from store to store searching for whatever it was that Alice was looking for.

We stopped for lunch at a restaurant with a menu that boasted they specialized in Mexican food. Thinking of Arizona Mexican food, I ordered the chili. It was not quite what I expected or was used to back in Phoenix. Chili in Canada was served over white rice and covered with a melted cheese sauce—tasty but unusual. It also came with several slices of white bread. They apparently didn't know about tortillas. Canadians are so nice...at least they tried.

After lunch, we continued our search for that undefined something for Alice.

Eventually, we stumbled upon an army surplus store. Perhaps we'd find a Canadian flag to wave around. A little patriotism can go a long way. We rummaged through racks of clothes and pins and badges and swords—no more swords, I silently prayed. We looked at caps and belts and all manner of military paraphernalia.

I'm not sure who spotted it first: a Riggs military grade all steel flare gun. Its barrel was at least twelve inches long with a one and a quarter inch round opening. The powerful charge needed to fire a projectile with a parachute would likely knock Alice to the ground, I joked. We made a close inspection of it anyway. It was large. It was heavy, and Alice could probably fit his whole arm into the barrel.

"Do you have flares for it?" I asked the clerk.

"I do," he answered.

A quick side conference with Alice. He was enthused, enraptured even.

"What do you want to do with this thing?" I asked him.

"At the end of the show, I'll fire the gun, the flare goes up, explodes, and lights up the whole stadium," he said, his eyes gleaming.

His excitement was palpable. Judging by the size of the shell, I was pretty sure that it would do exactly what he envisioned. We bought it and three flares.

"You're going to have to shoot this before the show." I said, "You have to know what happens when you fire this thing."

I had no idea what would happen with a flare pistol, never having fired one. What I didn't mention was he would be firing a 12-gauge shotgun shell from a hand-held pistol, not like a rifle or shotgun braced against his shoulder.

When we returned to the hotel with the flare gun, everyone was excited and said it would be the showstopper. We waited until it was dark, after midnight in fact, to test the flare gun.

The constant rain discouraged us from going outside and we decided to shoot the gun from the hotel room window. There was a large park nearby, and the rain, we thought, would make a burning flare less of a hazard. Anyway, the clerk at the army surplus store said the flare would burn out before it hit the ground.

The overhang of the hotel roof posed a problem. Alice couldn't simply stick his arm out the window and fire. Everyone broke out their calipers and slide rules to work on the trajectory problem. The solution was to put Alice on his back and hang half his body out of the window. He would need to hold his arms straight out and over his head to fire the gun and clear the overhang. We calculated that the shell would fly up and over the park where the flare and parachute would deploy. A perfect solution.

In theory the plan worked, except for one hiccup.

"I'm not doing that," Alice said resolutely. "You guys aren't hanging me out a window to fire that thing." He was dead serious. He looked at me. "Mike, you do it."

I was hoping he meant Mike Bruce, but I hoped wrong. All eyes were turned toward me. I guess now would be a good time mention our room was on the sixth floor. I completely understood Alice's reluctance to being dangled out the window.

"You want me to do it?" I asked, hoping somehow I had misunderstood.

Well, actually it did make some sense. Because of my height, I wouldn't need to hang as far out of the window, my arms were longer, and I kind of knew what to expect from firing the flare gun.

Questioning if this fell under my job description, I unenthusiastically agreed.

I slid the window open and put a couple of pillows on the sill to cushion my lower back. I laid my shoulders on the pillows and wiggled out the window until the small of my back rested on the sill. Everyone grabbed a piece of me—feet, legs, belt—as I shimmied through the opening. When I felt I was in a good position to fire, Neal handed the flare gun to me, which caused me to ask why wasn't he doing this, he's tall? I took in a deep breath, tried to forget I was hanging out a six-story window, raised my arms, and aimed the gun to make sure the flare would not come close to the overhang, and fired.

The first thing I noticed was the kick from the flare gun wasn't that bad. I reckoned it was because my elbows were locked in place. I was aware of the noise, a white flash enveloping my arms, and a bright streak shooting into the night sky. And I wasn't hurt.

I shouted, "Pull me in! PULL ME IN!"

The flare had rocketed upward two or three hundred feet. When it exploded, bathing the whole area in a bright white light, I was certain that I didn't want to be seen hanging out a window with the gun in my hand. That's why I was yelling, "Pull me in."

A white luminescence lit the sky for several nerve-wracking minutes before the flare began its descent. Just before hitting the ground, the flare fizzled out and fell cleanly in the park.

Excited reviews came flooding in. That was great! This will be the hit of the show! People will be talking about this for a long time.

Truer words were never spoken.

The night of the show arrived. We were third in line to play. When the first group finished, the equipment was promptly removed, and the next group's equipment swiftly set up. Alice Cooper was now in second position. The extinguishers—we had two—were ready, and everyone knew where I'd stashed the pillows. One of us would not have a pillow tonight for their bed. At the right moment, the plan was for me to hand Alice the loaded flare pistol. Everything and everyone was prepared. The group ahead of us only needed to finish. History was about to be made.

I was standing on one side of the stage during the next group's performance. Out of the corner of my eye I caught a glimpse of Glen's Acoustic amplifier being carried off. I hustled across the stage but all the equipment, cords and lights crowded together made it difficult. The amp was gone by the time I got there. From my position, I spotted two people carrying it into the bowels of the stadium. I did not need this trouble. After having Glen's guitars and our amps stolen in New York City and L.A., I was not about to let this happen again.

The amp-stealing men steadily made their way deeper into the building. As I watched, I wondered if I needed to get help and, if I was able to get the amp back, would there be time to set it and the rest of the equipment up. I followed them and hurried around a corner chasing the men and the pilfered amplifier down a long corridor. I was experiencing a fight or flight moment. I chose to fight.

The men disappeared into a room at the end of the corridor. I could hear several people talking inside. Reaching the doorway, I demanded, "I want…" but stopped, stunned, in mid-sentence.

In front of me were eight people, including the two who had taken the amp. The one who caught my attention, though, was John Lennon. He was sitting on a bench with Yoko next to him. Band members and others stood around him. John had plugged his guitar into Glen's amp and was playing through it. Eric Clapton stood next to him, waiting his turn.

I brought my tone down substantially. "I'm sorry, but I need that amp back onstage. We're up next," I said, almost apologetically to John.

Everybody looked at John Lennon as he spoke. "Sorry, mate. I wanted to try one of these amps out, and I haven't had a chance yet."

All I heard was that John Lennon called me "mate."

"After Alice Cooper plays, I'll be happy to bring the amp back down for you," I offered.

"Not necessary. Sorry for the bother. These guys will put it back," John answered.

"Thank you," I said.

Then John added, "I'm sorry I caused you problems."

He seemed like a genuinely nice guy. I wished I could have stayed to talk with him, but I wouldn't have known what to say. It would have been another Mickey Mantle and Yogi Berra moment.

The amp was returned with fifteen minutes to spare and without further complications, though a considerable amount of adrenaline pumped through my body long after that. I couldn't wait to tell Glen, "I caught John Lennon playing through your amp!"

That would have to wait, though. This night was destined for rock and roll history.

It was our turn now. Workers were removing equipment from the stage and bringing ours on. I pointed where things were to be set down and made final adjustments. I paused to view the crowd. It was minutes to show time, and the stadium was packed with more than 20,000 people in seats and on the field. Everyone seemed to be having a good time. The area in the front of the stage had been roped off so children from local hospitals could see the show. They sat in wheelchairs with nurses and attendants nearby to care for them. That was a nice thing for the concert promoters to do.

The band emerged and took their positions. Alice had complete control of the stage. Charlie used white lights throughout the show and the outfits sewn by Cindy gleamed and glittered in the intense light. All the band members on stage were super animated, each one vying for the attention of the audience. Alice pitched pieces of watermelon that he'd smashed with a hammer off the stage and kicked a football far into the cheering crowd. Dennis prowled the stage, worrying me that I hadn't attached enough cord to his bass guitar. At one point Neal climbed a towering bank of the sound system's speaker cabinets, and they began to sway dangerously. Below the stage, nurses on the floor with the kids noticed and began moving the children back. Neal climbed higher, up to the top, and did his best King Kong impression. For a moment I pictured a police negotiator talking him down, but he dismounted on his own, delighting the kids and nurses. Neal, still in great-ape mode, re-enacted the scene from *2001: A Space Odyssey* when the apes see the monolith for the first time. At one point he leaped on Alice and they mock-fought, rolling and wrestling around the stage for several minutes. After Neal returned to his drums, Alice ripped open the pillows, releasing feathers onto the stage. Mike Bruce grabbed a CO_2 extinguisher and blew a blizzard of feathers into the audience. Then Alice brought out the chicken.

I will pause here to clear up this chicken myth. It has been said that Alice caught the chicken. He didn't. If a chicken had wandered onto the stage, he couldn't have caught it. Alice would have spent the better part of the night trying to, and without success. Chickens have moves that would make a basketball player envious. It has also been written that Alice bit the head off the chicken and drank its blood. That never happened. If Alice had put his face close to an angry or terrified chicken, it would have been a very bad day for Alice--a very, very bad day. A terrible day he would remember for the rest of his life: the same thoughts repeating over, and over: *Why did I try to bite the head off that chicken? What was I thinking? If I had been raised in North Dakota, this never would have happened.*

This chicken was a Leghorn. A Leghorn can be seven pounds of pecking fury when it's angry. I hope you had a good life, because your hours were numbered. It was more likely if Alice hadn't tossed the chicken into the audience, the chicken would have tossed him. Also, chickens can fly. However, they don't do it well. They can fly vertically about ten feet, and maybe a distance of twenty or thirty feet. An interesting fact about this chicken was that it was a citizen of Canada. It was not imported from the U.S. The last thing I wanted was to get in trouble with the Agriculture Department for bringing undocumented poultry into the country. Those guys can be mean.

Alice tossed the chicken with an underhanded throw into the audience. This is true. Alice might manage to toss the chicken as far as the front rows where the nurses and the children in wheelchairs were. A bunch of crazed nurses jumping on the chicken and tearing it to shreds is doubtful, however. On the other hand, if the chicken flew high enough to get air under its wings it could travel further into the audience. The chicken was not torn apart by the crowd and the pieces thrown back on the stage—Canadians were far too nice for that.

Here's what I witnessed from my position on the stage. Alice tossed the chicken. It flew a good distance into the crowd, where a guy caught it and tucked it safely under his arm. He probably took it home and named it after a hockey player or after Foster Hewitt, the famous play by play commentator.

The time had arrived for the show's climactic conclusion. I brought out the flare gun and laid it on the designated spot atop an amplifier.

Alice grabbed the loaded gun as the last of the feathers fell on the crowd. He swaggered across the stage for a few minutes brandishing the gun. The extinguishers were empty. The music stopped. Everyone held their position. Suddenly, Alice moved to center stage, stepped forward, raised the flare gun above his head and fired.

The flare exploded from the gun narrowly missing the stage's overhanging canopy. It rocketed 300 feet into the sky bursting into a spectacular bright orange then sparkling white light. A collective OOOH! rose from the crowd. The audience tilted their heads back to watch the dazzling display and began yelling, whistling, and pointing. The burst had illuminated the entire stadium.

As the glowing burning orb hurtled toward Earth, the audience's delighted OOOHs! abruptly turned into panicked OHs! The parachute hadn't opened. It had been incinerated in the orange explosion and the white-hot flare was coming down fast.

It appeared that most of the concertgoers had advanced knowledge of math and physics, because they rapidly calculated the downward trajectory and retreated outward, forming a perfect twenty-foot circle around the projected landing zone. The fiery ball hit the circle dead center, bounced once, and stopped. A lumberjack-looking guy marched over and stomped it with his heavy boot, snuffing out the flare. He raised his arms in victory.

A deafening silence followed as 20,000 plus concertgoers tried to assimilate what they had just experienced. The concert announcer made his way onstage through overturned drums and microphone stands, fire extinguishers, feathers, and remnants of the smashed watermelon. He finally located a partially working microphone and spoke into it.

"Alice Cooper, everyone. ALICE COOPER! WHAT THE HECK WAS THAT!"

Then it happened. The silence was broken by an explosion, not literally, but figuratively, of pure joy. The crowd went nuts. They cheered wildly and yelled and stomped and jumped up and down. It was just great. The pandemonium might have been heard all the way to Detroit.

I leaned over the edge of the stage to look at the children and nurses who had come for the show. They were completely engulfed in wet sticky feathers. And they loved it. The children were giggling uncontrollably, and the nurses laughed at each other while trying to pluck wet feathers from their starched white uniforms, feathers clinging to their fingers as they worked. They would have quite a story to tell when they returned to the hospital. Their excitement was a joyous sight to behold.

Try following that, next groups up. Good luck. Who were the next groups? Oh right. John Lennon and the Plastic Ono Band with Eric Clapton, followed by The Doors. I think they'll do just fine. Before they could start, though, it took over an hour to clean up the pieces of watermelon and other debris left on the stage. Just before John Lennon came out, the Revival promoter had the stadium lights turned down and asked the audience to welcome to him with lit matches and lighters. It was the first time this tribute was ever given. John was visibly moved by it.

The show was a spectacular PR success. Everyone was talking about the Alice Cooper group's performance. By the next day it seemed all of Toronto had either seen it or knew about it. The events of the night had taken on a life of their own. The Alice Cooper show topped discussions on Toronto's radio and TV stations and was reviewed both in local and national newspapers. Radio stations that hosted call-in programs encouraged listeners who witnessed the show to call and let everyone know what they thought of it. Fans as well as shocked and outraged parents voiced their opinion. One caller reportedly said she was afraid for her children and meant to keep them home until Alice Cooper left town, which was the next day when we headed to Toledo for just another ordinary show. That Toledo show is not to be confused with their 1973 show where a riot broke out forcing the band to hastily exit the stage for their own safety. Fortunately for me, I wasn't there for that one. Unfortunately for them, they were.

The Toronto chicken incident developed as rumors of dismemberment grew exponentially, and rated highly on all news platforms. To this day it is a popular topic when discussing Alice Cooper legends. Recognizing a PR bonanza, Joey and Shep shamelessly promoted the story wherever and whenever they could. Frank Zappa, when he heard what they'd done, told the band, "Deny nothing." If the Alice Cooper group had intended to garner attention—job impressively done. In my mind it was, and still is, one of the greatest visual shows I've ever seen.

Sadly, this was the last time that the flare gun was used while I was with the group. We acknowledged that it was a dangerous prop, and employing it at the Toronto Rock'n'Roll Revival could have had a very different ending. I stored it away in the trunk with the cords and microphones, and smaller props. There was a single flare left.

The flare gun was used only once more that I know of. It was at the Hollywood Bowl concert in July 1972. I was no longer working for Alice Cooper. Neal kept the flare gun and has it in his personal collection.

Success, they say, doesn't happen overnight, unless you're an overnight success. And that overnight success might take years. Toronto was a start. A very good start. The best start.

After all the years and shows where audiences literally walked out of their performances and music magazines and newspapers carried negative reviews, it was an intoxicating feeling. At last, it appeared their fortunes were destined for change.

Toronto, with the performance, the chicken, feathers, CO_2 extinguishers, and the flare exploding over 20,000 people, would transform the band. But not right away. It would still take time. And my time was coming to an end.

We stayed on the east coast. Alice Cooper played in New York, Boston, and Philadelphia. In Philadelphia for a show with MC5, I was an hour-and-a-half late because of traffic. The trip started out fine, until we entered the Holland Tunnel. There had been an accident, and for once I wasn't involved. We were stuck, and because people hadn't turned off their engines, oxygen was being rapidly replaced with deadly carbon monoxide. The atmosphere inside the van was suffocating. I rolled down my window hoping the air outside the truck would be better. I was completely wrong. It was much worse. There were dozens of horns honking and desperate shouts to turn off engines.

Charlie and I felt nauseated, dizzy, and headachy. Finally, after more than twenty minutes being trapped in the tunnel, traffic started to move. We were thankful to be out—I really believed we were in serious trouble. As soon as I could, I pulled off the road and shut the motor off. We stumbled out of the truck coughing to clear the carbon monoxide from our lungs. Thirty minutes later we were feeling better, but our headaches persisted for a few hours.

Being delayed on the road was always a concern when there were back-to-back shows in different cities. New York to Philadelphia was less than a hundred miles, but it had taken more than four hours. Shep was agitated and annoyed. He tried convincing MC5 to go on first, but no dice. He waited for us in the parking lot.

"Where have you been?" he angrily demanded. "You're late."

I had a few snappy replies, but I didn't take the time to say them. I drove the truck inside the building and threw the equipment on the stage. Pressed to get set up, Joey and Shep helped. I should have taken pictures of that. All's well that ends well, I suppose.

After the Alice Cooper group performed, we drove back to New York City to our hotel. In the sixties, the Chelsea Hotel was the place to be seen: The Doors, Jimi Hendrix, Janis Joplin, Pink Floyd, and others had stayed there. The Chelsea was famous not only for who stayed, but also for who died in its rooms. It was where Sid Vicious murdered his girlfriend. The rooms were ok. There were porno magazines in the drawers. We had reading material if we were bored.

2-12-1970 1:00 a.m.

Dear Ellen,

This is our last night in New York City, then it's off to Detroit. We're beginning to play in Detroit as much as the VIP Club in Phoenix. Something exciting did happen while we were here. The police towed away my U-Haul truck. I had parked on the wrong side of the street at the wrong time. All it took was money and I got the truck back. Unfortunately, my cameras and film were missing. Never to be seen again. Now, I will have nothing to show you of our adventures when we get back to Phoenix.

After Detroit: the battle of the century, when two forces oppose each other for the title of where we will live: Phoenix or Buffalo. Why Buffalo? I have no idea. On the Buffalo side is the threesome of Alice, Glen, and Neal. On the Phoenix side, Mike Bruce, Dick, and myself. Charlie and Dennis don't seem to care—they would make the best of it no matter where they are. For that matter, so will everybody else. It's in our nature.

From what you sounded like over the phone, nothing too much is happening in Phoenix. Well, when I come back (positive thinking) every night will be dining and dancing till dawn. Sounds exciting right? Of course, there will be the usual movies and long drives to nowhere and back. I know how much you like long drives and movies.

It was nice talking to you, no matter what you say to frustrate me. It will never work, you know. I'm solid as a rock, and nobody trips me up. You should know that by now. Relaxed, that's my style.

I will let you know what's happening when I know.

Love,
Mike

Billboard from 1968

Truck Towed

There were a couple of theaters across the street from the Chelsea. Performances were in the evening, so parking after our shows was always at a premium. On certain nights, vehicles were required to be moved from one side of the street to the other for the street sweeper. I was forced to wait until the theater-goers and their cars left before I could move the U-Haul.

Unfortunately, one night I fell asleep before I could do that. Sleep was a rare commodity when you were on the road, and exhaustion was a frequent reality. In the morning, I looked out the window and the U-Haul was gone. I dressed quickly and in a panic bolted down the stairs to the front desk. I told the clerk that my truck was parked outside, and it was missing.

He said, "Yes. The police had it towed away."

Exasperated, I asked, "Why didn't somebody wake me?"

"Because they didn't know which room you were in. They left you this ticket and the address of the impound yard where your truck was towed. Just go down there and pay the fine and towing fee to get it back."

So, I went. With the fine, towing charge, and storage the bill was over $120 in 1969 money. To us that was a fortune. I paid the bill and checked the back of the truck. All the equipment was accounted for. That was good, and somewhat surprising. Back at the Chelsea, which was fast losing its appeal, I parked the truck in the proper location. It took another day for me to realize what was wrong. My still camera and an 8mm movie camera that I used to chronicle the band, their shows, who they played with, and things we did on the road was missing. I kept the cameras, along with all the movies and photographs, in a small suitcase. Some of the film was developed, some was not, and now it was all gone. The suitcase had been stolen.

Many of my favorite photographs and films were taken in 1968. One was of a billboard, a picture of a guy with an insolent smile, and unkempt not-too-long but needing to be washed hair. The message was, "Beautify America—Get a Haircut." I had taken several still-photos of the group standing beneath the sign, and a movie of them jumping up and down and throwing rocks and dirt at it à la the apes in *2001: A Space Odyssey*. I also had some other snippets of film, mostly of the group and other bands they performed with: The Doors, The Byrds, The Who, Ike and Tina Turner, Pink Floyd, Chicago, and of course Alice Cooper, and others. The list was endless. There were irreplaceable photos and film of the Alice Cooper group at our different residences just being normal people. Normal for them, anyway.

I phoned the towing and storage lot that had the truck. The guy I talked to said he would ask around about the cameras. He called back after a few minutes—nobody had seen them. The police may have them, he said, and suggested I call them. I knew that was going to be a waste of time. Whoever took the case probably just wanted the cameras and threw the pictures and film away. Even now, writing this and remembering it after all these years, it makes me sick.

I never felt sad about getting out of New York City. One time I left the hotel around 4:00 in the morning to get a jump on wherever I was headed next. The dirty streets were depressing and dark. Dim bulbs lit the doorways and stairwells of the apartment buildings I passed. Standing under the lights were ladies dressed in bright-colored sequined miniskirts or dresses, their hair and makeup all done up. Some had feather boas draped around their neck and a few wore long white evening gloves.

Now, that's something you don't see every day, I thought. One or two waved half-heartedly as I drove by, while others stood like statues or leaned against the grimy walls. It took me a few minutes to realize the women were not from the Chamber of Commerce to wish me a pleasant journey and thank me for visiting New York. They were ladies of the night, or early morning, prepared to go to work. I wanted to take their pictures, but I didn't have my cameras anymore.

> Spurlock, James. "Alice Cooper is, like, strange."
> *Chicago Daily News,* May 22, 1969
>
> *Alice Cooper was a witch who committed suicide when she was 13 some 200 years ago. Reincarnated as a male, he is now the lead singer for the rock group of the same name.*
>
> *Alice explains all this to you while throwing in a story of how he and his group were once chased out of a Western town by beer-bottle-throwing cowboys who kept up the chase for 20 miles.*

The Alice Cooper group was now known throughout the United States and Canada and their popularity continued to grow. We were bouncing from New York to Chicago to Detroit to Seattle to Portland to Eugene to San Francisco to Detroit to Chicago in a continuous circuit. On every trip I loaded up the equipment, took it to the airport, drove to the luggage cart, paid a skycap, and returned the truck. Most nights, I headed back to the airport until flight time, and stretched out on a couple of chairs in a mostly futile attempt to sleep. In the morning I'd catch the flight and repeat the whole process over and over again. I was tired. I think the term is "burned out."

On December 31, 1969 we found ourselves back in Toronto for a New Year's Eve show. The show would go on until after midnight. One minute before, Alice started the countdown. At the strike of twelve the Alice Cooper group was to play *Auld Lang Syne*. I was onstage but off to one side when the countdown reached one. Alice shouted, "Happy New Year!" and the song began. I felt a tap on my shoulder and turned to see who was tapping. It was a girl with shortish blonde hair wearing a one-piece body-hugging black jumpsuit with lots of zippers. It reminded me of Mrs. Peele's costume on *The Avengers*. The girl grabbed me around the neck, pulled my head down, and kissed me. At first, I thought she must have mistaken me for someone else. That would be embarrassing for her. Maybe she just wanted to kiss someone at the stroke of midnight. The kiss went on for fifteen seconds. Okay, I thought, it's time to wrap this up—I like to be courted first. I tried to separate my face from hers, but she was having none of it. The kiss kept going. Thirty seconds, then one minute. I opened my eyes to see what was going on. The audience was raptly watching the kiss marathon. Even the band members were looking at me, giving me a thumbs up. *When is this girl going to stop?* I wondered.

As soon as the band finished, the kissing ended. There was thunderous applause. I don't know if it was for me and the girl, the band, or for the start of a new year and a new decade. She stepped back, placed her hand on my chest, and said, "I will see you later." I didn't know when or where this later was supposed to be. My plan was to load the equipment and head back to the hotel room for some sleep. We were staying over an extra day because of a flight schedule and I didn't need to get to the airport.

I didn't see her again. Well, that's not entirely true. I saw the one-piece jumpsuit later that night when Mike came down to my room. He was wearing it. The jumpsuit looked much better on the blonde. Poor girl. She must have gotten tired of waiting for me and settled for Mike Bruce. At least that's what I told myself.

We finally returned to Los Angeles only to discover we were no longer living at the Quebec house. Joey and Shep had rented new places: three apartments on Ivar Street in a decrepit two-story building overlooking the Hollywood freeway. It was close to the Hollywood Hills and our old house, but not close enough. Being adjacent to the freeway offered a great view of the traffic, if you liked that sort of thing. The noise and noxious odor of vehicle exhaust did nothing to improve the situation, and simply opening a window was not the best idea. To sum it up, these rooms were depressing, and not just for me.

Everyone understood the reason behind our frequent moves: it was money. Even though the band had income, it went into a pot to keep us afloat, and barely that. Everything we did: rent on a house we only used part-time, hotel rooms, food, airline tickets, rental trucks, taxis, material for Cindy to sew new clothes, guitar strings, etc. drained our meager bank account. The list was infinite. Money was spent faster than it could be made. A lot of the time we walked around with nothing but the loose change in our pockets, if we were lucky. A salary—for any of us—was on semi-permanent hold. Even the promise of a salary was some nebulous future date. Being in a band, or working for a band, was a financially unfavorable prospect unless you made it big. And we had bet our futures on making it.

Mendelsohn, John. "Alice Cooper Is Cruel, Man! Tarzan, Chickens & monkey semen. Is this the future of rock and roll?" *Entertainment World,* 2/20/1970, page 9

The music, or its facsimile, having reached a deafening peak, Alice drops his microphone and begins dashing about, throwing into the now-madly-undulating audience what appear to be cardboard boxes and live, screaming chickens. He attacks a life-size female mannequin with a hammer, and then tosses the hammer, too, into the crowd. His bass player falls writhing stage-center, from which position he pounds out cascades of thundering bass chords. The two guitarists throw tennis balls at one another's instruments, filling the air with oceans of distortion, and then one unleashes a high-pressure fire extinguisher, first on his fellows and then on the audience, which is by this time beside itself with frenzied excitement and bewilderment.

21

The Death of Amp Boy

When we moved into the three separate apartments on Ivar Street in Hollywood, the loss of our sense of family was insidious. We still worked together but when we returned to Los Angeles we went to our shabby little apartments and stared at the freeway traffic through dirty windows. No more meals together. No more camaraderie or conversations late into the night. No more van to take us to the Sunset Strip just to hang out or have our pictures taken by tourists on buses. No more walking together to the Supply Sergeant to browse the merchandise, or stopping next door at Frederick's of Hollywood to be enticed by the girls who modeled the latest skimpy apparel. No trips to the Farmer's Market for fresh, hot bread, sitting together on the curb eating and watching people go by. No more listening to music at the clubs on Hollywood Blvd.

It simply ceased to be fun anymore. I knew they were going to make it. Toronto had shown me that. It was just a matter of time. We'd been together for nearly five years.

But our life together was at its end.

One important reason for my decision to leave was a credit card. My dad had given me a gasoline credit card, so I'd always have gas to get home, he said. The card was in his name, and the bills were sent to me. I would pass them to Dick or Joey or Shep, who were supposed to pay them. However, money was so tight Joey and Shep weren't, and my dad was getting collection notices. The gasoline bill by this time was over $2,000. The stress and guilt for the overdue bills was getting to me. I made the decision to leave the band and return to Phoenix to find a job so I could take care of that obligation. I didn't want to leave—these guys were my closest friends, my brothers— but I felt a responsibility to pay the debt and not burden my father any longer.

I confided to Glen what I intended doing. He asked me not to go. "Talk to Joey and Shep. Stay at least until the bill is paid," he said. I told Glen that I had already done that and they'd promised to take care of it. I didn't really blame them. They were paying bills as best they could manage. I blamed myself for using the credit card for every station wagon, van, and truck the band ever used. I cut up the card. Too little, too late.

I left all my worldly possessions with our friend Norma Greene from the séance, mostly my record albums. I owned two *The Beatles Yesterday and Today* albums with the butcher coat cover. Boy, I wish I had hung on to those. I also left a set of deer horns, and an antique clock which I later wrote to her about, and she sent it back to me. My possessions didn't really amount to much.

I don't remember if or how I said goodbye to the group, but I must have. I must have told Joey or Shep, because they needed to replace me. I don't remember how I got back to Phoenix—if I flew, took a bus, or someone drove me home.

I moved back into my dad's house for a while. He had remarried, and his new wife made it painfully clear I was not welcome and should leave sooner rather than later, a point she frequently brought to my attention. I told her I planned to comply with her demands as soon as I could.

With Ellen's help I found a place to rent and a new roommate. I was as happy to leave dad's house as his new wife was to see me go. After a few months my roommate Joe moved out, and another one moved in, who was found, again, by Ellen. His name was Mike, an easy name for me to remember. Now I only needed two things, a job and a car to get me to the job. I had saved a little money from the accident insurance claim. It amounted to about $1,500. $1,500 to start a new life. It could be worse, I thought.

My share of the apartment's rent was only $55 a month, but I still needed a car. One day I spotted it sitting in a used car lot. Fate brought it in the form of a red 1955 Jaguar XK 140 convertible. It didn't have a top—just the frame for one—or windows or air-conditioning, but it was mine, and the price was $800. Was it practical for Arizona? Not even close, but just look at it. It was beautiful. I paid $400 down and floated a loan from my dad for the rest. Thankfully, he didn't mention that to his new wife.

Now, all I needed was a job. I perused the newspaper's help wanted section—not much work for this 23 year old used-up Amp Boy. Eventually, I found a job for pizza delivery for a restaurant called Pizza Man. Their slogan was, "He delivers." I had a car and I had a job. It was a start, anyway.

Perhaps the best news of all came next. When I called Joey, he said they had taken care of the credit card bill, and my dad would be notified. I thanked him over and over again. Joey asked if I wanted to come back. I almost took him up on his offer, but my life was beginning to slowly turn around.

My 1955 Jaguar XK 140

Ellen Mitchell and me
at my 24th birthday

I didn't feel that delivering pizza in a Jaguar was meant to be my life's work and decided to look for another job. I had a car, a job, and no bills to pay other than my own. I was reconnecting with Ellen. My life kept getting better.

Ellen would be graduating soon from nursing school. I thought maybe I should look at something in the medical field. I tried bluffing my way into a job at a couple of hospitals, telling them I had been an orderly at one time. They saw right through me and sent me on my way. One helpful person suggested I apply at the Maricopa County Hospital—they will take anybody, she said. I went, and it was true. They took me, even sending me to classes for two weeks so I would know at least a little about hospital work. After finishing, I learned the director of the Emergency Room had requested me to work with them. Requested? Why would anybody request me? I really didn't know anything. But I went to the ER making $1.81 per hour. Delivering pizzas paid more.

On my first day in the ER, it became clear why they were so eager to have me. Maricopa County Hospital was a busy place, and the ER was the busiest. Most of the patients didn't want to be there, but there were also some who actually needed and wanted our help. There were regular old drunks and drunks who had been in car wrecks brought in by the police. Psych patients, heart attacks, drug overdoses, and those with an assortment of injuries, gunshot wounds, stabbings, and broken bones rolled through the doors.

The charge nurse explained the requirements of the job: hold patients down by any means necessary so they can be examined.

The ER was run by interns, residents, and an attending MD, but especially by the nurses. The doctors were learning, except for the attending physician, who was looking forward to retirement. If someone needed help or advice, they went to the nurses, who were efficient and cool under fire. Most days it was like working in a Mash unit. Many of the nurses had served in the military, so it was a fitting description. They, meaning the nurses, got the patients in, and they got them out. He/she goes to psych. He/she goes to surgery. He/she needs a medical consult. He/she needs a cast. He/she needs to go to the morgue. It was amazing to witness and be a part of. I acquired a new-found respect for the medical profession and especially for nurses.

The County hospital was made up of a bunch of Quonset huts situated over several acres in south Phoenix. They were rumored to be leftovers from the Japanese internment camp in Arizona from the Second World War. Except for the ICU, the buildings barely had heat and no air-conditioning. The wards used evaporative coolers, fans, and screen doors for ventilation. The entire hospital setup was pretty primitive. Example: after an operation the patient was moved on a gurney from the surgery building to their ward. This meant they were pushed outside into the heat, cold, dust storm, or rain on broken-concrete sidewalks to their assigned Quonset hut. Pushing and maneuvering a gurney was akin to pushing a shopping cart with a bad wheel and there was an occasional but inevitable accident. The pediatric ward's playground, which consisted of only a sandbox, was directly across from the morgue. Children watched as bagged bodies were wheeled in and out. It was quite a hospital.

The Burn Unit was one of the most depressing places. The stench of burnt flesh was overpowering, the pain those patients endured unimaginable. The nursing staff, though, was excellent, and they did their best with what they had, which wasn't much. The pay was lousy, and the work was hard.

Here are just a few of my experiences as an orderly working in the Emergency Room. Because there was no air conditioning in the ER, or in the wards for that matter, and not even a window in the ER, summer was particularly brutal for both staff and patients. One day a local company donated a very large industrial fan to help with cooling. The maintenance department constructed a wooden box with a chicken-wire screen to contain the fan and serve as protection from huge blades. At least that was the idea. They proudly arrived with the fan in its new box, as the grateful staff waited in excited expectation. The fan was plugged in and the blades began to turn, slowly at first, then faster and faster until the fan, with a tremendous roar, literally took off.

The vibration and wind it produced destroyed the box frame in seconds. Free of the cage, it shot through the ER with its blades spinning wildly. With each rotation, the blades crashed into the linoleum floor, causing the fan to jump and skitter across the room in every direction. Everyone, myself included, vaulted onto tables or patient's beds seeking to escape certain bodily harm. As I fled the deadly blades, I snatched a nearby chair and threw it at the fan. This only seemed to anger it, and the fan continued its threatening chaotic path through the ER. Only one thing saved the staff from being sliced to pieces by the runaway fan. The movement of the fan eventually stretched the electrical cord to its limit, and it pulled out of the outlet and slowly came to a stop. Humiliated, the men from the maintenance department gathered up the pieces and said they would work on it. Someone sarcastically remarked, "Take your time."

One night I was working in the ER when the police brought in an extremely large man for a psych evaluation. He had picked up his father and thrown him through a plate glass window. The man was handcuffed and taken into custody after being forcibly subdued. In the ER, he was put in a bed and the curtains were drawn around him. The overhead lights were turned off. The police must have taken a lot of the fight out of him, because he was pretty compliant at that point. The officers filled out their paperwork, retrieved their handcuffs, and left.

Almost immediately the cubicle came alive when the man simply got out of the bed and proceeded to tip it over. Then, he broke through the curtain defense and stood dazed and confused, staring at us, or at nothing.

The intern on-call blurted out, "Mike, take him!"

I thought, take him where? He's angry. Really, really angry. Not to mention really, really big.

The all-hands-on-deck alarm sounded, which brought a lot of people, mostly women, to help. The nurses tried to calm him while the rest of us kept one eye out as we tied several sheets together. Another person and I grabbed the tails of the sheets, which we had fashioned into a long rope, and we went at him crisscrossing behind and in front wrapping him up like a mummy. Several others rushed over then to wrestle him to the floor. He was angry and indignant at his present situation and made it known he would never come back as nurses holding syringes filled with sedatives approached. Soon he would be very happy, and so would we.

The hospital cafeteria was an interesting place where hot food and cold sandwiches wrapped in plastic could be had at reasonable prices.

Those sandwiches might have been in a refrigerated display case for weeks, possibly even years, who knew? This was way before the era of food expiration dating. The food, or its age, was not the pressing issue, though it sure should have been. The real worry was the large construction type trash bin that sat smack in the middle of the cafeteria. Diners were instructed to throw their garbage into the bin and set the tray on a nearby table.

Everyone who ate in the cafeteria was familiar with the bin. This included rodents, who could be heard scampering around inside searching for their own piece of the pie, literally. The neighborhood's feral cats were well-acquainted with the mice-delights in the bin and would jump in hunting for their own slice, so to speak. When a cat plunged into the bin, the mice leaped out, chased immediately by the cat. The cat and mouse raced through the cafeteria, dodging under tables and sprinting into the kitchen and back out. Dinner and a show. You just can't beat it. The animal cast presented three performances a day to shrieking-room-only staff and visitors.

One afternoon, a surgeon asked me to speak with a patient's family waiting outside the OR. I was to tell them the surgery had gone well and they could go in and visit when a nurse called them. I don't know if it was fatigue, or what, but I said, "He's doing fine, and you can come and visit him after the autopsy." They gasped and looked stricken. I quickly realized what I'd said and, after apologizing, corrected myself. It was time to find a new job.

I began taking notice of a group of hospital employees who always seemed to be sitting on a bench outside the ER eating ice cream.

I asked a coworker, "What do they do?"

"They are respiratory therapists."

I signed up for classes the next day. Before class started, the hospital's respiratory therapy staff showed me what they actually did. After a few weeks of instruction, I was a respiratory therapy tech making $4.50 an hour. I was rich! Two years later I would graduate from the Phoenix College respiratory therapy program and earn close to seven dollars an hour as a registered tech. I felt I knew how a Rockefeller must feel.

I went to Ellen's graduation from nursing school. I was very proud of her. I probably kept that to myself. At the close of the graduation ceremony, the class sang *Leaving on a Jet Plane*. A strange song for graduation, I thought, but I hadn't chosen the music. It turned out to be a perfect song for Ellen. Immediately after graduation she left for a three-week trip to San Francisco, coming back for her exams before leaving again to work at a kid's camp in Prescott, Arizona. She went off to Guadalajara, Mexico for another month after camp ended. "I will write," she said.

In early October she returned to Phoenix, and there was much rejoicing. She took a job in a hospital, but after eighteen months she and her sisters departed for Europe for a six-month long adventure. It was the trip of a lifetime. I wished her well, said I would miss her, and I would write. When she came home, there was much rejoicing.

I was working full-time by then and going to school full-time. She was also working full-time, so there wasn't much chance to see each other. I called her up for a date when I had a day off. Usually, though, she couldn't go because of work, or she was doing something else.

One night she came to my place while I was getting ready for work. I worked nights, and went to school during the day.

I said, "This is a pleasant surprise, but I have to leave for work pretty soon." She was standing on the porch, I hadn't invited her in yet.

I don't remember how the exact conversation went, but it was something like this:

"I need to talk to you." she said. "I'm moving to Seattle next week."

Stunned, I asked, "Do you mind if I ask why?"

"Do you really want to know?"

"Yes."

She hesitated for a moment then said, "I'm in love with someone else."

I felt sick. I don't know what I said in response. I was completely shocked, hurt, and devastated. I didn't feel anger, just overwhelming sadness. I tried to think what I could have done wrong. I knew that when I had called to ask her out, she would say she couldn't, and maybe we could get together some other time. It took a while for it to sink in, she had been seeing somebody else.

I couldn't grasp what I'd just heard. I just nodded my head and started to cry. She teared up. She came inside and we sat on the floor and talked and cried for more than an hour. I called work and told them I would be late.

I told Ellen that I didn't know what I would do without her. "Let's be friends and write to each other," she said. "You'll be alright."

She left. She'd left for good, and I got ready for work. I was in pain but did my job. When I finished my shift, I found an empty treatment room and curled up in a fetal position on the examination table. I remained there a long while. It was a very rough time.

We wrote back and forth a few times. It only made things worse for me. I knew I had to get on with my life and move on. Finally, I sent a letter telling her I didn't want to write anymore. Have a good life and goodbye. And that was it.

I would graduate from respiratory school, make $7 an hour, and move on. I thought about leaving town and taking a job in another state. But realized she had already moved, so what was the point? I really was a broken toy at this point in my life.

Months passed. I finally had a good talking-to with myself. She's gone. Get over it. You work in a hospital where there are seven females to every male. The odds are in your favor. Take advantage of the situation. I did. I started dating again, but I would only go out on two or three dates then move on. I guess I had trust issues, abandonment issues, rejection issues, or commitment issues. If there was an issue with a name, I probably had it.

There were dozens of single doctors at the hospital, and they had great parties. I went to every one I could to hang out and meet people. I still had the Jaguar. I bought a Volkswagen camper van for party trips to Mexico and camping trips. It was supposed to be my rebirth, but I didn't feel like I had been reborn.

There was one girl who I liked, not because she liked me, but because she didn't. She told me she only had weekends free to go on dates, and she wanted to make them special, with somebody else, if possible. That was fine with me. At least she was honest. I think I see anger there. We would meet up at night after work in the hospital parking lot and make out in my car or van. We even went out a couple of times—when she didn't have a date with that "special someone." At the time she was perfect for me: she didn't care for me, and I didn't care for her. She was looking for a doctor, and I was looking to keep from making a commitment. We would see each other at parties and acknowledge each other, but that was about it. It was a perfect non-relationship. I felt comfortable seeing other people, at least three dates worth, and she felt the same.

It had been just about sixteen months since Ellen left. One night there was a knock at my door. I opened it to see Ellen standing on the other side. It was good to see her again, but I knew she was probably in town for just a few days of vacation. I thought she only wanted to check on me and tell me how wonderful her life was. I was quite prepared to lie about mine. "It's great, going great." Instead, what she said, well the condensed version anyway, was the guy she loved and had moved to Seattle for was a jerk. She'd had enough of his abuse and was moving back to Phoenix.

"I called your roommate to see if you were dating anyone. He said not at the moment. I got up the courage to come see you," she said.

My roommate had told her, "He goes out on a lot of dates with a lot of different girls, but no one serious." She asked him if he thought I'd like to see her. He said he thought I would.

"If he doesn't want to see me, stand in the street and wave me by," she'd told him.

That night when I got home from work his car was not in the driveway. This worried her, but Ellen took a chance and knocked on my door. I remembered he had also been gone the night she'd left. I invited her in.

Ellen and I talked for a long time, into the early morning hours, about what I'm not certain. Her life and mine, I suppose. I remember she asked me a question. I replied, "You look old." What I'd meant to say is, "You look tired." But I'd said, "You look old." Had I meant to say that on purpose to hurt her, or had I said it accidentally?

Ellen said she was miserable with the guy in Seattle.

"You're not the only one who dealt with a devastating breakup," I said angrily. "I don't want to hear how miserable you are." That was totally unlike me.

Years after, she told me I had shocked her. I had never before spoken to her angrily or critically. It made her think about me in a different light.

Later, as I walked her to the car, she asked another question that I don't remember. I only hugged her, kissed her on the top of her head, and said, "You'll be fine."

She left to go to her parent's house. I went inside confused about what had happened. A girl I once loved had come back to Phoenix, and then had come to see me. Did she want to get back together, and why would I want to get back together with her? She could see another shiny object and be gone the next week, or tomorrow. I could not go through that again.

My old trust issues and fear of rejection resurfaced. I had gotten comfortable with my new normal, but I also wanted someone in my life. Over the next week we saw each other a few more times. On the last night before she left for Seattle to pack up, I walked Ellen to her car. We talked for a few more minutes then I put my arms around her, and I kissed her.

"I'm glad you're coming home," I said.

I was thinking about going back to school. I was thinking about anesthesia as a career—that would take more years of school, and all the schools were out of state. If we started seeing each other, would Ellen follow me, as she had followed the other guy? I didn't know, but there was only one way to find out.

Ellen moved home to Phoenix three weeks later. We got back together, each of us unsure of the other and ourselves. It was the biggest gamble I had ever taken. If she left me again, I knew I could never survive it. I would have given up like the people I saw sleeping on the streets in L.A.

I started school again. Ellen and I were good together. A year after she returned we bought a house. I sold my Jaguar to help with the down payment. We were married in March of 1976. Family and friends surrounded us on the altar—Ellen was afraid that I'd make a break for it, and she had everyone form a human chain. I was nervous, but I survived it. I may have even enjoyed it.

We didn't have much time off from work and school, so we honeymooned in Prescott, Arizona. Ellen's family had a cabin there. We arrived on a Sunday in the late afternoon to find the water pipes in the cabin were frozen solid. We couldn't stay in a place without running water, so we drove into Prescott to find a hotel. The only place open was the historic Hassayampa Inn. It had been a hotel, but was a retirement home now. Back then we called them old folks' homes.

Our wedding day 1976

The clerk felt sorry for us and showed us a room in a newly remodeled, but not quite finished wing. Just a few of the rooms were ready, but they were set up only to show potential residents, he said. We took the room even though it smelled of paint. The clerk handed me a key to the side door of the hotel to use if we went out to eat—they locked the doors after 9:00 p.m. to keep residents from wandering off. As we settled in, we discovered there was no heat and there weren't any blankets for the bed. I went to the front desk and told the clerk about the heat situation. He guessed the furnace had not been connected in that wing yet.

"I do have that," he said, pointing to a large alpaca rug that hung over the lobby fireplace.

He took it down and I carried it upstairs to show Ellen. That rug must have weighed fifty pounds. We definitely wouldn't be cold.

Years later I came to understand Ellen had always cared for me. It took a lot of guts to tell me to my face she was leaving me for another person. Facing me was a lot of pain for her to endure. It would have been so much easier to write a letter or just leave without saying anything. And, coming back, that also took courage, because she had no idea what to expect from me. We hadn't written in more than a year.

That was more than forty-six years ago. Taking Ellen back was the biggest gamble I had ever taken, but it proved to be the right choice for me, and her. She has made me very happy. We were young and unsure of ourselves. Well, she was unsure. It had taken a bad relationship with someone else for her to make up her mind that I was the one for her.

22

In the Beginning
There Was Glen

Glen
Courtesy Toodie Mueller

Glen Buxton was my friend. Our birthdays were two days apart. Truth be told, my dad would have adopted him, if he had known

Glen was born on the Marine Corps anniversary, like he hoped I would. I don't think Dad ever forgave me for that. I blame my mother. I had nothing to do with it.

Glen and I met while we were misusing our time in college, trying to decide what we wanted to do with our lives. I was completely unsure and didn't have a clue. Glen, on the other hand, knew exactly what it was he wanted. He wanted to be in a band that was famous all over the world, and he asked me to join him, and his friends, on the journey. I thought about it. I didn't have much going on at the time, only the confusion about what to do with the rest of my life. No big thing.

I said, "Sure. Why not?"

"Great!" he exclaimed. "It will be fun."

Life with The Spiders, The Nazz, and the Alice Cooper group was the single greatest adventure of my lifetime. I give Glen credit for meeting my wife, and to Toodie, who introduced us. If I hadn't been working for the band, I never would have met Ellen. I literally owe Glen and the band for everything in my life after the age of eighteen. Glen taught me about guitars and amplifiers; he taught me what could go wrong and how to fix them, and how to use a soldering gun. That knowledge came in very handy, because Dennis stretched guitar cords from here to infinity. He gave me a lot of soldering practice. Glen tried, in vain, to teach me to play the guitar, to my regret, I'm afraid.

When Glen and I traveled to Tucson in my old Plymouth Fury station wagon, he tried to entertain me with his Wolf Man Jack and W.C. Fields impersonations. Emphasis on the word tried. I would love to hear him do them again. We'd talk about our lives, our dreams, and what the future would bring. We'd stay in motels with porno magazines in the bedside table. Motels where we could check-in at 2:00 a.m. on a Saturday and stay until Monday.

Working for the band, I learned responsibility and the importance of being on time, whether it was across town or across the country. It's a trait I carry with me today.

In mid-1970 when I decided to leave the group, Glen asked me to stay. I said I couldn't, and he understood the reasons why. We wrote to each other, and he told me about the people they had hired to replace me, who weren't doing a good job. I thought he was just being nice.

"You hired *people* to replace me, as in the plural? You mean more than one?"

"Yeah. You're pretty dumb, aren't you?" he wrote.

"You just need to give them some time and they will be fine," I replied. "Remember you hired me when I didn't know which end of a guitar cord to plug in. Mike Bruce told me that I had to plug the cord in a certain way so the sound would travel from the guitar to the amplifier. I actually had to think about that for a minute or two before I realized he was kidding."

I wrote to tell Glen about a song I'd heard on the radio, "I'm 18. "

He wrote back that he was living the dream.

"Why don't you come back?" he asked.

On November 1, 1972 Rick Anderson, the bass player for The Tubes, sent Ellen a letter. He wrote in part:

> *"We were playing at the North Beach Revival a few weeks ago, on a Wednesday of all nights, and who should come in but Neal, Alice, and Mike Bruce, who had been told that it was the "happening" club in San Francisco. They gave us tickets to their concert the next night. They're really a good act now. A polished product pretty much, but you've probably heard about that. They got two Canadian and one American gold records. Glen said, at the party*

> *after the concert at Shakey's Pizza (just like Phx),*
> *that Michael Allen said he'd get stoned if they ever*
> *received a gold record, and he was going to hold him*
> *to it. Well, maybe."*

It was typical of Glen to remember such a thing. He never held me to that promise, though.

Eventually, I lost all contact with the band. Around 1974, I stopped receiving letters from Glen. I thought he was busy with his success. I didn't know that he had been gravely ill in a hospital in Phoenix. I never went to see him, because I didn't know. I wish I had. For a long time I didn't even know that Alice had parted company with the rest of the members of the band.

Out of the blue in 1976, Glen showed up at our wedding reception. It was great seeing him again. We hugged and slapped each other on the back and talked for thirty or forty minutes. It was like old times. Like we'd never been apart. Glen jokingly told Ellen that "she could do better." At least I hoped he was joking. He handed me a gift, a steak knife set, which we still use. Ellen wrote a note that they were a gift from Glen Buxton of Alice Cooper and put it in the box.

Then, he said he had to go, grabbed a bottle of champagne, and walked out the door.

That was the last time I ever saw him, but he wrote one last letter. He said he was starting a new band called Virgin, but the new members were not that keen about practicing. "They are young, but they will come around," he said.

The old man—Glen was only in his early thirties at the time—teaching these young kids what it meant to be in a band. I hoped they would listen. He finished by saying they would be playing some local clubs in Phoenix in the future and Ellen and I should come by.

I wrote back, "When and where and we will be there. Just as long as I don't have to carry anything!" I never heard from him again. John Lennon probably said it best. "Life happens while you're busy making plans."

I didn't learn of Glen's death in Iowa until four months afterward. I thought if I'd only known, maybe I could have done something. I regret it to this day. I felt that he had been a better friend to me than I to him. Years later, when I was making more money, I bought two guitars: one was an orange 1964 Gretsch Tennessean, and the other a 1965 Rickenbacker. I didn't realize the significance of buying these guitars until I started writing this book. They were two of the guitars Glen owned when I was working for the group. I keep them hung on my office wall, so I see them every day, and remember Glen.

Ellen's sister Carolyn gave me a Dick Phillips Spider's business card that years before Glen had given her, when we were all still kids. It's autographed by Glen, and he drew a little cartoon spider on it. It is framed now and in my office. I miss that guy.

When the Alice Cooper group was inducted into the Rock and Roll Hall of Fame, Dennis called to invite Ellen and me to a pre-event party at Cooperstown, a restaurant in downtown Phoenix owned by Alice. It was very nice of him to include us, and it was great to see everybody again. Everyone was there except Joey, Charlie, and of course, Glen. Even Dick came from L.A.

Glen would have loved the party, because Glen liked to party.

Acknowledgement by his peers that the original Alice Cooper Group was one of the greatest bands of all time would have made him happy. Being voted one of the top 100 guitar players of all time by Rolling Stone magazine in 2003 and then being inducted into the Rock and Roll Hall of Fame in 2011 were two of Glen's dreams. He would have joked about and downplayed those honors, but inside he would have been very proud. Glen always wanted to make hit records and become famous. He achieved both. As he wrote me years before, he was living the dream.

You were so right, my friend.

That's the story of Alice Cooper's Amp Boy. It was an adventure of a lifetime. I went places, meeting famous and interesting people, and some not so interesting. For nearly five years I lived in a family. And we were a family. A large boisterous, funny, adventurous, never-a-dull-moment family. I had seven brothers and a sister: Vince/Alice, Glen, Dennis, Mike, Neal, Dick, Charlie, and Cindy. Each with a unique talent and all with the same dream.

I was once asked, "Would you do it all over again knowing then what you know now?"

I thought about it for just a second, and replied. "Oh, Hell yes!"

* * *

Toodie Mueller

How I Met The Spiders 1966 by Toodie Mueller Mason

Dick Phillips was a good high school friend. He graduated one year before me, and somehow got to be manager of The Spiders. One day driving with a girlfriend, we were on our way to Dick's when he passed us on the road. After catching up to him, he told us he was on his way to Glen's house. Glen was the lead guitar player for The Spiders. He said he would introduce us. We were thrilled!!! Wow! They were the hottest band in Phoenix!

We arrived at Glen's home. He was listening to music, which was where Glen learned a lot of his guitaring from. We all went outside on the patio. Then, the doorbell rang. Mike Allen— Amp Boy—and the rest of the band entered. Mike asked if I, or my friend, knew how to cut hair. I said I did—I lied. I gave Mike a trim. He said he liked it! Mike liked it! Ha. And that's how I met and hung out with The Spiders. Oh, yeah, I ended up driving them a lot to Tucson, Albuquerque, California, and many more places, and to gigs in Phoenix in my car, a 1967 blue Ford Mustang. They were appreciative of the rides, and I have many memories of them back then.

The band played in Casa Grande Arizona one night. The western music lovers did not care for the band's long hair, and one "cowboy" approached Vince and stuck a knife in front of his face. Vince just kept on singing. When they finished playing, the band quickly packed up and left before any trouble could be started.

The Spiders always had a hard time finding places to practice. At least once, they went to Thunderbird Park in Phoenix, and with a picnic table, light pole, and one outlet they jammed for a couple hours. Pretty nice evening.

I remember, at the VIP Club in Phoenix, the popular Spiders wanted to show off their creativity. One night I put fluorescent paint on them, and the crowd went wild. Many future shows were duplicated with this paint.

Excerpts from Toodie Mueller's Journal 1967 to 1968

9/24/1967 Drove to Prescott, Arizona with the band and Mary and Ellen Mitchell to Mary and Ellen's grandmother's cabin. Some of us hiked around the mountains. Then the band practiced a bit. I drove into town to buy food for grilling burgers. Picked up a hitchhiker who wanted a ride to the Phoenix Airport. He agreed to eat with us. Then we headed back to Phoenix and to the airport. Hitchhiker left for New York.

11 / 3 / 1967 I drove to California to visit the band. Never saw Dick.

11 / 4 / 1967 The Nazz played at the Cheetah club with Smokestack Lightning. The band had a great set! I drove back to Phoenix.

11 / 8 / 1967 I sent Mike A. some brownies for his birthday in California.

11 / 11 1967 The Animals band went to the band's house but stayed in their cars. Didn't come into the house. Stayed a short time.

11 / 12 / 1967 John Speer left the group.

11 / 31 / 1967 The Nazz played at the Cheetah Club, with the Buffalo Springfield, The Seeds, and Smokestack Lightning.

1 / 5 / 1968 The Nazz played at the Mad Hatter.

1 / 6 / 1968 The Nazz played at the Mad Hatter.

1 / 19 / 1968 The Nazz played at my sister's birthday party. There were 30 13-year-old girls. It was really a practice session for the band, but the kids didn't care.

1 / 20 / 1968 The band had a gig in Tucson at a club. Mike A. was beat up. Back to Phoenix.

1 / 26 / 1968 The Nazz played with the "Music Machine" at the Beau Brummell Club.

1 / 27 / 1968 The band played at the Camelback Inn in Scotts-dale Arizona.

1 / 28 / 1968 Went mountain climbing with the band.

1 / 29 / 1968 The Nazz started recording their first record under that name.

1 / 30 / 1968 Another recording day. Then a party at the "Weeds of Idleness" house.

2 /3/1968 Nazz played at the Saint Francis Kino dance along with the Weeds, then back to the "Weeds" house for a party.

2 / 6 / 1968 Went horseback riding with Mike A. and Ellen. Then drove to Tucson for concert.

2 / 16 / 1968 The Nazz played at Mad Hatter Club. Glen and Neal got in a fight.

3 / 7 / 1968 Mary, Glen and Charlie and I went to Cave Creek Dam while Neal, Mike A. and Vince went hunting Neal shot himself in the foot.

3 / 19 / 1968 Nazz went back to LA. Band changed their name to" Alice Cooper."

3 / 29 / 1968 I drove to California to see A.C. They live in a house in Topanga Canyon now.

4 / 5 / 1968 Alice Cooper arrived back in Phoenix.

4 / 6 / 1968 A.C. opened their new club called "Alice Cooper."

4 / 12 / 1968 Alice Cooper Band drove back to LA. Got into an accident. No one was seriously hurt. I heard about the accident when Bonnie called me. She said she asked the Ouija board if the band got to L.A. safely. It answered "No." She asked what happened, and the Ouija board spelled "Accident." Freaky!

5 / 3 / 1968 I went to L.A. and The Cheetah Club then to The Doors recording studio with some band members. Cool!

5 / 4 / 1968 A.C. Band wrote Today Mueller.

5 / 11 / 1968 Back in Phoenix. Kathy, Charlie and I drove to Creek Cave Creek Dam to pick marijuana plants. Then to the Picture House.

5 / 18 / 1968 Went to see Alice Cooper play in Seal Beach, California. We got lost and stopped at a gas station for directions. Two very nice guys told us directions to get to the Seal Beach concert hall. Directions were very wrong and ended up at the Marine Corps base at the front gate. Some of the guys stuffed their joints in their mouths as we approached the gate. I died laughing. We got to the concert hall okay.

5 / 20 / 1968 A.C. band got their new van with the help from Jacque Memmott's dad.

6 / 1 / 1968 Drove to San Diego to see A.C. play at The Palace. It is a very nice place. The band played very well and loved "Today Mueller's" song.

7 / 12 / 1968 A.C. got a recording contract with Frank Zappa.

7 / 29 / 1968 Went to Phoenix Airport with Alice to pick up Dick. Alice was mistaken for Tiny Tim and signed autographs as Tiny. Very funny!

8 / 1 / 1968 My 20th birthday. I was in Phoenix. The Alice Cooper band called me and sang "Today Mueller" for me!

8 / 8 / 1968 I went to Charlie's house and frosted Alice's hair!

8 / 31 / 1968 I moved in with Nikki Furnier for a month while her parents were out of town for a couple of months.

9 / 7 / 1968 Drove to Fort Huachuca with the A.C. band. It was fun dancing with all the army guys! Blues Berry also played. Joey and Shep were there too.

Acknowledgments

There are some people I need to thank for helping me with this book. Their contributions only made it better.

I want to begin by thanking the band for the opportunity to live and experience the rock and roll life first hand. They might have harbored reservations about hiring me, but Glen could be very persuasive. I know I had reservations about working for them but, again, Glen could be very persuasive. Because of him, for nearly five years I was the proverbial fly on the wall: watching, listening, living, experiencing.

I am grateful to the following friends, without whom the book could not have been finished.

Len DeLessio for the best-looking image I've ever seen of Dennis's original bass guitar.

Monica Lauer for the use of her photograph of the three amigos: Dick, Charlie, and myself at the Whisky back in the day.

Jeanne Carney, thank you for letting me use your photograph of The Nazz drumhead that John Speer gave you. Nazz memorabilia is hard to come by as they were only a group for a few months.

Alice Cooper for the use of the hand drawn Nazz poster he made when they became Alice Cooper

Jane Ward, who gave permission to publish Scott's photographs of the Earwig days. They were essential in showing the early history of the band.

Janice Buxton Davison and Tom Buxton for contributing many photographs of the Spiders. Your photographs and memories helped tremendously in the telling of the story.

Paul Brenton, whom I had met at the Arizona premier of *Live from the Astroturf, Alice Cooper.* I had forgotten our conversation for more than a year. Despite my memory lapse, you have been helpful, supportive, and generous sharing your Alice Cooper memorabilia and offering opinions and good advice, which were always appreciated, on drafts of my book.

Toodie Mueller Mason, who is remembered in both song and word, and for groceries and transportation and photos. Thank you for being our friend. For cheering us on, feeding us, driving us around and immortalizing the days in Topanga Canyon and the freeway accident in photographs. As if that weren't enough, you introduced me to Ellen. And for generously sharing your journal. Just terrific contributions to the book.

Dennis Dunaway, a gentleman of the highest order, an artist, and from what I hear, not a bad bass player. You have been a friend and mentor during this long process and before. I was looking for help and reassurance. You were probably looking for peace and quiet. Your advice and guidance were excellent and reassuring—which I was in constant need of—and always spot on. You read my drafts, listened to my ideas, answered endless questions, offered insights, and continued, to the last, to give positive feedback and encouragement. You even found time to share your excellent design ideas for the book's cover, and literally used your coat for the background! I see why Cindy likes you so much. She's a good judge of character, even though she often called me a knucklehead.

And finally, Ellen, who happens to be my wife of forty-six years, for which I am thankful. Throughout my involvement with the band, and their many incarnations, you were with me whether near or far away.

One day a few years ago, I told her I was going to write a book about my life with the band. She simply said, "OK." I spent countless hours in the office speaking nonstop into the computer's headset and typing with two-fingers. Sometimes, the computer wrote better words than I'd dictated. She and I were a team, but one of the team had a problem. I prattled on without sentence structure or punctuation. Punctuation? I don't need no stinking punctuation! Who knew this stuff existed? Ellen became my de facto editor-in-chief. She corrected my spelling, or misspellings, and rearranged sentences, and occasionally paragraphs, so they made sense. When I reread pages and added something or rewrote a story, she followed right behind to tidy things up. She proved to be a good resource, especially with the letters she saved all these years.

It's because of her steadfast interest, support, and help that I have a book at all. She motivated me to continue writing, telling me the book was good and very entertaining. I might now believe her. Whatever I may have accomplished, it is all because of her encouragement and help.

And I love her for that.

CPSIA information can be obtained
at www.ICGtesting.com
Printed in the USA
BVHW042249200423
662738BV00002B/2/J